VEDIC INDIA

VEDIC INDIA
A History

M.P. AJITHKUMAR

KALPAZ

Vedic India : A History

ISBN: 978-81-7835-938-0

Published in 2013 in India by
Kalpaz Publications
C-30, Satyawati Nagar,
Delhi-110052
E-mail: kalpaz@hotmail.com

Lasser Type Setting by: Rudra Computer Graphics, Delhi
Printed at : Chawla Offset Printers, Delhi

Dedicated To

My Teacher
the late P. C. Menon, Formerly Professor of History and
Principal N. S. S. College, Kerala

Contents

Preface

History of ancient India is a subject of varied interests to scholars, each looking at it from different angles. Right from the early days of her history India has been preserving accounts on what happened in the past as seen from her ancient literature. India had a great tradition of memory from her past. Its *smruthi* literatures or the accounts of the values that guided life in India across the centuries were rich. India's *puranas*, *itihasas* and all the lore bristling with memories of past are helpful in unfolding to posterity the sublime and healthy tradition it developed over the millennia. The whole story of a people and their culture unrolls itself through their pages, all in its grandeur, glory and gaiety few ancient cultures could match.

But in many cases mistakes happened inadvertently to the writers of Indian history due to the paucity of research materials resulting in their improving little upon what was written before. Naturally, there came in stagnation of ideas, repetition of statements and redundancy. It was all an exercise within the circle already drawn by European Indologists. The development of Indology as a subject owes exclusively to the efforts of European scholars whose contributions to write Indian history cannot be underrated though most of them, as evident from many of their interpretations of India's past, had vested interests. While a few of them studied India's history as part of academic pursuit, colonialist interests prompted the majority. True, their lack of knowledge in India's early literature and unfamiliarity with an ancient culture and its heights which they could not scale combined with their colonialist interests resulted in many a folly and deliberate distortions. However, their efforts in laying the foundations of Indology as a special faculty deserve plaudits. But attitude of the later Indian indologists was almost deplorable, their having merely continued to parrot the opinions of European indologists rather than acting as corrective developers over the legacy the latter left behind. There was of course research on Indian history and many of its auxiliary subjects, particularly archaeology, which had unearthed facts in abundance that helped rewrite the history of ancient India. But such materials always remained at the level of high research, never reaching students of usual run through textbooks and general study materials. Besides, such novel findings did not get the acceptance of syllabi makers, academic councils and board of studies of centers of higher learning. Consequently for almost a century, old ideas and views held sway with the world of students at undergraduate and postgraduate levels remaining ignorant of these novel developments in Indian historical studies or unfamiliar with logics required to have the real understanding of Indian history.

Till the end of the later half of twentieth century many erroneous ideas including that of Aryan invasion and Sheet Anchor of Indian chronology dominated the domain of Indology. Most conclusions regarding the history of ancient India were predicated on this sort of premises, which lacked academic tenability. Hence the necessity of an intelligible recasting of ancient Indian history so that many confusions and misunderstandings could be avoided.

This book covers the long historic period of Vedas which may well be called Vedic India or India of the period which effloresced into knowledge systems, all having their roots in Vedas and Vedic tradition. Evidences speak volumes about the similarity of cultures and their ideas that sprang up in India. Teachings of the Vedas, Mahavira and the Buddha and new findings from Saraswati-Sindhu valley speak of a commom culture. Hence the conclusion that they all belong to the same tradition and that they are not mutually contradictory and conflicting as described in some writings.

Here a humble attempt is made to present things in a right perspective. Differences are within the law of nature. Multiplicity and diversity bring about the beauty of universal order. 'From multiplicity to unity or diversity to harmony' is the only desirable law of universal progress. The aim of any type of study must be to evolve coherence out of de-coherence in such a way as to realize the oneness latent in humanity and universe. This rule is applicable to all faculties of knowledge including historical studies though the present trend as seen in many areas of historical research, especially Indology, is the pursuit of differences, decoherence and disintegrations and resultant anarchy at all levels, mental, material and what not. Thus as one of the prime faculties devoted to the cause of universal unity the faculty of historical studies is commissioned with the duty of making an enquiry into this oneness and actualizing it to the most possible extent. This being the mission of historical studies, it is desirable to have an enquiry into the elements of unity in India's ancient history and culture.

May I extent my hearty thanks to those who helped me write this work. I am indebted to my undergraduate students at my College whom I have been teaching Indian history and culture for the last few years. In fact the lecture notes I have prepared for them constitute the chapters of this book. I also express my thanks to Dr. V.R. Manoj, Deputy Director, Chinmaya International Foundation, Adi Sankara Nilayam, Kochi who helped me give diacritic notes to the Sanskrit verses. Thanks are also to Smt. T. S. Kartika, Associate Professor of Philosophy, N. S. S. Hindu College, Changanacherry, Kerala who contributed the appendix, 'Buddhism : A Continuation of the Vedic Religion'.

Thiruvananthapuram **M. P. Ajithkumar**
12 January, 2012

Introduction

It has been habitual to early as well as later historians to write history of ancient India following the track laid by the European indologists. Seldom has it been taken note that new discoveries in the field of Indology have greatly changed the very subject as well as its perspectives, and that the writings of these European indologists were partly the products of ignorance as they were partly of European bias. It may also be noticed that later half of the 20th century have produced a profusion of scholarly works, which remained beyond the pale of academic institutions. Their works, though did not contain as much as what modern archaeological discoveries have brought out, however, were pointers to many anomalies found in the European writings on Indian history. But it has been characteristic of those described as 'modernists' to pooh-pooh these nationalist writers disparaging them as fascists. Their works, though studded with gems of knowledge and high research values, were obscured from the knowledge of general student community because of the absence of fans in academic bodies and boards. In an academic world bristling with such modernists, post modernists and their dilettantish and comic interpretations of wise counsels on Indian history got frozen or were left unnoticed.

These aspects are thus to be born of in mind while addressing the many problems involved in the study of ancient Indian history. Indeed research in some cases has taken so worse a turn as to fan the flames of regionalism, communalism and all other associated narrowness. The fight between antinationalism on the one hand and overzealous patriotism on the other has also not lagged behind in distorting and disfiguring India's history. The question whether Euro-centric, the Indo-centric or the Marxian approach is to be applied to Indian history has greatly overlooked the need and possibility of an objective approach. And unfortunately modern Indian historians have become the camp followers of different ideological groups on to whose intellects many old and orthodox ideas still cling as dead weights. They are still not daring enough to come out of their ideological grooves, lest it should irritate their political and official mentors. What would happen if the tree were, even after its having come out of the shell, not ready to receive more than what it got while in the seed It would only stunt. This is the case of many peter pan or if to use new synonym, bonsai intellectuals. And the result; India's history is not properly understood or studied. This pathetic condition of Indian history writing makes one think whether there is not a desirable alternative or an objective approach possible.

History of ancient India has been a topic of controversy right from the beginning of Indian historiography. It has been the issues of decoherence, as noted earlier, both at intellectual and ideological levels that made it controversial and marred its beauty which once evoked wonder in the minds of scholars world over. Since coherence is better than decoherence, it is necessary to understand how much there developed in ancient India the elements of coherence and unity or how much India succeeded in maintaining that balance between unity on the one side and variety on the other, between confluence and the seeming conflicts.

But it should also be seen that this assimilating mind of India has during the past three or four centuries been looked down upon by undesirable forces as means to alienate India from her original moorings. Indeed what Arnold Toynbee meant when he described India as an epitome of the world, i.e., the accepting and assimilating mind of India is now almost being done away with the forces of alienation and westernization dominating every sphere of national life. The result was the emergence of conflicts instead of convergence and confluence. Unfortunately, the present day India, as a thinker has stated, has gone far away from its original moorings. India, he said, is Bharat divested of its cultural and spiritual values.[1] Bristling with opportunism, communalism, terrorism and barbarism couched in modernity, India is becoming different from what it was centuries ago, almost an epitome of the world's unholy side.

And history writing down from the time of European Indologists has been used as a tool hell-bent to develop cancerous elements of conflicts. Divide and destroy being their policy, writers with vested interests overlooking the elements of unity, endeavoured to give out an inflated picture of the seeming disunity, and the readers caught in mirage took it for truth. Consequently, the present India was written off as a conglomeration of foreign migrants down from the time of Aryans, leading to the thesis that all Indians are originally foreigners who are historically bound to accept many more foreigners likely to come in future. This is nothing but denationalizing a nation of hoary antiquity, subjecting it to all kinds of exploitation and dehumanizing. Hence the Arya-Dravida conflict, which is bereft of any theoretical background or Hindu-Jain-Buddhist differences and their sectarian outlooks though all these faiths belong to one common tradition with common religious tenets, beliefs and often practices, too. It was indeed a deliberate distortion of history, which served the vested interests with the result that actuality was curtained up with misinterpretation and twisted logic. It is from this angle history as an academic subject is to be saved, reviewed and objectively rewritten.

Reference

1. T.R. Somasekharan, 'Gita and Our Nation', *Bhagavad Gita and Modern Problems* (P. Parameswaran. Ed), Thiruvanantapuram, 2001, pp. 231-237.

PART – I

VEDIC CULTURE

1

Vedic Literature : Source for the Study of the Vedic Age

Vedas are the only literary source of information for the study of ancient India prior to the emergence of *mahājanapadas.* Vedas with their root *vid* or *vidya* (knowledge) were the vast collection incomparable to any other coeval literature. Though the term Vedic age is referred to in modern writings in history, it is very difficult to fix the chronology of Vedas owing to the very nature of Vedic collections. They had lain collectively and at random before the coming of Krishnadvaipayana, far-famed as Veda Vyasa. Tradition has it that Krishnadvaipayana collected the Vedas and divided them according to the nature of Vedic hymns rather than their chronology. However all these notwithstanding, it has been characteristic of historians to describe them as early and later Vedas basing on unsubstantial assumption that some were written earlier and some later. Such an approach in the study of Vedic literature has become stereotyped.

Divided into four, the Vedas are repositories of knowledge adequate enough to sustain both ancient and modern societies. With no aspect of human life left untouched, Vedas have down the millennia disciplined and perfected life in India. *Ṛk, Sāma, Atḥarva* and *Yajur* Vedas are seemingly different in nature but have no fundamental ideological difference in their vision and spiritual background. Whereas *Ṛk Véda* is fully spiritual and divine just as in case of *Sāma Véda* which is a collection of songs mostly taken from *Ṛk Véda, Atḥarva Véda* is a collection of spells and charms.

Ṛk Vēda contains 1028 *suktas*, divided into ten *mandalas* and again in eight *ashṭakas*. Each of them is ascribed to the family of priests like Gritsamata, Vamadeva, Atri, Bharadwaja and Vasishta. The ninth *manḍala* is a collection of hymns addressed to Soma. The *Puranas* refer to thousand *samhitas* of *Sāma Vēda*. But we have not got all these except the one in three recessions, like *Kuthuma* current in Gujarat, *Jaiminiya* in Karnataka, and *Raṇayāniya* in Maratha country. These hymns are 1810 in number. *Ṛk* and *Sāma* are full of prayers for attaining knowledge and enlightenment whereas the other two often pray for material welfare and prosperity. *Ṛk Véda* envisions a world of enlightenment as revealed when it prays to lead man from "untruth to the ultimate truth, from darkness to light, from death to immortality," or when it refers to stories of *Gora Angirasa* or *Kutsa Angirasa* which point to the attainment of the world of celestial light or a life divine as the ultimate aim of all human endeavours. *Yajur Véda* is full of *samhitas*, which are a collection of sacrificial formula. Patanjali speaks of 101 schools of *Yajur Véda*. However, at present we have got only five like *Kaṭhaka Samhita*, *Kapishtḥala-kaṭha Samhita*, *Maithrayani Samhita*, *Thaittiriya Samhita* and *Vajasanayi Samhita*. *Atḥarva Véda* is mostly terrestrial with the spells either to charm away epidemics and physical ailments and some time even for material prosperity. Scholars like Dayananda and Sri Aurobindo have interpreted the stories of *Ṛk Vḍa* as symbolic of the high metaphysical truth visualized by ancient bards who were hearers of Truth (*kaviyā satyasrutāḥ*). While taking the nature of *Ṛk Védic* hymns, the opinion held by European Indologists like Max Muller or William Johns that *Vedas* were materialistic, holds no water. *Ṛk Véda* is full of prayers to divinities like *Agni* who is both *Purōhita* and *Ṛtvik*. *Agni* is the God of prime importance, saviour, benefactor, purifier of mind and soul, destroyer of all sins. There are also a host of Gods like *Indra, Varuṇa, Pushān, Ushas, As'wins, Brihaspati, Araṇyāni,* etc. With different functions, these Gods and their names are often used in the same context, and with same duties. Or why the Vedic bard prays, "Salutations to thee oh *Indra* who appears in the form of Sun God and shatters the *śāradīyapura*"- perhaps the notion that the same Godhood has its different manifestation through different incarnations must have made Vedic seers use the names of different Gods in same context or the same God for different functions. God is the same though he is told differently in scriptures (*ékamsat vipraḥ bahudhā vadantiḥ*), they realized. The unity of god-hood was well conceived.

These four *Samhitas* constituted the basis of four *Védas*, which were accompanied by their annexure and appendices viz., *Brāhmaṇas*, *Āraṇyakas* and *Upanishads*. The cases of *Aitaréya Brāhmana* and *Satapatḥ Brāhmaṇa* are well known. The *Āranyakas* were authored and chanted amidst the forests and as their name implied intended to serve as objects of meditation for those who live in forests during their vānaprasthạ. "They form the transition link between the rituals of the Brahmanas and the philosophy of the Upanishads."[1] Finally there are *Upanishads* or *Vedanta*, which are the conclusions of *Vedas*. Innumerable are the *Upanishads*, and the generally studied principal *Upanishads* are eighteen in number. *Upanishad*, which means 'sit near', was taught to the disciple who sat near the *Guru* or spiritual preceptor engaged in helping the seeker to have his final sitting near God. The spiritual teachings and highest metaphysical expositions were often couched in the flowerbed of poetic conversations as seen in the *Kaṭha Upanishad* where Yama, the God of death, explains to Nachiketas a hundred and more mysteries of the nether world. The discourse in *Chhandogya Upanishad* on the Gross-Subtle monism by Uddalaka to Swetaketu with the aid of a *nyāgrōdḥa* seed is definitely the most effective and simple way a highly complex subject could be discoursed on lucidly and unambiguously.[2]

Every single work of this vast literature belongs to the category of *Vedas* whose authors are *Ṛshis* or Poet-seers to whom Vedas were the truths revealed or *srutis*. *Apaurushéya* (impersonal and springing from the highest values) *Vedas* were considered *nitya* (existing in all eternity) and *Ṛshis* the *mantradrashṭa* or inspired seers who got ultimate light from supreme creator. Thus we come to hear of the seers like Viswamitra (or the friend of the entire universe as his name means) and others as the authors of Vedic hymns.

Besides these, there is another class of works belonging to Vedic literature. These are called *Sutras* or *Vedangas*, which are six in number. They are not six distinct books or treatises, but six subjects the study of which was necessary either for reading or understanding the real connotations of Vedic literature. They are *śiksha* (pronunciation), *chhandas* (meter), *vyākaraṇa* (grammar), *nirukta* (explanation of words), *jyōtisha* (astronomy), and *kalpa* (ceremonial). The first two are necessary for reading the *Vedas*, the next two for understanding it, and the last two for employing it at sacrifices. Though these subjects were originally dealt within the *Brahmanas* and *Aranyakas*, later separate texts were written on each of them. Couched in a peculiar style, they are called *sutras*, which consist of a series of extremely concise formulae noted for their algebraic brevity.

There is another class of literature called *Upavedas* or subsidiary Vedas, which deal with medical science (*āyurvéda*), military science (*dhanurvéda*), music (*gandḥarvavéda*), architecture (*sthāpatyavéda*) and many other analogous subjects.

There are *Puranas* and *Itihasas* which give details on the life and culture of the period when Vedas were authored and that followed. Though we cannot fix a precise date they were written on, it can easily be inferred from their description that they speak about the Vedic period. The *Vishnu Purana* and the *Harivamsa Purana* inform us a lot about the period of Vedas and also the chronology thereafter. Likewise there are *Vayu* and *Matsya Puranas. Itihasas* like *Ramayana* and *Mahabharata,* too, are highly elaborate on the life in times of the Vedas. Though compiled only later, they speak about a society that existed millennia ago. *Ramayana*, the earliest one, speaks about kingdoms of *Ayodhya, Mithila* and *Kosala* and the socio-political life that flowered around them whereas *Mahabharata* is narrative of the very age of Vyasa. According to tradition Vyasa was an eyewitness of the Battle of *Kurukshetra* that took place by the end of *dwapara yuga*, and that the age of Veda Vyasa, battle of Maha*bharata,* life and death of Krishna and collection and classification of the four Vedas had almost synchronized. And if all these writings are parts of Vedic literature, it can be easily inferred that age of Vedas covers a very long period that witnessed the elapsing of *yugas*, each *yuga* consisting millennia. Archaeology as well as geology and space studies, too, give us some idea about Vedic age through many artifacts discovered from North-Western India, which was the homeland of *Védas.* The recent photographs sent by the Landsat and other space cameras of NASA and ISRO confirm the historicity of many costal cities and sites referred to in Vedas and allied literature.

References

1. S. Radhakrishnan, *Indian Philosophy*, New Delhi, 2008, Vol. I, p. 41.
2. See chapter on Vedanta.

2

Political Ideas and Public Institutions : Vedic Phase

Political ideas and public institutions were as old as the very origin of civilization in India. Its ancient literature is replete with references to many democratic bodies and political ideas, which made public life easy and smooth functioning. In Vedic literature one can see mention of political institutions getting crystallized. We come to hear of the designations like the *Raja*, *Ganapati*, *Jyeshṭa*, etc., though the literatures as well as its interpreters do not convey the exact connotations of these terms. Besides, the *Vedas* speak of *sabha*, *samiti*, *vidata*, *vis*, and *gaṇa*, which appear to be some public bodies or assemblage of administrative top brass.

On the role of *sabha* and *samiti* scholars have adduced different views. *Ṛk Véda* mentions *sabha*, *sabhāsid*, *sabhéya*, *sabhā-pāla*, *sabhāpati* etc. While *sabha* is generally described as the body of administration, *Sabhāsid* and *Sabhéya* were the members who participated in *sabha* and its deliberations. The *sabha-pala* as its meaning conveys, was the keeper of assembly while *sabhapati* was lord of the assembly.[1] In later times there were *sabhas*, which were administrative bodies or councils of eminent public figures whom the chief administrator presided over and also consulted. These *sabhas* were indeed parliaments of rulers. We come to hear of *parishads* as well as *sabhas* referred to in later political treatises and popular literatures. *Arthasastra* and *Mahavamsa* allude to *mantriparishad* along with the *Chandraguptasabha*, which were top bodies of Mauryan government. There are also references to *rājasabhas* or royal councils in *upanishads* and *itihasas.* Perhaps *sabha* of Vedic times might have been the assembly of kings who with its support and advice dispensed royal duties. However, its reference in some context other than mere material makes one doubt a bit about its worldly connotations, too. For instance the *sabha* of Vedic gods as well as *Indra,* the supreme god of celestials, is bound to cast a little doubt on its mere political importance. However, its temporal importance also cannot be denied when it comes to the political set up of various kingdoms. The only one conclusion we can come up with is that *sabha* was an assemblage or a political forum, which the rulers sought help of in matters of statecraft. Scholars differ in their opinions regarding the nature of *sabha.* According to some scholars the *sabha* was an association of kinsfolk, 'of men bound together either by ties of blood or local contiguity', 'an advisory body of the king', his 'political council' or 'a standing stationary body of selected men working under the authority of the *samiti*'. The King's council referred to in Mahabharata appears to be composed of the members of Royal family, ministers who are real protectors of the king, priests and eminent and intelligent (*vidushi* or *vidūshaka*) advisers and philosophers of highest caliber like Vidura (*rājānō mantribāndḥava*).[2] Some scholars opine that *samiti* was a gathering of people of the community, the assembly of the *rashtra.* Jayswal describes it as national assembly of the whole people. Altekar has it that *samiti* was a political assembly of the central government.[3] It is, however, difficult to distinguish between *sabha* and *samiti. Samiti* may provisionally be said to have been 'an assembly of large groups of people for discharging political business while s*abha* was 'a more select body, less popular and political in character.'[4]

Another term noticed is *vidata* - a word of obscure sense confined mainly to *Ṛk Véda.* Baji Nath Puri has it that extreme caution has to be taken in drawing conclusions regarding the working and significance of these bodies, or in trying to explain them in the light of modern concepts of political theories and organizations. We are still not sure of the functions and role of the *vidata* in the political context of the life related in Vedas. However, it is generally believed by scholars that *vidata,* too, was one of the political bodies of Vedic times like *sabha* and *samiti.*

Altekar opinionates that Vedic society in its early period was divided into families, *janmans, visas* and *janas. Janmans* seem to have corresponded to a village consisting of people claiming a common descend. A number of such villages joined together by a bond of kinship seem to have constituted a *vis*, which was headed by a chief, designated *Vispati.* He opines that *visas* were closely knit together which often contributed even the battalions in war. Several *visas* made a *jana* or tribe, which had its *janapati* or the Chief. Altekar even goes ahead with his comparative study of Vedic *Jana* with the early Greek and Roman bodies. He says, "Védic *jana* probably corresponds with the tribe, *vis* with the Curia and the *janman* with the gen."

These various political bodies in their long run of evolutionary process seem to have constituted the bedrock of ancient India's political life and the cradles of its manifold political ideologies. The Vedic literature is replete with references to the emergence of polity in early India. They speak of a social set up, the kind described later in the political thought of modern Europe. What Rousseau or Montesquieu theorized in their revolutionary political ideas was visualized in ancient India way back in times of *Vedas. Mahabharata* speaks of an early society ruled by the principles of justice and truth or *satyayuga* wherein there was neither the ruler nor the ruled, neither the wielder of rode nor the punished, where people living in with *dharmic* principles helped each other. But as time passed, the literature says, the society plummeted to disorder and chaos, which made people think in terms of a new political set up. Narada and Brihaspati postulate the original existence of a golden age and point out that it soon came to an end and was succeeded by a political chaos. Sukra, however, does not seem to believe in the theory of Golden age or Social Contract though he recognizes the quasi-divinity of a virtuous king. But the general belief goes after Narada and Brihaspati. According to many authoritative Indian traditions, Manu was the first king whom the people selected and agreed to pay tributes and tax to.

Taking all these references it may not be far from reality that there existed a matured political system in the Vedic phase. This political system consisted of many administrative units ranging from village units to large kingdoms. The titles and designations like *rāja, visvasya bhuvanesasya rāja, samrāt, janapati, vispati,* etc., give us a hint to various ruling chairs whereas references to *Sabha, Samiti, jana, vidata, vis,* etc., confirm the existence of various administrative bodies and units. There are also allusions to *virat, gana* etc., the exact connotations of which are still a matter of dispute though scholars like N N Law defines them as self-governing groups without a ruler (*virāt*). Vedas no doubt speak of a highly advanced political set up, not experienced or experimented in other parts of the coeval world.

References

1. Narendra Nath Law, *Aspects of Ancient Indian Polity*, Bombay, 1960, pp. 26-27.
2. *Vidura*. 34. 38.
3. *State and Government in Ancient India.*
4. U N Ghosal, *Studies in Indian History and Culture.*

3

Kingship

Institution of kingship in India is very ancient. Vedic literature alludes to how the gods defeated by demons because of their having been leaderless thought on the need of having a king. The story tells that they made Soma their king and leader and vanquished the *Asuras.* Similarly the gods at certain times accepted Indra and Varuna as their kings.[1] *Ṛk Véda* refers to Raja. The term *daś arājña* meaning (battle of the ten kings) is mentioned. Deemed the representative of the divine, king was Indra, Brihaspati, Mitra and Varuna combined. He embodied the ruling power, eloquence, truth and law. The lore emphasized the protection of law or dharma as the foremost of kingly duties.[2] Manusmruti accords divinity to king when it says that king is an incarnation of the eight guardian deities of the world like Moon, Fire, Sun, Wind, Indra, Kubera, Varuna and Yama and that God had created King as an embodiment of the eternal essence of these deities to protect the world.[3] Obviously Manu makes it obligatory on the person of the king to be the guardian deity of the ruled. Manu compares king with the sun with dazzling luster and supernatural abilities.[4] According to Yajur Véda, king's essential task is to fight evil forces and enforce law of justice. Thus goes a Yajur Vedic hymn:

> Self-ruler art thou, conquering foes;
> Ruler forever art thou, conquering aggressors;
> Ruler of the people art thou,
> Destroyer of the wicked powers;
> All ruler art thou, destroyer of enemies.[5]

In this respect king according to Yajur Véda shares the function of Indra, the slayer of evil powers. King's power represented the collective power of people because his power is derived from the power of people, says *Yajur Véda.*[6] From the Ṛk Vedic reference even to the election of king it may be easily assumed that king was bound to act in with the collective will and wishes of the ruled. Mere hereditary succession overlooking weakness of the person of the ruler was not often favoured. Some times an efficient one was selected instead of less qualified as testified by legend of Devapi and Santanu referred to in *Yaska.*[7] There are instances of unpopular kings having been expelled. *Śatapatḥa Brahmana* refers to Srinjaya king, Dushtartu Paumsayana who was deposed. *Panchavims'a Brāhmaṇa* says that Dirghasravas was banished from his kingdom and that king Sindhukshit remained in exile.[8] The case of Vena being deposed and killed in later times may also be mentioned.[9]

It was King's right to rule the mother earth with its unlimited space. Perhaps Vedic people even envisioned a universal sovereign when Vedas speaks of a *viś vasya bhuvanéśasya rāja.* Here is another Yajur Vedic hymn related to this:

In us may there be your power,
in us your valour, your wisdom,
in us be your mental splendour,
Obeisance to Mother Earth,
Obeisance to Mother Earth,
This is thy sovereignty,
Thou art the controller, ruler,
Thou art steady, firm.
Thee for culture of the land,
Thee for peace, thee for wealth,
Thee for nurture.[10]

The king accordingly tried his level best to be the greatest patron and benefactor of the ruled; the well being of his subjects was his main pursuit. He therefore undertook to unite and defend his people. Hence the following prayer of the king:

Satisfy my mind, satisfy my speech,
Satisfy my vital power, satisfy my eye,
Satisfy my ear, satisfy my spirit,
Satisfy my progeny, satisfy my herds,
Satisfy my people, let not my people thirst.[11]

Yajur Véda makes it obligatory upon the ideal citizens and leaders of society to support king and keep constant vigil over people. In fact, Véda envisioned an enlightened ruler guided and aided by leaders of the people. If the lore expects of the ruler an enlightened performance, it fixes certain criteria regarding an ideal citizen also. Hence its dreams regarding one who is *karmaṇya* capable of *karma* or work, *śadanya* capable of household work or discharging domestic responsibilities, *vidatya* or fit for *vidata*, the Assembly, i.e. capable of discharging his duties to community or social group he is the member of; and *Sabhéya*, fit for *Sabha*, the political body guiding the king in administration, conduct of warfare, etc. An ideal citizen therefore was primarily to be a man capable of work, doing duties in the widening spheres of action, to his household, society and state.

Ancient law giver Manu envisions a king who is free from the ten vices springing from love of pleasure and the eight proceeding from wrath, which include hunting, gambling, drinking, excess with women, treachery, violence, slandering etc.[12] He says:

> The king must work day and night strenuously to control his senses; for only he who has command over his senses can command the obedience of his subjects.[13]

Another law giver Vidura advices king to abstain from the seven evils which strand the kingdom in chaos like "woman, gambling (dice), hunting, drinking and harshness of speech, great severity of punishment and misuse of wealth."[14] He says that the qualities like wisdom, high birth, self-restraint, learning, valour, moderation in speech, charity according to one's capacity and gratitude add luster to a man.[15] Vidura further sublimates the ideal of kingship when he discourses to the king of Kurus:

> Oh Dhritarashtra! Ten do not know what virtue is. These ten are intoxicated, inattentive, the racing, the hasty, the covetous, the terrified and the lustful. Therefore a wise man should not take to these moods or conditions (or should not be attached to these men).[16]

The king's means and ways must always be virtuous, righteousness should be governing principle in the state affair. Hence Vidura's dictate to the king that:

> "One should acquire the kingdom through righteousness, and through righteousness one should govern it. Having

won a prosperity founded on virtue one has neither to forsake it nor is forsaken at any time.[17]"

Manu has it that only a ruler who is morally strong deserves the right to be the wielder of rod (*danda*) because if danda is applied forgetting *dharma* or adherence to truth it would destroy men of this and other worlds.[18] These law-givers insist on the high sublimity and ethical state of mind for the ruler. Because they believed that only by a man of enlightenment and highest perfection can the society be led towards a harmonious perfection of life on earth. Being above the lower limitations, he can view everything from an exalted plane. Having a complete inner knowledge and a higher surpassing knowledge, he can guide the world humanly as god guides it divinely. Because like the divine, "he is in the life of the world and yet above it."[19] Such a man is "neither conquered nor wishes to conquer. He is neither a foe nor a retaliator to any. He remains even in praise or in censure. He does not grieve nor rejoice."[20] He is the foremost of men who wish for prosperity of all and never sets his heart on anything opposed to it, who is truthful in speech, gentle by nature and restrained of all passions.[21] Leadership combined with sublimated ideals thus proves most desirable. For a person of controlled self who moves about amidst sense-objects with the sense governed by the self and free from attachment and aversion attains serenity and helps the society he leads to attain it, says *Bhagavad-Gita.*

rāgadvéshaviyuktaistu vishayānindriyaścharān
ātmavaiśyair vidhēyātmā prasādamadhigachhati.[22]

Kingship in ancient India was thus a highly sublime office which catered to the all round social progress.

Vedic literature makes mentions of *samraj, rajan, adhiraja, maharaja, rajadhiraja, sarvabhauma* and *ekaraja* and the various royal ceremonies like *aśvamédha, rājasūya* and *vājapéya* in connection with the coronation and conquest. While *rājasūya* conferred upon the king a prospective blessing, *vājapéya* invested the king with overlordship whereas *aśvamédha* asserted the power and political authority of the ruler over the neighbouring kings and territories. Ramayana and Mahabharata refer to Rama and Yudhishtira as performers of *aśvamédha* or horse sacrifice. Skanda Purana refers to the latter as having performed a *rājasūya* and five *aśvamédha* sacrifices. Brihadratha the king of Anga, Bharata the son of Dushyanta, Yayati the son of Nahusha, Ambarsha the son of Nabhaga are a few among the kings who performed royal sacrifices.

King, though was the sole ruler whose will prevailed over all state matters, was expected to be benevolent, popular and democratic in his dealing with the ruled. Ramayana refers to *sabha* or council of princes, military officers, ambassadors and consuls which king had to take into consensus while taking decisions including the nomination and coronation of a new king.[23] Dasaratha is referred to as having speedily summoned the 'Rajanah' or his councilors for discussing and getting their permission for crowning Rama as Yuvaraja or Heir Apparent. It may again be noticed that when Bharata went to the forest to get back Rama on to the throne he requested the latter to be crowned by all the subjects, priests, and citizens who were the different units of Ayodhya's *sabha* or administrative council. Bharata was accompanied on this occasion by the representatives of all classes of subjects, councilors, and members of the *saba.*[24] The nature of coronation of Yuvaraja appears to have assumed the nature of election because king's nomination of a particular individual as his successor required the approval of people through their representative assembly, the *sabha.* It is interesting to learn that Dasaratha after expressing his desire to be free of his burden as king, proposed the election of Rama as his successor and even requested the Sabha to suggest alternative names if his proposal be not approved.[25] King was so much committed to the people that he was to identify himself with the ruled. "Oh king! People would be pleased with the ruler who pleases his subjects with his glance, words, mind and deed (*chakshushā manasā vāchā karmaṇā*), said Vidura to Dhritarashtra. King should not hamper the progress of the subjects in any way, says the Mahabharata. Even the collection of tax by the king, it says, should be like bee sucking honey without causing any harm to the flower.[26] King should be sworn to protect, promote and patronize the people, their progress and prosperity. Manu has it that king should entrust tax collection to trusted and just ministers and extent paternal care to the subjects (*vartēta pitruvanrusha*).[27] Also having been bound to act in with the directions of the science of polity and social ethics, he could not be an autocrat. King as all political literatures attest had a council of ministers to advise, assist and attend on him. And he had to consult this body of expert whenever an important matter was to be decided. The council usually consisted of eminent ones like *purohita, mantri, yuvaraja* and *senani* along with representative of the tributaries in case of an emperor, and other officers including the chief advisor and *vidushaka* or an intelligent friend who pleased the king with meaningful humours.

Manu says, King had to observe the laws of tradition and *dharma*, and makes it obligatory on the ruler to undergo certain routine. His day beginning with his saluting the scholars of highest knowledge including laws of justice went on falling in line with their dictates. He was bound to cater to the interests and needs of the old and get their blessings. He should be a man of humility so that with non-ego as his highest quality he would grow and his kingdom would flourish. Manu even cites examples of kings whose humility helped them regain their lost kingdoms. King should keep himself in touch with people belonging to all walks of life and get from them knowledge about different aspects. He should amass knowledge of Vedas from Vedic scholars, law of punishment from those who know it, art of argument from good logicians, spiritual knowledge from seers and economic science from traders and agriculturists. This practice, Manu believed, would update king's knowledge, helping him in daily administration of state.[28] Manu gives the king certain guidelines in selecting his ministers. His Council should be filled with seven or eight ministers who were well versed in jurisprudence, heroes and experts in warfare who are born of aristocratic families and of so much an aristocratic nature that they would not torture the subjects or cheat the king.[29] With them king should discuss matters of state's welfare, law and order, finance, state's security and expenditure and consult their personal and collective opinion. In addition to these cabinet ministers, king should recruit the required number of high officials who might be deputed to areas of administration their character and nature would fit them in. For instance, those with heroism, efficiency, aristocratic birth and free of economic temptation may be deployed in areas like gold mines and of production. Those born of noble families, good natured, well versed in sciences, experts in understanding others' words and tone and reading facial expressions, intelligent enough to create dissensions among the enemies, efficient in performing duties irrespective of time and place may be selected as messengers, emissaries and spies.[30] It is interesting to note Rama's query to Bharata at Chitrakuta whether he was keeping himself informed through the *chāra* or spies of how his ministers and officials act.[31] Ramayana again makes mention of Ravana's spies mixing innocently with people and soldiers with nose for secrets. Rama, too, made use of them to ferret out public opinion and gossip of his citizens and also to shadow the various Tirthas or officials. The Vedic kingship thus appears to have been one of benevolence, catering to the needs of the ruled, always considerate to popular will. To all extent monarchy performed in line with the principles of democracy, or it was democracy in the mantle of monarchy.

References

1. *Aitareya Brahmana*, I. 14.
2. A. S. Altekar, *State and Government in Ancient India*, p. 78.
3. *Manu.* VII. 3, 4.
4. Narendra Nath Law, *Aspects of Ancient Indian Polity*, Calcutta, 1960, p. 152.
5. *Yajur Veda.* 24.
6. A C Bose, *Call of the Vedas*, Bombay, 1988, p. 274.
7. *Nirukta.* II. 10.
8. *Panchavimsa Brahmana.* XV. 3. 25.
9. *Ibid*, XII. 12. 6.
10. *Yajur Veda*, 9. 22.
11. *Ibid.* 6. 31.
12. Manu. VII, 45, 47, 48; G. Buhler, *The Laws of Manu*, Delhi, 1988, pp. 222-223.
13. Manu. VII. 44.
14. *Viduraniti*, Vivyaratnam P N Menon (Ed), Palghat, 1962, p. 38.
15. *Ibid*, p. 40
16. *Ibid*, p. 41.
17. *Ibid*, p. 63.
18. *Manu*, VII. 29.
19. Sri Aurobindo, *The Human Cycle : The ideal of Human Unity : War and self-determination*, Pondicherry, 1985, 9. 169.
20. *Viduraniti*, Vivyaratnam P N Menon (Ed), p. 125.
21. M. P. Ajith Kumar, 'Philosopher King', *Quarterly Journal of the Mythic Society*, Bangalore, January-March, 1998, pp. 52-59.
22. *Gita*, II. 64.
23. P. C. Dharma, *The Ramayana Polity*, Bombay, 1989, p. 17.
24. *Ibid.*
25. *Ramayana*, II. 2. 8.
26. *Vidura*, 34. 17.
27. *Manu*, VII. 80.
28. *Ibid*, VII. 43.

29. *Ibid,* VII. 54.
30. *Ibid,* VII. 62-63.
31. *Ramayana,* II. 100. 36.

4

Republics in Ancient India

Ancient Indian literature bristles with references to the republican governments, with dominant role in India's early polity. Variously known as *Ganas*, *Sanghas* or *Arājavishayas*, these republican people ruled their territories all by themselves. In all the cases these republics had in their seat of authority people hailing from aristocratic groups of society. Organized with a central council, which manned the administrative machinery, these republics were strong and determined to resist any infringement on their authority by external powers. They represented the idea of self-government and democratic elements in ancient Indian polity and stood side by side with monarchical governments.

From literature we come to hear of the *Ganas* of *Mālavas* and *Yaudhēyas* whose governments were republican in nature. A well-known passage in *Aitarēya Brāhmana* says that countries north to Himalayas like Uttaramadras and Uttarakurus had *vairājyas* or non-monarchical states whose people were called *virats*. *Bhagavatapurana* and *Mahabharata* mention the *Vrishnis* and *Andhakas* led by Srikrishna. It is mentioned that the council of *Andhaka-Vrishni* was so powerful that even its president Srikrishna had complained to Narada that he is no master but slave of the central assembly as he had to listen patiently to bitter criticisms from different parties.[1] Members of various political factions who were representatives in the governing council of Madhura, according to literary sources, had been very powerful in administrative matters of that state till Kamsa silenced them with muscle power. Later literatures speak in volumes about the republics. *Avadānaśataka* speaks about a group of merchants from Madhyadesa who introduced themselves to a local king of Deccan as belonging to the state ruled by *Ganas* (*kéchiddeśé gaṇādhīna*). The republics of the trans-Gangetic region during the reign of Magadhan kings, Bimbisara and Ajathasatru are mentioned as highly powerful. Strong and pugnacious, these *gaṇarājyas* were not ready to genuflect before the Magadhan imperialism however much they might have been coaxed and threatened. Indeed the warnings given by Ajathasatru to submit proved ineffective before the republican combine of Vajjis, Mallas, Lichhavis and Jnatrikas. They were so well knit a group that they would not be brought to heels by usual threat from Magadhan Empire. Even the Buddha, belonging to line of Lichhavis (*Lichhavikula*), advised the council of these trans-Gangetic people to preserve their republican tradition without succumbing to dictatorial threats though he was frequent visitor to Magadha, too. And it took many years of effort by Magadhan spies headed by Suninda to create dissention among these republics and subdue them.

The Greek writings, though their actual time in Indian chronology is a subject of dispute, also throw light on the Republics of India in early times.[2] Arrien, Strabo, Plini, Curtius and others wax eloquent on these ancient governing formations, which were noted for their power and pugnacity. They say that Macedonian Phalanx under Alexander had tough times when it fought with these non-monarchical governments who would not succumb but fight to the last soldier. Thus the fighting groups of *Musaknois* (Mushikas), *Oxidrakis* (Kshudrakas) and *Assakenois* (Aswakayenas) are referred to as very powerful people whom Alexander found difficult to bring to heels. Mentioning about *Assakenois*, the Greeks wrote that they were led by their chief upon whose death his wife took over the command and carried fire and sword into the enemy rank and fought relentlessly before falling in battle. The Asokan edicts are also informative on these republics. They speak on republican territories like those of the *Yonas*, *Nabhaka*, *Nabha-panktis*, *Bhojas*, *Pitinikas*, *Andhras*, and *Paradas*, which are described as the "dominions of his majesty."[3]

These republican groups, as already mentioned, were so powerful that no body could just beat them. So strong was their solidarity and fraternity that even powerful monarchies could not defeat them quiet easily as revealed from the stories of Magadha-Lichhavis conflict or from the writings of Alexander's historians. Their council of administration consisted of representatives of different influential lord families and dynasties who formed a powerful clique. According to Kautillya in some republics of *Kambhoja* and *Saurashtra*, both military and trading classes (*Kshatriyas* and *Sréṇis*) shared power. Also there were rules and regulations about the conduct of the councilors. *Arthasastra* says that the councilor found guilty of misconduct and irresponsibility should be dismissed.

These republican governments were however not in the good books of monarchies or even the ideologies of statecraft, which favoured monarchical form of government. That they upheld the philosophy of freedom did not occur to the merciless monarchical theories of these political thinkers who advocated the idea of political unification under a powerful monarch. Typical monarchical hatred towards republics can thus be had from the writings of Chanakya who thought that republic is a thorn in the flesh of a state getting unified under the leadership of an ideal king. According to him the republics some times prove states within a state and hamper the unity of the empire. Of course, the Mauryan Empire allowed independent existence of republics, which accepted imperial supremacy. However the imperial policy referred to in *Arthasastra* was averse to independent existence of republics. Kautillya thus says, "Acquisition of a *sangha* is more desirable than an alliance of goodwill or military aid. Those which are united (in a league) should be treated with policy of subsidy and peace, for they are invincible. Those which are not united should be conquered by army and disunion." "In other words," says KP Jayswal, "the Mauryan policy was to allow an honourable existence to those republics which were strong and united in leagues (for these were difficult to be conquered). Those which were isolated were to be weakened by a policy of internal division and then reduced by force."[4] Perhaps to Chanakya, the idealist of unification, these small republics might have appeared stumbling blocks in the way towards a greater unity of the cultural location he dreamt to give cohesion and unity. He would not endorse the idea of a state within a state, as it would be inconsistent with the principle of sovereign constitution he endorses in his political treatise which envisions a monarchy sworn to protect democratic values and public interests.

But this would not underrate the importance of ancient Indian republics and democratic values they stood for. It is interesting to notice that K. P. Jayswal, the most noted writer on ancient Indian polity, dedicates his work on Hindu polity to the ancient Indian republics like Anus,

Dhruhyus and other ones who proclaimed the philosophy of freedom descending from Gods to the ordinary people. They were, no doubt, the early torchbearers of the ideals of freedom and self-Government, which have been the main characteristics of Indian polity down the centuries.

References

1. A.S. Altekar, *State and Government in Ancient India*, p. 127.
2. See Appendix - I.
3. Rock Edict - XIII.
4. K.P. Jayswal, *Hindu Polity*, Bangalore, 1924, p. 116.

5

Social Formations and Caste

Social scientists have interpreted historical developments variously. Some have focused more on the history of different formations in society down the centuries than other aspects. History of social formations in India as explained in line with the economic interpretation deals with such aspects as mode of production, theory of Surplus Value and class formation. According to Marxian school of thought, an interpretation on this line would help understand the real meaning and purpose of history.

In the long history of production there came up different aspects like 'elite', 'status', 'hierarchy', 'decision-making', etc. According to RS Sarma, it is always the surplus that sustains society. He says that it is the extra produce that supports the whole-time administrators, professional soldiers, full-time priests, craftsmen and other similar specialists who do not produce their food all by themselves. And the compulsion of an organized coercive authority made peasants to work for this extra produce. It is this surplus that "plays a key role in the formation of class and leads to the erection of an entirely new type of power structure called the state," says Sarma.[1] Idea of class is an integral part of the materialistic approach in history. While one class owns means of production, other is deprived of it. Dispossession of capital and denial of the fruits of production are the prelude to class formation. Those who control the fruits control the roots, too. Superior communities had control over producers' community like those of Sudras in ancient India. Having claims over the taxes and tithes from peasantry, the priests, and warriors' communities formed an upper class whose interests were always pitted against peasants' interests. Class conflicts basing on this difference must have surfaced in ancient India though the literature of the ages concerned, do not refer to them. In ancient India even intellectuals never got chances to develop their potential since intellect had to work and flower in line with certain social and economic situations.[2] Naturally, intellectuals became a submerged class whose ideas are "hardly articulated in ancient texts."

While developing his theory Sarma gets on with the Base-Super structure theory, which is relevant in Marxist discourse. Base means "factors of production including ecological environment which conditions human activities." "Superstructure means social and political arrangements that are based on these factors" of production. They serve to maintain, modify or alter the modes of production. Artistic, literary, ritualistic, philosophical and similar activities are considered to be ultimate products of the base. But Sarma says that "not everything is explained by adopting such a postulate" because of so many 'imponderables in history' and so many 'extra-super-structural' problems which he describes as 'enigmatic.' But he believes, this approach is still useful in historical studies.

It is interesting to notice Sarma's acknowledgement regarding the 'imponderables' and 'enigmas' of history, which the base-super-structure theory cannot explain. Meanwhile he says that this approach is still useful. But it is difficult for an ordinary intellect to believe in the utility of uselessness though Sarma believes otherwise! Besides, Marxian idea of Asiatic mode of production was not based on Karl Marx's direct knowledge of Indian condition or reading in any Indian literature directly. It is interesting that Marx never visited India nor read any ancient Indian text but studied about India through the descriptions of the British writers he loathed. Hence the necessity to enquire whether such a type of social formation as Sarma believes ever happened in ancient India.

In the history of ancient India we come across so many types of formations in society. Literature abounds in references to the social segregations based on different trades and occupations. Indeed trade was an important factor that determined the social status of a person. But this trade was not the monopoly of a particular social group though certain groups were traditionally engaged in some professions. *Ṛk Véda* never makes mention of any group as monopolizing a trade or any field of activity though it cannot be denied that certain classes of people were traditionally associated with some jobs. And at certain times professions the people followed resulted in the formation of new classes. For instance *Ṛk Véda* refers to the class of people called Panis who were carrying on trading activities abroad, especially in Mediterranean regions which was the trade emporium of Europe in ancient times. If to cite the opinion of A. Kalyana Raman, these Panis were the founders of the civilization of traders called Phoenicians on African coast. In Indian history one comes across the trading groups bearing similar names with similar meaning with only slight variations in pronunciations. Thus there are Vaniks, Baniya, Vaniya and the like groups engaged in trading activity in different parts of India. Probably they might be the descendents of the early trading group of India. But it can hardly be believed that Panis were a cloistered group tabooed and alienated from the rest of the society. It never formed a class all by itself, which was like a watertight compartment. *Ṛk Véda* indeed speaks of a classless society and extens its philosophy of philanthropy to all men alike. It envisions the ideal of *lōkāsamgraha* or holding together of all. In that classless society people of even same family followed different occupations irrespective of high and low status of job. Author of one of the hymns of *Ṛk Véda* refers to his family members as doing different professions unmindful of their caste.

The society described in *Ramayana* and *Mahabharata* is more or less similar to the early societies. By the time of *Itihasas* caste-based class difference was getting social imprimatur, which was, however, overlooked on innumerable occasions. There were formations of trading people moving all around. The fisher folk are specially mentioned, as are the flower sellers. There were goldsmiths, blacksmiths, stonecutters, sellers of gems and people with cattle-rearing profession. We come to hear of the community of cowherds. The terms like *gōpāla*, *gōkula*, *vraja*, etc, are worthy to be mentioned; and pastoral people, along with cattle rearing, practised agriculture, too, making them almost compatible. But here, too, professions were never the monopoly of certain classes. Though *Kshatriyas* were the traditional ruling class there were others who, crossing the borders of communities they were born in, took to different professions usually described as the monopoly of certain classes. Thus we hear that Sri Krishna though born of the community of cowherds, itself a part of the republican combine that ruled Mathura, became king of Dwaraka and king maker in the battle of Kurukshetra. Yadus formed an important ruling group among the republican formations headed by Vrishnis and Andhakas. Duryodhana was the son of Dhritarashtra, the son of Veda Vyasa, himself the son of a fisher woman, and even Krishna himself did not hesitate to say so when challenged in the open durbar. In an age when handling the lofty philosophy of *Vedas* and *Upanishads* by a *S'ūdra* was considered rather forbidden Sri Krishna made his sermon on the highest metaphysics : the *Gita*. Even *chaṇḍālas* had their own kingdoms, and the case of Guhak, king of the country of Sringivera referred to in Ramayana is a significant example. His devotion to Ram, the prince of Ayodhya, is of much celebrity. Eklavya, another nishada was well at home in the art of archery. And Drona, the Brahmin teacher in archery, denying Eklavya right to wield bow under the convenient excuse that Eklavya was lowborn only expresses his personal affection to Arjuna, his dearest ward whom he did not like to be second to any one. Thus in most cases caste was unimportant, often relegated to tertiary importance.

That spirituality and metaphysics were never monopolized by any particular community is testified to by examples of many *Kshatriyas* who were adepts in spiritual knowledge. Janaka Videha, the king of Mithila who initiated great scholars into *Brahmajñāna* or supreme knowledge about *Brahman* was *Kshatriya* by birth. It was Vyasa born of a fisher woman who collected, compiled and divided the *Vedas*, and composed the great *Itihasa*, the *Mahabharata*. Even to attain seer-hood there was no caste bar. Quiet often we come to see Brahmins as well as Kshatriyas becoming *Ṛshis* or seers unmindful of the caste they were born in. Besides, Manu says Brahmin is one who learns and teaches, performs *yajna* and makes others to do *Yajna* and moves in the world of Knowledge of Brahman or Supreme Being. *Varnadharma* is particularly emphasized. Manu makes certain duties obligatory on Brahmanas for the well being of humanity. Parasurama though born a Brahmin, mastered the art of archery and even annihilated Kshatriyas in many rounds and Drona the royal tutor of Kurus in *dhanurveda* or archery who denied knowledge of archery to Eklavya under the pretext that the latter was baseborn, was Brahmin by birth. Indeed it needs not to be said that there was not caste-based class. It would be relevant to remember the opinion of Sri Krishna in the *Gita* that *chāturvarṇya* is based on one's tastes and interests, and occupation one follows (*chāturvarṇyam mayāsrushṭam guṇakarma vibhāgaśa*). This philosophy of social life came from the one who combined in him all the pursuits: agriculture, cattle rearing, a higher political life with all the required scruples and tact, the highest knowledge as enunciated in *Gita* and what more. Trades never formed social classes though peoples of different trades had their own groups and formations.

In later literature there are references to occupational groups. *Arthaśāstra* speaks of *āṭavikas* and *śastrōpajīvasrēṇis* who took to warrior profession and formed themselves into a class of fighters. *Kautillya* opines that soldiers recruited from this class were most heroic.[3] The republican community of *Yaudhēyas* continued to be professional fighters during the time of *Kautillya* and Panini.[4] Trade groups thus formed separate classes. It is interesting to notice that even a particular trade group in early times got themselves divided into two basing on slight difference related to the techniques they adopted in their work. Radha Kamal Mukherji cites the instance of oil squeezing people who got themselves into two groups, because one group employed the use of bullocks for pulling machine while the other worked it out manually. There are people with identical group names like medieval Nayaks and Naidus of Andhra, Naiks of Tamilnadu and Nairs of Kerala with more or less same social status in their respective states and times. But these were never the castes or classes of the kind Marx believed or Sarma opines. They had nothing to do with 'race' concepts, too, which European historians and sociologists equate with *vamsa. Vamsa* in Sanskrit means bamboo, which shoots and branches off from the same root. It is genetic group, not the race of European concept. Any interpretation of ancient Indian condition or concept, applying European parameters can only misinterpret.

Early literature of India refers to *Jāti, Varṇa* etc. However, the exact connotations of these words have not still been agreed upon by scholars of Indology. The Four *Vedas, Brahmanas, Dharmas'astras, Puranas* and *Itihasas* refer to various social systems and institutions among which the fourfold division of society looms important. This division of society into *Brahmanas, Kshatriyas, Vaisyas* and *Sudras* seems to have been a later development. *Ṛk Véda*, the earliest of Indian literatures, never generalizes caste as a social institution. Only once it refers to the emergence of *Brāhmaṇa, Kshatriya, Vaiśya* and *Śūdra* from the *Purusha* or the supreme God. This according to many scholars including Swami Dayananda and Sri Aurobindo is the symbolic interpretation that God manifests as knowledge, physical protection, wealth and service. More over these divisions again answer to four cosmic principles, "the wisdom that conceives the order and principle of things, the power that sanctions, upholds and enforces it, the harmony that creates arrangements of its parts, the work that carries out what the rest directs."[5] Even if it is otherwise, a single instance cannot be generalized. Also there is more than one instance in *Ṛk Véda* to point out that no kind of social division prevented people crossing over to other social sections or doing work generally assigned to a particular group. One author of a *Ṛk Vedic* hymn, as mentioned above, says that his father is a physician (*bhishak*), mother grinds corn (*upala-prākshiṇi*) and he is a poet-seer (*kāru*, or 'maker of hymns') and speaks of the differences of mental aptitudes and occupations (*nā nānam dhīyō vartāni janānām*) like those of the carpenter (*thaksha*), physician (*bḥishak*) or learned man (*Brahmaṇa*).[6] The Véda recognizes the creativity of the Sudra's work by calling him a *kavi* or poet and *dhīra*, a sage.[7] Yajur Veda finds divinity in all irrespective of their caste difference and prays seeking brilliance for all types of workers: "Give luster to our *Brāhmaṇas, Rājanyas, Vaiśyas* and *Śudras* ..." It is clearly implied that one cannot pursue divinity in isolation and definitely this is why the Veda prescribes *brahmacharya* or path to Brahman or highest knowledge for all growing youth, boys and girls, irrespective of their parents' professions. There are again many references to inter-caste marriages and inter-dining without any fear of social ostracism. *Ṛk Véda* refers to the term *Daṣa* or *Dasyu,* which means servant. Neither word connotes caste. This is only the meaning of the term *Dasa* or *Dasyu* taken in ordinary sense. But *Ṛk Véda*, which uses the word about 86 times, at times giving a lofty meaning to it, does not subscribe even to this. The *Dasyus* are called *anyavrata, amānusha, ayajvān* and *adēvayu.* The word *amānusha* indicates that the *Dasyus* were not human beings. *Anyavrata* means those observing alien or non-Vedic rites or no rites, *adēvayu*, godless and *ayajvān*, non-sacrificer.[8] Some time adjectives like *akarmaṇaḥ* and *abrahma* are used to denote the *Dasyus.*[9] *Ṛk Veda* is highly vocal on the non-human or superhuman character of the *Dasyus* who are referred to as of non-earthly regions. According to one statement Indra-Dasyu conflict occurred at beyond the earthly regions while in another context it is said that Indra burnt the Dasyus in heaven and that thanks to Indra killing the Dasyus water and sun were released.[10] These make it clear that Dasyus were non-human and non-earthly obstructers of light and water whom Indra did away with to bring light and water to earth.

Of course it is true that people were following different trades and professions. But this never channeled the society to organize itself into caste formations. People followed different professions according to their interests and ability. One could thus peruse in ancient Indian literature the prevalence of something similar to division of labour, which might have led to trade and profession-based social formations.

In the other *Védas* and allied literature like *Smrutis* and *Upanishads* the words denoting social divisions abound too much. According to them the *dharmas* differ from group to group. True, the term *varna* has different meanings like colour, letter etc. *Chāturvarṇya* system according to some interpretations means the different stages in chanting the *mantra* or magic spell. Again Goddess Saraswati is described as the embodiment of *varna* (*varṇavigraha*) or letter. Besides, one is bound to think that how such a heinous system as *varṇa* which distinguishes man from man can come compatible with *asrama* system expected to discipline and perfect human life. It can thus be presumed that the system of *varṇa* must have developed side by side with *asrama* to perfect social life. *Varṇa* was indeed one of the types early India developed to guideline society. Thus we come to hear of *varṇadharmas* prescribed by *dharmas'āstras*. Accordingly each *varṇa* was assigned a particular duty or *dharma*. It was also not unoften that a person belonging to a certain *varṇa* by observing the duty of another *varṇa* identified himself as of the latter. True, Brahmin learnt and taught, Kshatriya ruled and fought, Vaisya went on with his economic pursuit and Sudra with his manual labour. But instances abound which tell that people performed many duties irrespective of *varṇa* differences. They crossed over from one occupation to the other.

There were also cases of inter-caste marriages. Though the lawgivers of different times speak about certain *varṇa* rules to be followed in marriages the same jurists allow inter-caste marriages, too. Thus Manu and Yajnavalkya prescribe *anulōma* (high caste groom marrying low caste woman) system though they proscribe the reverse (*pratilōma*). Instances abound. Stories of marriage between Santanu and Satyavati or the like are well known. Thus in almost all walks of life caste was not strictly binding. Criss-crossing caste borders continued all throughout Vedic times.

It is however believed that caste system became more rigid during post-Vedic age and that caste rigidities led to the birth of new religions in India. But to ascertain this argument literature or archaeology does not give any clue. Here, too, the picture remained almost same. There were different professions, which people followed unmindful of their caste and birth. According to *Mahavams'a*, Mauryas were peacock tamers,

Mayūrapōshakas or *Mōriyas.* Literature makes mention of Chandragupta Maurya as born of the Moriya Kshatriya community (*mōriyāṇam khātiyaṇ ām vams'e' jātam*). All the Jain canonical texts mention Moriyas as being engaged in peacock taming. It is thus interesting to note that the first imperial family of India belonged to a group doing Vaisya job. In scholastic and spiritual pursuit there was no caste preference. Saints and scholars were recognized irrespective of caste and birth. Even if there was any barring the Buddhist Order overlooked it with the result that people belonging to any caste could take to asceticism. There was no caste prerogative. Before law every one was equal. *Kautillya* says that any one found guilty of treason should be severely punished even if he is a Brahmin. The reign of Mauryas contributed to a feeling of equality. Emperor Asoka recruited persons belonging to all castes to the department of *Dharmamahāmātras* or ministers of charity. Following this, there came the age of Sankaracharya. This sage from Kalady in Kerala who propagated the teaching of *advaita* or monism could not see any difference between man and man. To him all human beings were the manifestations of the same *Brahman* or God. Hence his emphasis on *varṇadharmas* or duties of different people. It is *dharma* that licenses *varṇa* or that *varṇa* is based on the *dharma* one performs, he believed. *Dharma* and *karma* are both compatible and identical with each other. Sankara thus once again took Indian society back to its old moorings, where Srikrishna, its high priest, declares that *varṇa* is based on interest, taste and duty performed. The society thus lived in line with the rules of *varṇa* as told in *Dharmasastra.* It would therefore be erroneous to hold that caste was highly rigid and that it hampered the emergence of a civilized society. Caste never stood in the way of cultural or spiritual progress of ancient Indian society.

It was indeed through the path set by early ages later Indian society moved. *Chāturvarṇya* ruled the society, and people belonging to various social groups went on with their different professions. As usual changes were brought in according to changing attitude of the times. And it is found that Sudras and even Brahmins took to agricultural activities. New occupational groups, too, added to existing social divisions. It is said that Vardhanas and Gupta rulers were vaisyas. Likewise Maratha Pewshwas were of the Brahmin stock. Cheras, Cholas and Pandyas are said to be of Vellala origin. Even from the early Sangham period there was no rigid caste system in South India. Indeed the great poets like Paranar, Kapilar, Nakirar and Kannanar who sang and sublimated the age belonged to lower castes. It is also interesting to note that Brahmins ate meat and drank toddy without any fear of social ostracism during the Sangham age. The Naiks of Madhura were traders by caste. A Sanskrit inscription of AD 5th century speaks about the silk weavers who took to different trades and castes in course of their migration to Gwalior. Indeed as time elapsed many of the caste privileges plummeted, and from medieval period onwards Brahmin predominance declined. Assimilation became more pronounced than before.

The religious upheaval of Maharashtra in 13th century AD and after brought about sweeping changes. The age produced saints and scholars in Sudra community. Non-Brahmin saints like Namadev and Tukkaram were renowned religious teachers. Brahmin saints like Jnanesvar and Eknath discarded Brahmin prerogative in spiritual field. Kabir sang, "It is needless to ask a saint the caste to which he belongs". Many of the Brahmins, crossing religious barricades, came out to serve the downtrodden. The spiritual leaders like Ramanuja took bold steps to improve the social and spiritual condition, of people. The story of Kanakadasa is well known. Also in later times there sprang from the outcaste, leaders who took up social reform as their mission. Indian society thus through the centuries presented almost the same scenario. It is as Sardar KM Panikker very rightly puts: "The society described in the Mahabharata is not different from what exists in India today".

References

1. R.S. Sarma, *Material Culture and Social Formations in Ancient India*, Bombay, 2000, Introduction, p. XVII.
2. *Ibid.*
3. *Kautillya*, VIII. 14.
4. R. K. Mukherji, *Chandraguptha Maurya and His Times*, Delhi, 1988, p. 23.
5. Sri Aurobindo, *The Human Cycle, The Ideal of Human Unity, War and Self-Determination*, Pondicherry, 1985, p. 6.
6. *Ṛk Ve'da*, IX, 112. 3.
7. *Ibid*, III. 17. 1.
8. *Ibid*, VIII. 70. 81
9. *Ibid*, IV. 16. 9.
10. *Ibid*, I. 100. 18.

6

Education

No society could be described as educated as that of the Vedas, which paved the very foundations of all educational and cultural developments India achieved down the millennia. *Véda* itself means Knowledge. *Véda*, *vid*, *dyo*, *dyuti*, *déva*, etc., have the same root which means education, knowledge, light, enlightenment, the shining one, etc., In fact the very aim of education was the attainment of knowledge and enlightenment and finally Supreme light, the divine. All the Vedic literature is replete with references to educational accomplishment of the time, and the end of Vedic education was to lead man from darkness to light and from mortality to immortality.

It is desirable to start with the ideals of education, teacher taught relations and the idea of supreme *guru* who was deemed supreme God. It is also interesting to note that a direct communication and intimacy between teacher and disciple was essential for proper imparting of knowledge. It also points to the highly secret and intuitive nature of teaching that should be imparted only to an earnest student worthy of receiving it. A true aspirant of knowledge would spend the whole life span, if required to attain supreme wisdom from the teacher. The story of Indra and Virocana who approached Prajapati for self knowledge narrated in *Chhandogya Upanishad*, of Satyakamajabala who as directed by his guru Gautama looked after four hundred cows whose number he increased to a thousand through years' effort and also Upakosala who approached

Satyakama who initiated him into a twelve years preliminary discipline are clear examples of the test of earnestness in knowledge conducted by the teachers before imparting the supreme knowledge.[1] Indra spent about hundred years of celibacy before Prajapati imparted to him divine knowledge. Criteria of accepting disciples, too, were based on a sense of equality. The student could be of any age, caste, sex or profession and might be a *brahmachari* or an ascetic, a king, a housewife, god, and even an *asura* or one born of the family of demons. So also the teachers, too, could be kings like Janaka, Ajatasatru, gods or goddesses like Indra, Yama and Uma, or learned ladies like Gargi and Maitreyi. This suggests that Upanishadic Sheers believed in equality and unity of humanity and in the divinity inherent in all men irrespective of mundane differences. It was all the more a divine relation based on principles and their unfailing practice. The programme of academic give and take was marked with perfect mutual love and reverence. Teacher and the taught, seeker and the sought, subtle and the gross, all are thus presented in their perfect harmony in Upanishadic scene.

Guru was nothing other than *brahma* and student or *brahmachāri* was the one living and moving in the supreme spirit. Likewise the earthly *guru* or teacher was looked reverentially as the incarnation of God. Teacher-taught relation was thus a God-soul relation in miniature. The student in ancient times was wholly the product of the teacher who was both the father and mother in his rebirth into the world of knowledge. This process is called *upanayana* or bringing one near to one's own inner and informing ultimate knowledge which is sublime, sacred and highly spiritual. *Atḥarva Véda* thus says:

āchārya upanayamāṇō brahmachāriṇam kruṇuté
garbhatamanta tam rātrīstrīsra udaré bibharti
tamha jātam drashṭum abhisamyanti dévāḥ[2]

The teacher or *Acharya* conceives his disciple in his womb of knowledge [Sayanacharya translates this as *vidyāśarīrasya madhyé* or at the center of teacher's knowledge body or the teacher's supreme knowledge] Teacher then keeps him three days there. When he comes out after having lived in his teacher's womb of knowledge Gods descend to earth to see him.

Thus initiation performed by *āchārya* or teacher with the injunctions of *Sruti* makes him a Brahmana or Brahmachari. According to Manu, in the second birth that comes through *upanayana* or initiation *Sāvitri* is the mother and *āchārya* the father to the *dwija* or *brahmachari.*

tatra yat brahmajanmāsya maunjībandhana chihnitam
tatrāsya mātāsāvitrī pitātvāchārya uchyate[3]

Thus thanks to his teaching Vedas to disciple the Guru becomes father to the disciple in his second birth to the world of knowledge.

védapradānādāchāryam pitaram parichakshate[4]

The teacher thus fathers him in his whole life of knowledge. Hence the relevance of the lore advising students to look to their master with as much reverence and service as one does to his father. The scriptures suggest a highly ethical code of conduct, which the disciple is expected to observe in his relations to the master, too. They were particular that education should not be given to the undeserving and to those who do not seek after it. "Even in times of dire distress a teacher of *Veda* should rather die with his knowledge than sow it in a barren soil," says Manu.[5] Manu refers to the story of sacred knowledge i.e. Goddess of learning who approached the scholarly Brahmin and said: "I am your treasure, preserve me, deliver me not to a scorner who is envious to all. If you preserve me thus I shall be supremely strong. But deliver me as to the keeper of your treasure, to a Brahmana who you shall know to be pure, of subdued senses, chaste and attentive."

vidyābrāhmaṇamétyāha sévadhishṭésmi raksha mām
asūyakāya mām mādāstadḥā syām vīryavatta mā.[6]
yamēva tu śuchim vidyānniyatam brahmachāriṇam
tasmaimām brūhi viprāya nidhipāya pramādine.[7]

Therefore, what was needed as precondition for Vedic education was the development of a life wedded to ethics and disciplines, and hence the scriptural prescription regarding certain moral codes a student was bound to observe. Even in acquisition of knowledge scriptures prescribe noble means. One should not take knowledge from a teacher without his know and permission lest it should incur the guilt of stealing *Veda* and shall sink him into hell. A student shall reverentially salute the teacher from whom he receives material and spiritual knowledge. A Brahmana who is completely in control of his senses, though he knows *Savitri* only, is better than he who knows the three Vedas, but does not control himself, eats all sorts of food and sells all sorts of goods. Character formation rather than acquisition of vast and highly informative knowledge was held in esteem, and education was considered to manifest itself in man's perfection. It may be taken that education bereft of noble qualities and moral and ethical standards was always looked down upon just as the one who, though educated, was immoral. It is interesting that the later Kamandakiya *Nītisāra* abhorred an educated but immoral man, who, it opined, should be kept at a distance (*śūdramaksharasamyuktam dūratā parivarjayét*). The student was to respect and attend to the needs of his teacher and salute him. According to Manu he who habitually salutes and constantly pays reverence to the aged obtains an increase in longevity, knowledge, fame and strength (*āyurvidyā yaśō balam*).[8] Apastambha and Baudhayana also hold the same.[9] Manu was also to extend utmost respect to the fair sex, addressing her with reverence-filled words like *bhavati* (respected lady), *subhaga* (beautiful and blessed) and *bhagini* (beloved sister), and this must be observed particularly to a female who is wife of another man and also one who is not a blood relation. Likewise he was to respect the wife of his teacher who was to be looked on with as much reverence and salute her as towards his mother. Manu again prevailed upon the *brahmachāri* or the student to honour a maternal aunt, wife of a maternal uncle, a mother-in-law and paternal aunt. He was to respect the wife of elder brother, touching her feet in reverence on the eve of any auspicious occasion including a journey, and consider his elder sister like his mother. In fact the disciplines and practices a student was to undergo at the feet of his teacher sufficed to transform his very life. It was really a rebirth.

This rebirth makes the student a *dwija* or twice-born. Described as *brahmachārin*, he guards the earth, heaven and the entire world with his *tapas* or meditative power. In him the Gods are harmonized.[10] Even he is referred to as carrying the streaming effulgence of *brahman* into which all Gods are woven.[11] The most common system of education was *gurukula* wherein students had their schooling at the house of the teacher so that the former got all-round care and attention of the teacher in all walks of life. Unlike modern school system wherein the teacher does not get adequate time to cater to the student's all-round growth, in *gurukula*, which was residential, teacher could attend to the versatile growth of the disciple. It was for the teacher to ring out darkness from his disciple's mind and ring in infinite light. *gu* in Sanskrit is a one-letter word, which means darkness or ignorance, and *ru* means that which obstructs or does away with darkness. Thus *guru* is one who eradicates ignorance and enlightens. *Guru* or *acharya* was a daily practitioner of his knowledge who turned his life itself into his message, which his disciples were expected to imbibe and emulate. Therefore the teacher by his own holy life or *brahmacharya* sought the *brahmachārin* or disciple.[12] *Āchārya* was bound to keep himself on the path of observance or *ācharana*. The lore thus defines an *acharya*:

āchinōti hi śāstrāṇi
hichāré sthāpayatyapi
svayamācharatéchāpi
tasmādāchārya uchyate.

> Along with imparting to students the spiritual knowledge he has imbibed, the teacher sees his disciples strictly observing and practising it. But for this the teacher, too, must continue to move in his spiritual path. He alone is called a real *āchārya*.

Observing in line with the spiritual tradition is *dharma* and what is opposite is *adharma* or irreligion. Therefore the greatest duty or *dharma* of the *āchārya* is to observe great values in his own life so that his life itself would be a role model for his disciples to follow. A teacher cannot force on his pupils what he himself does not observe. Thus through strict observance and disciplining the teacher was to attain a higher plane of mental and spiritual maturity so as to lead the entire society in its pilgrimage to knowledge. The teacher was thus considered the incarnation of God or earthly God. Hence the Ṛk Vedic address *āchārya dévō bhava.*

Early method of teaching seems to have been oral, and Vedic hymns (*mantra*) were only chanted rather than written. They were handed down from generation to generation by words of mouth, lest phonetic errors should creep in. Pronunciation was much stressed since Vedic hymn was the harmonious conglomeration of sacred syllables and letters, each an abstract carrying a definite meaning. The word *akshara* meant that which has no destruction (*kshara*), and hence infinite. Letters were thus symbols of the eternal, the divine and therefore they were to be pronounced with all perfection, which the divine called for. We may also take for instance another Vedic notion that the Goddess Saraswati was the symbol of knowledge and was eulogized as *varṇavigraha* or the icon of vowels (*varṇa*). Therefore the divine should not be pronounced fallaciously and the Vedic Sheer or *mantradrashṭa* insisted on phonetic accuracy. It is interesting to note that Vedic seers had already fixed certain laws that would preserve the purity of the Vedic chants against the changes or corruptions in time. Thus the technique *pada-pāṭha* (word-text) by which "every single word is shown in its independent and phonetically unmodified form and compounds are separated into their elements" and *karma-pāṭha* (Step-text) which emphasized that where every word of *pada-pāṭha* appears it should be pronounced twice i.e. both after the preceding, and before, the following one. Full scheme of Vedic recitation thus finally led to development of many distinctive forms, ensuring preservation of Vedic texts and their verbal purity.[13] Jaimini in his *Pūrva-mīmamsa sūtra* mentions the *vākyaniymāt* according to which Vedic recitation must be in the prescribed manner because the slightest lapse in pronunciation of Vedic *mantra* would be ruinous to those who recite them.[14] But a mere recitation would not suffice. More important was the contemplation and comprehension of the meaning of the text recited and *Ṛk Véda* often condemned and ridiculed such *dilettantish* and blasphemous approach to mere recitation without a clear insight into it. *Ṛk Véda* refers to the value of such contemplation, which enlightens the Brahmana, and holds that out of contemplation comes the *vāk* or speech or the word, which is God himself. Descending from the highest plain of ultimate knowledge *vāk* or speech takes different steps like *para, paśyanti,* and *madhyama* to the world of man where it is called *vaikhari* or audible speech. *Para,* the stage of sound remaining as *jyōtirūpa* or *paramarūpa* is the supreme stage of bliss. *paśyanti* and *madhyama* are second and third stages of sound's evolution. Inaudible to ordinary senses, sound in these stages becomes a part of realization or experience or *darśana,* supreme vision accessible to men of highest spiritual faculty. Finally it is *vaikhari* or sound in the plain of ordinary human beings. Different expressions and stages of sound or *vāk* are those through which supreme energy or *parāśakti* comes down to the world of man as sound (*parāpratyak chitīrūpā paśyantī paradévatā madhyamā vaikharīrūpā bhaktamānasahamsikā*). To realize these different stages of the *vāk* percolating down to ordinary level one must be a real ascetic, a *yōgi.* The real meaning of the *Veda* would always remain far from comprehension so long as one is bound by sense organs.[15] Yaska disparages mere reciting the *Veda* without knowing its meaning. He endorses the view of *Samhitopanishad Brahmana* that he who studies *Veda* without sensing its real purport is like an ass carrying the load of sandalwood without enjoying its fragrance (*sthāṇurayam bhārahāra*) and opines that learning without understanding is called cramming and would be like dry wood on ashes that would never blaze.[16] The process of learnin g again involved *ayan, avindan, abhritya, adadhu,* i.e. attainment, mastery, collection and propagation of words known only to *Ṛshis* or Vedic Sheers who brought them to the learned assemblies. *Ṛk Véda* makes mention of the assemblies where scholars united in fellowship of Vedic learning, deliberated on and developed further the knowledge they realized.[17] "The highest stage of education is represented in what are called the Brahmana-Sanghas, the Assemblies or Academies where the more successful students flocked together, as we have seen, for the advancement of knowledge by discussing their respective contributions to it. Thus the conference method for the promotion and diffusion of learning, the method of discussion in seminars and academies, was first evolved in India, as evident from *Ṛk Véda*," says R.K. Mookerji.[18] Consequently suitable methods were developed to conserve and teach the coming generations this sacred knowledge. Vedic hymns were thus committed to memory and recited in the form of meters, stressing every letter, syllable and word in line with the rules of accent so that every sound vibrates to express its inner sense. Verbal stress was cared much, and hence the chanting of the Vedic hymn. Thus the young ones chanted Vedic hymns in repetition after their teacher as referred to in one hymn that alludes to the frog in rainy season which "repeats the word of another like students echoing the voice of the teacher" forming a chorus when they loudly croak.[19] Vedic education, as noted earlier, was wholly spiritual, and its final aim was to know the ultimate reality, the *Brahman.* Naturally the student was referred to as *Brahmachāri* or one who lives and moves in the *Brahman.*[20] It seemed that children of many families had their fathers as teachers and children of these families taking lessons along with those of the neighbouring families were not rare. Just as the attainment of the ultimate enlightenment, sharpening of intellect and character development, too, were aimed at as seen from the *Gāyatri* verse invoking grace of *Savitṛ* or Sun god to stimulate and sublimate the intellect - *dhīyō yōna prachōdayāt.*

Subjects of learning ranged from high spirituality to ordinary material science, all forming parts of Vedas. Knowledge in totality was called *Brahmavidya*, which was ever broadening and was divided into *ātmavidya* or spiritual knowledge and *bhūtavidya* or knowledge of matter. The former was called *vidya* and the latter *avidya* and their harmonious rendezvous made life perfect (*vidyām chāvidyām cha yastad védōbhayam saha*).[21]

First it was the study of the Vedas which loomed important, and the rules that help learn them constituted another class of literature called

Védangas. Vedas could not be pronounced the way one liked since it would do away with the inner substance and exact meaning of *Sruti.* Hence the set rules by different seats of Brahmanical learning for pronouncing and understanding Vedas. Thus the *Védangas,* which are six in number, were formulated. Earliest reference to their number as six, is found in *Shadvimśa Brāhmana* of *Sāma Véda.* Similar references are found in *Mundakopanishad* also.[22] Manu, too, speaks of the *shadangavid* or scholar in *shadangas* (six limbs of the Vedas) or *Védāngas.*[23] Composed for the most part in *Sutra* (aphoristic) style, they are ascribed to authors known as *sūtrakāras* or *sūtra* authors.

Among *vedangas, siksha* comes first. Earliest reference to *Siksha* or phonetics appears in *Taittiriya Upanishad,* which refers to the six elements that constitute it like *varṇa* (individual sound), *svara* (accent), *mantra* (quantity), *bala* (organs of pronunciation), *saman* (delivery) and *santana* (euphonic laws). Later there developed the *pratiśākhya* literature or treatises formally embodying peculiarities of accent, *krama* or the order of reading vowels and separation of words. *Pratiśākhya,* literally means 'belonging to each *śākha* or branch' *śākha* denotes a particular tradition setting recessional style. As important as *śākha* was *carana,* the body of people with wider curriculum, which included texts like law books, too. There were also the *parishads* or assemblies of the Brahmanas competent to give decisions on all points regarding phonetic rules. *Śiksha* or phonetics evolved later into more perfection and we come across a number of *Śishas* like *paṇinīya śiksha, manḍavi śiksha, siddhānta śiksha, yājñāvalkya śiksha, samana śiksha, narada śiksha,* etc. In number they come up to around sixty-five in all.

Next was *Nirukta* or etymology. Student of Vedas along with reciting its verses had to learn the origin and history of words and their meanings. *Nirukta* ascribed to Yaskacharya states that "without this science there can be no understanding of Vedic *mantras.*" But it may not be construed that Yaska's *Nirukta* was the maiden attempt on this line. There was an older list of Vedic words called the *Nikhantu* or *Nikhantuka,* which illustrates each word with the help of a Vedic passage. *Yaska* himself mentions Sakapuni, an earlier *Niruktakāra* whose line must have started the branch of etymology the time Vedas began to be chanted. Vedic literature offers as many as 600 etymologized words. The *Samhitas* of *Sukla Yajur Véda, Brahmanas* like *Satapatha* and *Aitaréya, Āranyakas* like *Aitaréya* and *Upanishads* like *Brahadāraṇyaka* and *Chhandogya* contain synonymous expressions, explanation of one word by another and contextual explanations of all verses and hymns. Myths and legends were also employed to throw light into the derivation of different words so as to make them less dry to the Vedic students and priests. The study of phonetic and semantic history of words stressed the value of both sound and sense. This often led to the understanding of semantic changes that gave rise to metaphor and transference. A look into the phonetic similarity between words of the same language as well as different languages helped a good deal in etymology (e.g. *angarā angiras; purisaya purusa*). Etymology helped studying the history, too, of many things. Often a word's root and meaning would be studied to ascertain whether they agree together and fall in line with grammatical rules. Some times words were explained through their resemblance to the verbal and nominal form of a root. For instance, "*hasta* (a hand) should be derived not from *has*, 'to laugh', apparent in it, but from *han*, 'to strike', because the hand is quick at striking"[24]. While explaining an obscure Vedic word etymologists even resorted to imagination to suggest a number of roots to get clue to the sense. Thus psychological means, too, were of great importance if they would help derive the exact meaning of words since meaning or *artḥa* was the principal element to which all other elements stood second. *Nirukta* also helped the Brahmanical schools define a word (*nirvachana*) as well as many spiritually important abstracts of Vedas.

Vyakaraṇa was another branch of knowledge essential to the study of Vedas. In case of *védānga vyākaraṇa* there were a number of scholars during Vedic time. Panini, whose work was a culmination of grammatical studies of early times makes mention of about sixty-four grammarian predecessors like Apisali, Kasakritsna, Gargya, Bharadvaja, Senaka, Sphotayana, etc. Vedic literature refers to parts of speech, analysis of speech, speculations on letters and speech and terms like *akshara*, *varṇa*, *vachana* and *vibhakti*, etc. *Satapatḥa Brāhmaṇa* differentiates between singular and plural and Chandogya Upanishad classifies letters and technical terms. *Samhita* texts of Vedas were reduced to *pada-pāṭha*, which exhibited each word with its grammatical analysis and distinguished the four parts of speech - noun (*nāman*), verb (*ākhyāta*), preposition (*upasarga*), and particle (*nipāta*), and separate parts of compounds, prefixes and suffixes. *Sarvanāman* or pronoun also occurs in Vedic literature. According to scholars Patanjali's commentary on the terms like *dhātu, upasarga, avyaya, samāsa, tatpurusha, bahuvrīhi, dvandva, karmadhārayan, anunāsika, lōpa, hrasva, dīrgha,* etc., infer that these terms already existed. It may thus be concluded that grammar was an important subject of study during Vedic times.

Another limb that helped study the Vedas was *chhandas* or metrics. Authors of *Ṛk Véda* were well at home in the art of metrical expression and they could cast such fine poetic moulds for their expressions of the ultimate truth as to impart the hearer a celestial experience. Hence the poetic beauty of Vedic chants. *Ṛk* was the *yōni* (womb) whence came the *sāman* (tune or melody), which made sound musical and dulcet. To those ancient bards poetry bereft of music was meaningless since it could not impart to the hearer the message of the infinite. Poetry was to them, if to quote Sri Aurobindo, not a mere dancing girl of mind but a priestess appointed in God's house not to spin fictions but to image the hard and secret realities deriving from the mystic vision. And the music consisting of *swarasthānas* or dwelling places of Gods should be so beautifully couched as to carry the loftiest of such truths, reducing the intensity of its abstractness, to hearers. Naturally the bards often designed new meters required to give poetic mould to their innumerable compositions. Technical names used in later times for meters like *gāyatri, ushṇi, anushṭubh, bruhati,* and *virāṭ* had already been mentioned in the *Ṛk Véda. Gāyatri* is said to have originated from *agni, ushṇi* from *Savithṛ, anushṭubh* from *Sōma, bruhathi* from *Brahaspati* and *virāt* from *Mitravaruna.* Indra created the most used meter *trishṭubh* and Viswadevas the *jagati.* Vedic seers believed that harmony and charming rhythm of meters are mystically and mysteriously the fundamental cause of world's harmony. Like the universal soul created the harmony of the world, word power too which is the outcome of universal spirit put in an orderly manner contributes to the universal harmony and fundamental unity. According to *Śatapatḥa Brahmana, Prajapati* among his various creations caused the birth of meters, too.[25] *Gāyatri,* the *Śatapatḥa Brahmana* says, soars up in the form of a bird to the world of celestials and fetches *Sōma,* the nectar of immortal bliss or the divine *ānanda. Gāyatri* is here the vehicle that carries down to terrestrial plain the sweetness of musical notes that God the Master Poet pants forth. Bird was often to the mystic bards a symbol that conveyed to man the message from a higher plain, a blithe spirit, as it appeared to an English poet, which pours down in profuse strains "a flood of rupture so divine."[26] In *Brahmanas* as well as *Upanishads* one comes across innumerable speculations on the mystical significance of meters.

Brahadaranyaka Upanishad thus says: "The words *bhūmi*, *antariksha* and *dyu* (pronounced as *diyu*) make up eight syllables; *Gāyatri pāda* consists of eight syllables; therefore he who knows the *Gāyatri* gains control of the whole world." Inquiries into the beginning of the science of metrics often led to formulation of the principles of versification, too. So divine were they to Vedic bards that they raised them to the position of deities to be adored with sacrifices. Texts abound in their references to the *Chhandas*. Last three *Patalas* (chapters) of Saunaka's *sākalapratyaksha* describes about the meters while *Nidāna Sūtra* of *Sāma Véda* refers to various aspects of this musical *Véda*, like *ukta*, *sthōma* and *gāna*. *Ṛk Véda* consists of the *chhandōnukramaṇi* (index on *chhandas*), enumerating the meters of *Ṛk Védic* hymns and the numbers of meters in each hymn. We have also the *sarvōnukramaṇi* (general index) which contains metrical *pādas*. *Anukramaṇi* or index of *Sukla Yajur Véda*, attributed to Katyayana, consists in its fifth section a brief account of meters found in that *Véda*.

Another important branch of study, the science that helped Vedic people in calculating time and position of stars and planets was *Jyōtisha Védānga*. *Jyōtisha* as taught by Lagadha speaks of 36 verses in the *Ṛk Védic* recension and 43 in the *Yajur Vedic* with 30 common to both. *Atharvaṇa Jyōtisha* that dealt with *muhūrta* (a particular division of time), *karaṇa* (an astrological division of day), *yōga* (leading star of a lunar asterism; a variable division of time), *titi* (lunar day) and *vāra* (week day) was a noted branch of *jyōtisha*. It dealt with *jataka* (astrology), too. It helped select time and place for sacrifices by determining the *solstice* position of sun and moon, and of the latter in the circle of twenty seven *Nakshatras* or star-groups of zodiac. Vedic hymns betray an accurate knowledge of the months, seasons and year required to regulate sacrificial ceremonics. They refer to the conduct of *satras*, which lasted for one year in line with sun's yearly course divided into two sessions of six months between which came *vishuvat*, the equatorial day dividing the whole *satra* into two halves. The *Brāhmaṇa* passages identify the *samvatsara* (year meant the cycle wherein all the seasons dwell) with sacrifice, and elsewhere reference is made to *ṛt-vij* (*ṛtūyaj* or one who performs the season sacrifice). Vedic literature mentions solar year also. "The adjustment of the lunar year to the solar year was effected either by adding the intercalary month every two or three years, as *Ṛk Véda*, I.25.8 shows, or by the insertion of twelve (intercalary) nights at the close of the lunar year, as is suggested by the *Ṛk Véda*, IV.33.7, which tells us that the *Ṛbhus* (the genii of the seasons) slacken their course and rest with the sun for twelve nights at the end of the year."[27] *Brihadaranyaka* and *Chhandogya* Upanishads equate *dévāyana* to the six months of solar movement starting from vernal equinox.[28] There are references to solar eclipses of which one was total as observed by sage *Atri.* The later part of Atḥarva *Véda* enumerates the lunar mansions by name. *Védas* again refer to such names as *nakshtradarśa* and *gaṇaka* for astronomers. The five year time unit is mentioned as *yuga* in *Taittiriya Brāhmaṇa* and it speaks of the names of months derived from seasons, namely *madhu* and *mādhava. Śatapatḥa Brāhmaṇa* again refers to *Krittika* (Pleiades) as the starting point of the *nakshatra* series as opined by Bal Gangadhara Tilak who takes the *Śatapatḥa Brāhmaṇa* passage *krittikā ha vai prāchyai diśōna chyavante* as "*krittika* rose due to the east." All these speak aloud of the heights the age attained in astronomical and mathematical knowledge.

References

1. *Chhandogya Upanishad*, 8.7, 4.4.1 - 4.15.6.
2. *Atharva Véda*, XI. 5. 3.
3. *Manu*, II. 170.
4. *Ibid*, II. 171.
5. *Ibid*, II. 113.
6. *Ibid*, II. 114.
7. *Ibid*, II. 115.
8. *Ibid*, II. 121.
9. *Apastambha.* I, 5, 15; *Baudhayana.* I, 3, 26.
10. *Atharva Veda*, XI. 5. 8.
11. *Ibid*, XI. 5. 24, 25.
12. *Ibid*, XI. 5, 17.
13. Radha Kumud Mookerji, *Ancient Indian Education*, Delhi, 1974, p. 21.
14. *Jaimini*, I, 2, 32.
15. *Ṛk Véda.* I, 164, 37.
16. *Nirukta*, i, 18. Quoted in RK Mookerji, *Op. Cit*, p. 31.
17. *Ṛk Véda.* X, 71, 8.
18. R.K. Mookerji, *Op. Cit.* p. 37.
19. *Ṛk Véda*, VII. 103.
20. *Ibid*, X. 109.5.
21. *Isavasyopanishad.* 11.

22. V.M. Apte, *Cultural Heritage of India*, (S.K. Chatterji Ed.), Calcutta, 2001, Vol. I, p. 265.
23. *Manu.* III. 185.
24. V.M. Apte, *Op. Cit*, p. 280.
25. *Satapatha Brahmana*, VIII. I. 1, 2.
26. PB Shelley, *To a Skylark.*
27. VM Apte, *Op. Cit*, p. 290.
28. *Ṛk Véda*, I. 72. 7; X. 2. 7.

7

The Philosophy : Shaddarsanas

Among other subjects of academic and spiritual prominence were the *shaddarśanas*. *Darśanas*, as they are known, were of highest on to logical significance as all of them aimed at giving man vision of the Ultimate. *Darśana* means the highest vision, vision of God. All the subjects which helped the seeker towards that realization were looked with adoration, and hence their names *darśanas*. Six in number, all of them are as old as Vedic literature. Highly scientific, they are the gems of Indian philosophical thought, each stream with a long drawn tradition and a teacher or an *acharya* who was a *ṛshi* reputed in Vedic tradition. They begin with *Nyaya*, deemed to be the basis of *shaddarśanas* and attributed to Akshapada Gautama, the first known authority to systematize *Nyāyaśastra* or science of logic by putting it into a *Sutra*. *Nyāya* seems to have had a long drawn tradition in the history of Indian thought. Mahabharata and allied literature are replete with references to philosophical and logical debates and disputes in the sacrificial assemblies and hairsplitting arguments relating to spirituality and metaphysics. The logical dialogue between Uddalaka and Swetaketu in *Chhandogya Upanishad* on the nature of soul and Brahman and their interrelation, the heated arguments between Yajnjavalkya and Gargi Vachakhnavi as found in *Brahadāraṇ yaka Upanishad* and the highly convincing metaphysical discourse as seen in *Gita* or any such lofty metaphysical literature of ancient India bear, witness to the existence of a science of logic, argument and concluding ascertainment. Mahabharata alludes to different *Nyāya* texts by different debaters. It refers to Narada as an adept in the five limbs of *Nyāya* and enumerates different aspects of *Nyāya* like *vāda* (debate), *jalpa* (disputation), *vitanḍa* (destructive argumentation), the four *pramāṇas* or sources of knowledge, *nigraha* (vulnerable points) and *prētyabhāva* (afterlife).[1] Calling *Nyāya* as *anvīkshiki* or logical science, Mahabharata refers to the one-lakh-chaptered work by Brahma covering a wide spectrum of subjects including Vedic teachings, *anvīkshiki vārta* (commercial and economic sciences) and *danḍanīti* (administrative and judicial science). Presentation of facts with documentation and evidences, logical argumentation raising them beyond dispute and establishment of one's point with beauty, simplicity and sequence was thus a perfect art the entire gamut of the world of knowledge and life required and felt presence of.

Gautama, the teacher of *Nyaya* was so judicious and intelligent that *Mahabharata* speaks of his birth as a jackal. *Yājnjāvalkyasamhita* counts *Nyāyasastra* of Akshapada among the *Vidyāsthanas* (knowledge systems) and deems it as an authoritative *āstikadarśana* (spiritual science) studded with many gems of knowledge, a bunch of fruits which pours out nectar-like juice in abundance.

Nyayasutras are divided into five chapters each having two daily lessons (*ahnikas*). The first lesson of the first chapter details the sixteen *Nyaya* categories like sources of knowledge (*pramāṇa*), objects of knowledge (*praméya*), doubt (*samśaya*), purpose (*prayōjana*), illustrative instance (*drushṭānta*), accepted tenet (*siddhānta*), members of syllogism (*avayava*), argument (*tarka*), ascertainment (*nirṇaya*), debate (*vāda*), disputation (*jalpa*), destructive criticism (*vitanḍa*), fallacy (*hētvabhāsha*), quibble (*chala*), futile rejoinder (*jati*), and points of defeat (*nigrahasthāna*). It again divides and defines the first nine items which are epistemologically and logically significant while the second lesson defines the remaining seven categories of special significance in debates and disputations. First lesson of the second chapter deals with doubt and four sources of knowledge like perception (*pratyaksha*), inference (*anumāna*), analogy (*upamāna*) and verbal testimony (*sabda*) in addition to the composite substances and time while the second lesson includes other *pramāṇās* among the recognized ones, discussing the verbal testimony in detail. Third chapter in its first lesson deals with the four objects of knowledge like soul (*ātman*), body (*śarīra*), sense-organs (*indriyas*), objects of senses (*arthạ*). The second examines intellect (*buddhi*) and mind (*manas*) and deals at length with the merits and demerits determining the association of souls with specific bodies. The first lesson of the fourth chapter analyses such aspects as endeavour (*pravrutti*), rebirth (*prétyabhāva*), result (*phala*), sorrow (*duhkha*) and salvation (*apavarga*) and deals with the eight theories (*prāvādukavāda*) on the creation of entities while the second discusses on the composite bodies, indivisibility of ultimate particles (*paramāṇus*), reconsiders the refutation of eternal objects and suggests means to enhance and preserve true knowledge. The two chapters of the fifth lesson subdivide and define the last two categories, *jāti* and *nigrahasthāna* respectively.

Being of prime importance among the *darśanas*, *Nyayasutra* analyses only those categories that help attain the highest good (*nisréyas*) which are of two kinds : the higher one attained through the true knowledge of the *praméya* and the lower one known through *pramānas*. *Praméya* means what is to be known. According to *Vedas* what is to be finally known or the *praméya* is the highest spiritual subject, the God. *Pramānas* are theories that help one know the *praméya*. With a two-fold scope, it is thus both a *mokshaśāstra*, a science that helps attain the eternal salvation and an aid to know other branches of knowledge in *śastras*. The subject is thus two-in-one, spiritual and intellectual, helping one in intellectual perception of the Ultimate truth, the God. Giving importance to both spiritual and empirical considerations, *Nyāyasutra* thus focuses on the replacement of false knowledge (*mithyājñāna*) with true knowledge which removes the *dōshas* or vices like attachment, aversion and delusion.[2] Removal of vices finally leads to the removal of rebirth which in turn annihilates misery (*dukha*) and helps one attain ultimate salvation (*apavarga*).

Another important subject, the twin brother of *Nyāya*, was *Vaiśéshika darśana* which is indispensable to the student of Indian culture and philosophy. It is ascribed to Kanada, differently called Kanabhuk, Kanachara, Kanabhaksha, Kanavrata, all showing their association with *kaṇa*, which is defined also as grain, particle, atom, etc. His other epithets Pailuka, Pailukantha (*pilu* means atom) also support this. An adherent to the highest wove of asceticism, Kanada, if to believe the *Nyāyakāndāli* of Sreedhara, lived on unclaimed grains in the fields after harvest. His practice of begging for his food at night, resembling that of an owl, earned him the name Uluka as he is referred to in many texts. Later literatures inform us that Lord Siva, in the form of an owl, appeared before this sage and taught him *Vaiśéshika* tenets. *Mahabharata* refers to the sage Uluka who was beside Bhishma at the time of his death. The place of Kanada in the history of *Vaiśéshika darśana* is so important that innumerable have been the works later scholars wrote basing on the system he developed, the works like *Padārthaḍharmasamgraha* of Prasastapada, *Kaṇ ādasūtranibanḍha* of Bhatta Vadindra and *Vaiśéshikasūtrōpaskāra* of Sankaramisra being only a few. *Bhāshyas* or emendations on *Vaiśéshika darśana* had begun being written as early as the period of Vedas and we come to hear from reference of the *Bhāshyas* of Ravana, Atreya, etc.

The treatise of Kanada, the *Vaiśéshika darśana*, is a collection of aphoristic sentences called *sūtra* divided into ten chapters, each *chapter* consisting two daily lessons or *ahnikas*. Hence its name *Daśalakshaṇi.* All later commentaries and digests that evolved into the present *Vaiśéshika* materials including the discussions on duality, chemical action and derivative disjunction, made the subject so vast and complex that it is very difficult to distinguish the works of Kanada from those of later scholars.

The first chapter elaborates on all the categories inherent in substances, its first lesson dealing with the properties of those wherein the universals inhere and the second examining the universals as well as the particularity or *viśésha.* But the sole aim of *Vaiśéshika* is explaining virtue or *Dharma* which helps one attain prosperity (*abhyudaya*) and salvation (*niśréyas*) and to establish the validity of Vedas in guiding man to these heights. Salvation is reached through the real knowledge regarding the dharma of different substances, qualities and aspects inhering universe. Thus Vaiseshika Sutras speak about substances (*dravyas*) like earth, water, fire, air, ether, time, space, soul and mind. The qualities (*guṇ as*) include colour, taste, odour, touch, number, measure, separations, contact, disjoining, quality of belonging to high genus or species, etc.[3] Then it speaks about karma cr action and interactions among these aspects, bringing in new things and effects like contacts of atoms producing a substance or many colours in fusion producing another colour. If there is no cause there is no effect, says Kanada and he thereby introduces the relative nature of things and events. According to him genus (*sāmānya*) and species (*viśésha*) are relative to understanding. But beyond all these relativities there stands the being of all as the ultimate genus. All-pervading, it is in all objects and qualities, as identical entity in *dravya*, *guṇa* and *karma.* This Kanada calls the *satta* or potential aspect which takes its manifestation and expresses itself in a manifold manner. Essential unity comes to have its diverse forms. The idea of change from unity to diversity and vice versa which modern science speaks of was thus already envisioned by *Vaiśéshika darśana.* We had better take the Vedic saying *ékam sat* or the inner content is the same in all and compare it with the statement of a modern physicist that "what is more important is the force of this super-personal content and the depth of the conviction concerning its overpowering meaningfulness."[4]

The second chapter in its first lesson examines the five physical substances or *bhūtas* while the second lesson deals with such aspects as space and time. He elaborates the qualities of substances such as the earth possesses colour, smell, taste and touch or the water has colour, taste, touch, liquidity and smoothness. Fire has colour and touch and the air has touch. But ether possesses none of these qualities. He also deals with natural qualities and those that are created. For instance, Kanada says that liquidity is the special quality of water because butter, wax, lead, iron, silver, gold become liquids if only they are heated whereas water is naturally liquid. Similarly each and every substance both inanimate and animate has got its own quality that makes it difference (*viśésha*) from the other. Time is that which gives notion of youth, old age, simultaneity and quickness, and is the cause of all non-eternal things, whereas notion of time is absent in all that are eternal. Space, Kanada says, is another construct of mind which is referred to in relation to a specially marked point such as something is far away or so much near to a particular location.[5]

The third book deals at length with soul (*ātman*) and mind (*manas*) respectively in its first and second lessons. Knowledge of sense objects (*indriyārtḥa*) helps one know the existence of things different from senses and objects which are related to them. Cognition derived by contact of soul, senses and objects provides one with inference of the soul, and even if senses and objects are shed one after the other there still remains the 'I' as different from 'mine'. This cognition regarding one's own soul helps one know the soul in others. The 'I' according to Vaiseshika therefore refers to the self and nothing else. Hence the inference regarding 'soul' that 'I' am.

An account of the physical body (*sarīra*) and its accessories (*tad-upayōgin*) are the subjects of the first and second lessons respectively of the fourth chapter. It deals with the eternal things (*nitya*) which do not have causes behind and are different from the non-eternal things which are called ignorance or *avidya.* That alone which was born of itself or primordial energy is eternal and knowledge regarding it alone is *vidya* or real knowledge. All the rest are non-eternal, the knowledge of which is not real but only something other than knowledge or *avidya.* Here *Vaiśéshika* deals at length with the aspect of cognition of many things which are both visible and invisible. While dealing with air and colour, Kanada says that it is the quality of compounded things. Air has colour in its unmanifest form and becomes visible only when there is colour with special qualifications and conditions. In this way he goes on explaining the cognition of taste, smell, touch, number, measure, separateness, contact and disjoining, pleasure, pain, etc. by use of senses. It again mentions atoms of different elements combining with one of them acting as the central radicle.

Action or *karma* is described in the fifth chapter, its first lesson dealing with physical actions (*sarīra karma*) and the second the mental ones (*mānasa karma*). Among physical actions many aspects as movements including special types of movements, contact among different sense organs, heaviness, etc., are dealt with. Citing the process of threshing corns, it says that the movement of hands happens from their contact with soul and mind and the movement of hands results in the movement of flail. If not held by hand the flail would fall down owing to its heaviness (*gurutva*). Besides, special kinds of movements (*nōdanaviséśha*) may result in upward and sideward movements. Even without any mental or conscious effort there may be movements like that of the body during sleep. There is also the *végasamskāra* or inertia which keeps moving a body which has already acquired motion. There are again references to happenings whose causes are unknown (*adrushṭakāritam*). Pleasure and pain are due to the contact of self, mind, senses and objects. They are feelings both physical and mental. Each action translated into physical is thus mind-born. Once the mind is separated from body through strict spiritual control there would be no more pleasure or pain. To attain this, *Vaiśéshika* advises the practice of *Yōga.*

The sixth book elaborates on the principles of *Dharma* related to giving gifts. Gifts should be given only to the deserving in accordance with scriptural injunctions and in accompaniment of Vedic performances. This certainly would result in some invisible purification and refinement of soul with its work leading to *Mōksha* or ultimate salvation. The seventh book deals with eternal and non-eternal qualities of things, change of qualities in relations to the effect produced by different phenomena and the causes of visibility and invisibility of atom and huge objects respectively. It then goes on explaining ideas of unity and separateness, which are inextricably intertwined. They are as if neither one nor distinctively separate. Indeed the notion of unity is related to the notion of duality, separateness and diversity and vise versa because without diversity there cannot be unity. They are coexistent as the opposite but interactive poles of a united whole. They are like cause and effect with no independent entity from one another. Everywhere there is unity, and duality is only a delusion born of ignorance. The idea of non-duality or monism both at material and spiritual levels thus proves an interesting theme of *Vaiśéshika* thought.

Another great name in the history of Indian spiritual thought is Kapila the exponent of *Sānkhya darśana* to whom every system of India owes much. Kapila's historicity is referred to in many ancient Indian writings. Deemed a great sage or *siddḥa* by the author of *Bhagavad-Gita* (*siddḥānām kapilōmuni*), Kapila even after millennia continues to be a prominent figure in India's philosophical tradition.[6] Son of Kardama Prajapati and Devahuti, sage Kapila was characterized with unlimited knowledge and boundless compassion. Perhaps it may not be unnatural that the place associated with his name, Kapilavastu had later given birth to another great man of compassion born to relieve humanity of its sufferings, Gautama the Buddha who, too, like Kapila believed that knowledge of the ultimate truth is the only panacea to end worldly pains. Considered by the lore as supreme knowledge, *Sānkhya darśana* is the spiritual discourse by Kapila Vasudeva who according to traditional belief was Vishnu incarnate, to his mother Devahuti (onc who was born as offering (*havis*) to God or *déva*). With *apavarga* or eternal salvation as its whole aim, *Sānkhya* tops all other knowledge systems of India. With sympathy for the world plunged in ignorance, Kapila is said to have been after disciples ready to imbibe his teachings which could bail the world out of sufferings. One such disciple was a Brahmin householder wedded to the cult of sacrifice but renounced everything to practise strict celibacy as advised by Kapila. This Brahmin householder, Asuri, thus became his disciple to whom Kapila first communicated the principles of his system.

Unlike the later or classical *Sānkhya* which is generally said to be atheistic, Kapila's teachings were purely spiritual. It enunciates the philosophy of oneness of all things in universe including human beings.

Kapila is indeed an *adviaitin* or a pure monist who surpasses the naive world view that highlights strife and divisions of ordinary material plane. He theorizes that the realm of objects is in truth a scene of continuities and differentiations, all dependendant on and integrated with an underlying basic oneness and unity. The foundation of objective realm Kapila calls *prakruti* which is rather invisible, *avyaktam*. And this basic reality is a composite entity made up of three gunas like *sattva*, *rajas* and *tamas* which are not qualities but substances, a group of active entities manifesting both in physical and psychic plains as pleasure, pain and delusion; illumination, action and restraint; buoyancy, mobility and inertia. Kapila thus points to psychic and physical entities as manifestations of the single aspect, the *prakruti* which is both quiescent and emergent or potential and kinetic. Quiescent is the state of dynamic equilibrium called *samya* while in emergent state, the *vaisamya* the *gunas* or constituents vibrantly interact, clashing and cooperating in the process of progress and ascendancy. Since the visible is the manifestation of the invisible and objects in the world are limited in time and space, Kapila looks beyond the material existence for their source and cause. This in fact leads one to the ideas of universal causal energy and substance which find themselves in a state of unity of all forms or *vaiśvarūpyam*. *Sānkhya* which denies the independent entity of substances theorizes on the interconnectedness of things and events which find themselves in an unbroken continuity from the lowest inorganic to the highest organic forms. Everything forms inseparable part of the cosmic web or originates from and returns to the common source of universe which Kapila calls *prakruti* which is *avyakta* or undifferentiated from the universal energy and existence. This is further illustrated by Srikrishna in Bhagavad-Gita which states that all are in their beginning undifferentiated from the infinite and hence without a separate identity, a state which they again attain on their return to the undifferentiated whole. Every form, if to quote Sri Aurobindo, "tends towards a harmonized complexity and totality which again breaks apart into various channels of special effort and tendency, only to unite once more in a larger and more puissant synthesis."[7] Things and beings come to have their differentiation and separate identity only when they are between the beginning and the end, i.e. when they are in their manifest form. Thus says the Gita:

> *"avyaktādīni bhūtāni vyaktamadhyāni bhārata*
> *avyaktanidhanānyéva tatra kā paridévana.*[8]"

It is thus the state between existence or *sat* which is the real cause of all manifestations and its reverse, non-existence or *asat*. It is *jagat*, the moving and disappearing state which Sankara calls *mitḥya* which is neither existence nor non-existence. It is only a stage in the cyclical process of universal movement wherein existence (*sat*), visible world (*jagat* or *mitḥya*) and non-existence (*asat*) come recurring one after the other. In fact an ancient Indian counterpart of modern theories of Unified Field and Quantum interconnectedness, Sankhya pointed to the primordial cause or the existence of effects in their material or any other causes which express themselves differently through the process of evolution or *pariṇāma*.[9]

It thus points to an ultimate reality as well as unity as the sole cause behind the entire universe and its phenomena. There is only unity behind all verities which in an ultimate analysis proves just delusion. How then one can attain this eternal salvation or *apavarga* or the state of becoming one with the universal soul or energy Answer is in the *Gita* which elaborates on so many aspects of spiritual life and *sādhana* or preparations for higher life. It exhorts one to live a totally unattached life or a balanced life between attachment and detachment or walk the borderland between hate and love so that one may be free of the both. As world itself, as noted earlier, is the state between existence and non-existence, so is human life a path between the two extremities of pleasure and pain, attachment and detachment, love and hate and birth and death. Therefore *Gita* exhorts one to lead a perfectly balanced life wherein lies the beauty of life which gives eternal pleasure. Balance makes the beauty and a balanced life helps one attain the ultimate beauty. Hence the Vedic injunction to follow the middle path so that one may be free of mundane allurements even while alive. Man of this mental state is called *jīvanmukta*. This in fact is the state of *samādḥi* wherein *dḥi* or intellect is well balanced, wherein one, totally untouched by externalities, is the master of himself. This is the state of *Buddha,* or according to *Gita* of the *Yogi,* or the one endowed with 'Wisdom' which takes one beyond Good and Evil. Thus says *Gita*:

"buddhiyuktō jahātīha ubhé sukrutadushkruté
tasmādyōgāya yūjyasva yōga karmasu kauśalaṃ."

Endowed with this wisdom, one gets rid of both good and evil; therefore take to *Yoga*; *Yoga* is the skill in work.

Gita further explains the nature of man with well established intellect. "He who is free from affection everywhere, and who getting whatever good or evil neither welcomes nor hates them, has steady wisdom," it says. He who is with well established wisdom is called *sthitaprajña.* Thus says *Gita*:

> *"yadāsamharaté chāyam kūrmōngānīva sarvaśā*
> *indriyāṇindriyārthébhyastasya prajñā pratishṭitāḥ."*

> "As the tortoise tucks its feet and head inside the shell, and you may kill it and break it into pieces, and yet it will not come out, even so the character of that man who has control over his motives and organs is unchangeably established."

It is the attainment of this wisdom that determines spiritual height and helps one to get eternal salvation or ultimate unity with the universal soul which Kapila calls *Prakruti. Prakruti* is thus the cause from which all effects come. Existence is born of existence. Nothing comes out of nothing (*nāsatō satjāyaté*). Discarding the unscientific notion of creation out of nothing and basing on the idea of causation or *satkāryavāda*, Kapila, gets on with the idea of evolution or *pariṇāma.* According to Kapila, evolution is a cyclical process with *prakruti* as the beginning and end and is determined and willed by what he calls *buddhi* or *mahat* or intelligence inherent in the universal being which is compounded of three aspects, *sāttvik*, *rājasik* and *tāmasik.* What is seen thus outwardly is the manifestation of the unseen. As Sri Aurobindo points out, "we have therefore two fundamental facts... a fact of being, a fact of becoming. To deny one or the other is easy, but to find out their relation is the true and fruitful wisdom."[10] *Buddhi* or *mahat* in simple terms is the cosmic principle of the wisdom that conceives the order and principle of things. It is the primordial and ultimate wisdom.[11] It is this wisdom that determined to manifest itself into manifoldness.

This idea that universe with its manifoldness originated from cosmic soul which decided itself to be 'the many' is interesting from the cosmological point of view which now comes almost in perfect agreement with the Big-Bang theory of modern physicists at least in the sense that everything proceeds from and recedes to a zero volume singularity. Though there are a lot of disagreements between Vedanta and modern physics on aspects like the evolution, involution, withdrawal and manifestation, and that the very theory of the Big-Bang has been called to question, the both agree on this idea of oneness.[12] According to Konrad Rudnicki, an extragalactic astronomer, cosmologist and philosopher of science, "the first culture of which we have definite information concerning its cosmological ideas is ancient India," whose "Rishis - the great teachers" led to an efflorescence of Hindu spirit, "when Indian nation lived peacefully in the northern part of what is now India ... as early as about six thousand years before Christ." This former senior research fellow of the California Institute of Technology continues, "if we are to find, through the ancient Hindus, the roots of modern science, then we can say that what is natural science today was in those days elaborated on the one hand with the highest principles of universal existence, and on the other with the finest sensory perceptions." That the soul of the cosmos expresses itself with extraordinarily streaming effulgence is well illustrated by *Gita* thus:

> *"divi sūryasahasrasyā bhavédyugapaduddhịtāḥ*
> *yadi bhā sadrus̄i sāsyādbhāsasastasya mahātmanaḥ.*
> Even if a thousand suns at once
> rose on the horizon, yet the light
> would not compare to that glory
> and splendour of that great form.[13]"

It was thus the cosmic soul that manifested itself into the many. On the eve of creation, which is an eternal phenomenon, the scriptures say, the universal or cosmic intelligence decided to divide itself into the many so that manifoldness of the world appeared.

> *"sōkāmāyata. bahusyām prajāyēyēti.*
> *sōtapōtapyata. sa tapastapa tvām idam sarva masrujata*
> *yadidam kimcha tat srushṭvā tadévānuprāviśat.*[14]"

The universal soul desired to be born into the many. It sank into a long meditation. Out of the energy thus acquired it created everything and entered into all creations pervading them with itself.

This idea is further underscored by *Aitaréyopanishad* which says:

> *"ōm ātmā vā idaméka évāgra āsīd,*
> *nānyat kinchana mishat sa īkshata lōkānnusruja iti.*[15]"

"Before the creation of the cosmos truly there was only one soul,
There was nothing as either active or inactive.
That cosmic soul decided, "I may create the worlds."

The unity thus expressed itself into the verity. Unity and diversity are thus one and the same like cause and effects which are inextricably intertwined. Cause is born for the effect just as effect is within the cause. Every thing is predetermined and things happen as are due. True, theory of causation gains significance in ordinary human contexts but this, too, is just a medium in the hands of destiny so that what are already in store must have their terrestrial expression. Causes are just factors that bring about an incident and it is for the happening of an incident the cause surfaces. What is already in store must happen either due to one cause or the other. Thus before an intuitive and penetrating analysis even the theory of causation itself gets relegated to secondary importance, the cause being just a means to serve the divine end.

Then how the ancient sheers realized this ultimate reality, the sole energy which is latent in as well as the cause of everything. This indeed is an area even modern science stands puzzled because to it this is still a world of experiment that includes ideas from that of the Unified Field to the still unrealized Quantum computer which if actualized, the physicists say, could be all-knowing. The Quantum Computer, the modern physicists say, if developed could know many things at a time. It would be an all-knowing device. To Indian seer the all-knowing knowledge is part of the highest spiritual experience. Indian seer says, *yat jñānāt sarvavijñānam :* "the knowledge of 'This' [One] brings knowledge about everything." Knowledge of this energy or the reason behind all creations gives man knowledge of everything. This knowledge the Indian sages attained not through laboratory apparatus but through austere spiritual practice called *Yoga* or higher spiritual preparation that makes one communion with the ultimate spirit or the all-pervading content of the universe. If this spirit knows everything, by becoming one with it, the seeker could know everything. Naturally the sage sitting in meditation on this universal spirit and becoming one with that which is the inner spirit of everything was inferred of everything. To him there is even no division of time which stretches infinitely before him and he sees the future as he sees the past. Time is to him just a part of the infinite entity of which his vision is clear and complete. He is the *trikalajñāni* to whom there is no past-present-future division. Just like is to him the space. He has crossed the limitations of both time and space. The sage was thus the Seer or *drashta* and knower of all; he was universal consciousness manifest.

It is *Yōga* that brings one into unity with the ultimate energy. *Yōga* is the most ancient of Indian sciences which is widely referred to in Vedic literature. This system traditionally associated with the name of Patanjali, had its beginning prior to his time. *Yōga* had an ancient origin with many lines and stages of development as evident from the innumerable references in Vedic hymns to different paths pursued by seekers of the infinite. Some verses of *Swétāśvatara Upanishad* mention certain steps in *Yōga* practice which were formulated later, and refer to the posture of neck, trunk and head of a yogi seated in meditation. Thus says the *Upanishad* :

> *"trirunnatam sthāpya samam sarīram*
> *hrīdndriyāṇi manasā sannivéśya*
> *brahmōḍupéna prataréta vidvān*
> *srōtamsi sarvāṇi bhayāvahānī*[16]."
>
> Keeping body erect with its three limbs unmoving and
> controlling the limbs with the mind and withdrawing
> to the hearts innermost recess, the man of knowledge
> must cross all the turbulent currents in the boat of *ōm.*

Referring to the development of coherence through concentration, it speaks about men of knowledge who bring mind and other sense organs into perfect harmony and come into communion with *Brahman* through meditation or *dhyāna.*[17] It speaks of the scholar, adept in the path of meditation, who controls psychic and sensual pleasures just as a charioteer his horses. The *Upanishad* advises a *Yōga* practitioner to select a plain, serene and hearty place cooled by gentle breeze or a solitary cave to sit and control his breath, one of the primary steps of *yōga.* If the yogic practitioner comes to have the vision of mist, smoke, sun and fire, the *Upanishad* says these could be taken as good indicators or prelude to progress in practice. Thanks to the yogi concentrating on the five constituents of creation these five elements in his body would become effulgent and the *yōgāgni* (glow) that pervades his body would keep it strong, steady and free of all physical illness. And the soul realizing its real nature by identifying itself with the entirety or universal soul becomes undifferentiated, dynamic and free of all sorrows. Realizing the auspicious vision that one is Brahman itself through coming face to face with the streaming effulgence of the infinite, yogi becomes free of birth and death and all knots of attachment and detachment to be a *mukta.*[18] Upanishadic dictates as R.D. Ranade says, have already set the disciplines of *Yōga* even before the time of *Bhagavad-Gita* and Patanjali composing *Yōgasūtra.* He writes:

> "It may be seen that in the first place it calls our attention to the posture of the body at the time of practising the yoga. Anticipating the Bhagavad-Gita, it tells us that we should hold the trunk, the neck and the head in a straight line at the

time of meditation. Secondly, we are advised to control our senses by means of mind, or a process equivalant to *pratyāhāra.* Thirdly, we are told to regulate our breath implying that it should be made rhythmical, which practice may be called the precursor of the later *praṇāyāma.* Fourthly, we are told that the environment in which one should practise meditation should be pure...the meditation should be practised in the recesses of a cave. Fifthly, we are informed of the harbingers of a spiritual day-light to come, namely the forms of mist and smoke, sun and the fire...Sixthly, we are led into the secret of the physiological effects produced by the "fire of Yoga." We are told that one who practises Yoga becomes ageless and immortal... Lastly, the *Swétāśvatāra* immediately carries us to the highest result secured by the practice of *Yōga,* namely to the state of *samādḥi,* where the individual soul sees the Universal Soul and becomes one with it[19]."

Other steps of Yoga are also mentioned by Upanishads. While *dhyāna* is already referred to by *Swétāśvatāra Upanishad, dhāraṇa* is given in *Kaṭha Upanishad.* Both *dhyāna* and *dhāraṇa* being mutually complimentary the Upanishads often take them together. Hence the *indriyadhāraṇam* as found in *Kaṭha Upanishad.* Permanent control over sense organs, according to this Upanishad is called *Dhāraṇa.* And this state leads the seeker to perfect righteousness.

tām yōgamithi manyanthé sthirāmindriyadhāraṇām
apramattastatā bhavati yōgōhi prabhavābhyayau.[20]

Thus the system of *Yōga* as already mentioned was almost well conceived and systematized prior to the coming of Patanjali, the author of *Yōgasutra* and as R.D. Ranade observes, "if we add the *yama* and *niyama* of the later Yogic philosophy to the various elements of *Yōga* as mentioned in the old Upanishads...we have the full fledged eight fold scheme of *Yōga,* or the way to spiritual realization."[21] Upanishads also allude to the psychological as well as physiological significance of *Yōga* as found in *Kauśataki* and *Maitri* Upanishads. A soul refining subject apart, *Yōga* is related to the study of physical aspects as found in *Maitri Upanishad* which enumerates the seven *dhātus* or elements of the body like bone, skin, muscle, marrow, flesh, semen, blood, four excrements like mucus, tears, faeces and urine and three other *dhātus* or constituents of body like *vāta*, *pitta* and *kapha* or wind, bile and phlegm. *Yōga* had thus been a science as well as an art of life aimed at developing a perfect man who sees and handles everything with a balanced approach and equanimity of mind. A more sublime explanation in this regard is given by *Bhagavad-Gita* which is all the Upanishads collected and condensed. Sri Krishna according to the *dhyānaśḷōka* of *Gita* had milked all the cows that are Upanishads and churned out from them the nectar that was the *Gita* to enlighten Partha, his dearest devotee. He, as Swami Vivekananda has rightly opined, was the first ever teacher to accomplish the task of collecting all systems of *Yōga* or the paths to salvation, and threaded them together into a single garland i.e., *Bhagavad-Gita* or the song celestial in so commendable and sublime a style that few before and after his time could match. Therefore any study of *Upanishads* and their content without reference to *Gita* would prove incomplete. The study on *Yōga*, too, calls for an Upanishadic background.

Gita thus discourses on the hindrances resultant of worldly attachment and desirability of *Yōga* in salvaging man from temporal bondages. In the temporal world man is bound to become the slave of sensual pleasures. Any kind of involvement in mundane activities makes man attached to them, and *Gita* elaborates on how this worldly attachment leads man to the final destruction if this involvement is not guided by principles of un-attachment. It says:

> *"dhyāyaté vishayānpumsā sangasthvéshupajāyaté*
> *sangāt samjāyaté kāma kāmātkrōdḥābhijāyaté*
> *krōdhātbhavati sammōha sammōhātsmrutivibhrama*
> *smrutibhramśādbuddhināśō buddhināśātpraṇaśyati.*[22]"

> For a person thinking of the sense objects there grows an attachment for them, from attachment desire arises, from desire results anger, from anger results delusion, from delusion results confusion of memory, from confusion of memory results destruction of intelligence and from destruction of intelligence he perishes.

Hence the scriptural advice to work with unattachment to get mental equanimity which, according to *Gita* is another name for *Yōga*. Therefore it says:

> "Established in *Yōga*, O Dhananjaya! (Arjuna) perform actions, giving up attachment, and unconcerned as to success or failure; this equanimity is called *Yōga*.[23]"

Srikrishna advises Arjuna to perform actions guided by wisdom because far inferior is the work prompted by desire to work done through wisdom (*buddhau śaranānviścha krupaṇāphalahétava*). This earliest of the Buddhas of Vedic India thus stressed the need of taking refuge in wisdom or enlightenment because those who are impelled by results are miserable.[24] And this wisdom helps one get rid of both good and evil and from the bondage of birth and death and attain indifference to what is to be heard and what is heard. This state of wisdom is equated again with *samādḥi*, a state wherein *dḥi* or intelligence becomes balanced thanks to one's having established a balance between all the extremities. Srikrishna further explains this wisdom thus:

When a man gives up all desires
of the mind, O Partha and himself
delights in his Self, then he is said
to be a man of steady wisdom;

He who is unperturbed in misery
and free from desires amidst pleasures,
who is devoid of all attachment, fear and anger,
that sage is said to be of steady wisdom,

He who is free from affection everywhere,
and who getting whatever good or evil
neither welcomes nor hates them
has steady wisdom.[25]

But it is the turbulent senses which forcibly lead astray the mind of a seeker of the ultimate. Therefore Srikrishna instructs the *Yōga* practitioner to control all the senses and sit in meditation or *dhyāna* with his mind concentrating on the Ultimate. Because his wisdom is steady, whose senses are under control, says the author of Gita.

'tāni sarvāṇi samyamya yukta āsīta matparaḥ
vaśō hi yasyéndriyāṇi tasya prajñā pratishṭhitāḥ.[26]'

And such a self-controlled person who moves amidst the sense objects with freedom from attachment and aversion sheds all the misery and attains serenity. Srikrishna further says, "That person who is giving up all sense objects goes about unattached, devoid of the idea of ownership and free from egoism attains peace," and he concludes:

éshā brāhmī sthiti pārtḥā nainam prāpya vimuhyati
sthitvāsyāmantakāl épi brahmanirvāṇamṛchhati.[27]

> "This is the Brahmi state, O Partha, the attainment of which erases all the delusions; one who rests in it at the time of death, attains *nirvāṇa* in the Brahman."

This is in fact the state of total *Yōga* when one comes in complete communion with the ultimate ever-expanding entirety by attaining equanimity of mind and balance of intelligence or Wisdom. Such a person even while physically alive is free of mundane existence. *Nirvāṇa* or the *brahmi* state could be either of a living person who is free of the worldly attachment or *jīvanmukta* or of the soul which finds itself in total identification with the unmanifest *prakruti* (as described in *Sānkhya*) which gives the vision and sense of the infinite being. In fact as Mahayogi Sri Aurobindo points out, *Yōga* helps one return from de-coherence to coherence or unity from which all diversities manifest. And a Yogi who has successfully passed through all stages of *Yōga*, his having realized the vision of unity must take back in the right relation to the world of the manifested existence. If he was so far bound to them in wrong relation and "in the poise of a falsehood created by Time by the principle of divided consciousness with all its oppositions, discords and dualities," he has after having attained the *apavarga* or the salvation to "take back all things and beings into his new consciousness but as one with all, not divided from them by an egoistic individuality."[28] By becoming cosmic consciousness itself one identifies his being with the infinite which, as the base and content of the world, dwells in all existences. He, by attaining the complete cosmic consciousness sees all existence in the self and self in all existences. Having become one with the infinite, time and space lose their frontiers in his world. He sees past, present and future as one entity and everything in time as preset. He goes beyond the spatial limitations, too. Hence the power of a yogi to see what happens in distant places and in distant future. It is *Yōga* that endows him with this power. Therefore the scripture prescribes the practice of *Yōga* to know the reality which is unity in totality. Hence the duo *Sānkhya-Yōga.*

The last but not the least, the two *Mīmāmsas*, *Pūrva* and *Uttara*, attempt to lend philosophic and scientific credence to the teachings of Vedas, trying to prove that *Srutis* are in perfect line with Vedic philosophy. *Pūrva Mīmāmsa*, earlier of the two, is ritualistic and interprets Vedic texts and discusses the doctrine of eternity of sound which it identifies with the ultimate reality, the Brahman. It enquires into the nature of *sabdabrahman* and interprets the *mantra* portion of Vedas. Performance of sacred rites according to *Mimamsa* is the prelude to the pursuit of wisdom leading to *mōksha.* Thus just like any other *darśana*, the aim of *Mīmāmsa*, too, is to help one attain ultimate deliverance. Origin of *Mīmāmsa* could be traced to the Vedas and was wholly related to the performance of religious duties including the performance of sacrifices based on correct interpretation of Vedic hymns down the ages when Vedic text and oral tradition were the only two authorities on the performance of sacraments. *Mīmāmsa* thus continued to be prominent throughout Vedic and post-vedic times though it was only later that Jaimini, Kumarila, Bhaskara and Sabara attempted at systematizing its rules.

More practical than speculative in its interest, the *Pūrva Mīmāmsa* examines the nature of *Dharma.* It affirms the reality of Soul which it regards as a permanent being, possessing a body which benefits from the performance of duties. It is *Dharma* which is the authority that licenses the performance of duties and the Vedas affirm that such duties would produce beneficial results. *Mīmāmsa* is thus purely Vedic in character with transcendent importance of *Dharma* as its central theme. It was a system that disciplined life, bringing it in line with the principles of *Dharma* or strict observance of duties. *Dharma* is not a physical existence or a subject of sensual perception but manifestation of the supreme truth of which the knowledge is derived from Vedas which is the only source of inference about it. Repudiating the traditional blind view that Vedas are the works of God, *Mīmāmsa* emphasizes the importance of *ātman* which according to it is nothing but consciousness (*bōdḥa*) or reflection of cosmic consciousness. Hence the *Mīmāmsa* viewpoint, that the self stands independently of and separate from body, senses and understanding. The body is only a means to an end, i.e. to serve the soul which directs it. The ultimate *Dharma* has its reflection in human plain in the form of right living. What provides one with the ultimate happiness alone is *Dharma* and is expected to bring about order, and the action resulting in loss or pain or disorder is not *Dharma.* And it is to tune human activity in line with principles of the ultimate *Dharma,* that the *Dharmaśāstra* originated. It is to be noted that the Vedic injunctions lay down details of *Dharma,* i.e., good actions to be followed as prescribed by *Veda* and all the *sruti* literature including *Upanishads* and *Gita.*

Mimamsakas or teachers of *Mīmāmsa*, being the staunch advocates of Vedic infallibility, do not accept any tradition that goes against Vedic injunction and believe that *smruti* texts (documents on traditions and customs) must have corresponding *sruti* texts (Vedas). According to them no *smruti* is acceptable unless supported by *sruti* or *Véda. Véda* which is revelation about the ultimate truth should be the guideline even for the minutest aspect in social life and therefore the view of *Mīmāmsa* that no *smruti* which runs in contrast to the teachings of *Véda* is genuine and hence something to be refuted. If certain *smruti* is known to have no matching *sruti*, it indicates that either the corresponding *Sruti* was lost over time or the particular *smruti* is not authentic and is to be disregarded. For instance there may be *smrutis* written with selfish and vested interests. But these *smrutis* according to Mimamsakas must be thrown out. What is based on *Véda* alone would establish *Dharma* in the world, *Dharma* being the terrestrial reflection of the ultimate truth the *Veda* speaks of. *Mīmāmsa* thus gives great stress on Vedic infallibility even in ordinary social activities and customs.

Salvation being the ultimate aim of human life, regular daily duties were to be observed to attain it. Daily duties like *sandḥya* (evening observances and prayer) and *naimittikakarma* (duties on special occasion) were recommended. But to attain salvation these duties were to be unconditional and unselfish or *nishkāma.* Any work done with selfish end, i.e., *kāmyakarma* is undesirable since it hinders one's progress towards attaining salvation. By keeping clear of *kāmyakarmas* one frees oneself from selfish ends and by observing the *nitya* and *naimittika* karmas or duties one attains salvation.

Vedanta means the end or final stage of *Véda* or knowledge, i.e. ultimate or supreme knowledge. The main sources for Vedantic study are the Upanishads. Upanishads, generally hailed the end portion of Vedas, contain basic as well as final or the ultimate teaching of all Indian knowledge systems. Hence the term *Vedanta* applied to them. Upanishads, given in the form of dialogues regarding the secrets of this as well as the nether worlds, contain gems of highest metaphysical thought few other branches of knowledge could deal with. Direct derivates of Vedic thought, Upanishads are prominent in Vedic literature or the entire range of Indian metaphysical texts. Reflections of an age with its never ending quest for knowledge, they are couched in the flower bed of poetic diction bristling with imageries, stories, parables, apothegms and dialogues, all in their effort to seek the ultimate reality of everything. Even the God of the world of death unrolling before an ordinary mortal a thousand secrets of the realm beyond terrestrial plain, sometimes forms an Upanishadic theme. The style of the dialogue elucidating the highly complex and complicated subjects is so inimitable that it forms the most effective method of academic instruction, too. *Upanishad,* literally meaning 'sit near,' presents the picture of a disciple 'sitting near' the teacher in his earnest desire to sit near the ultimate reality which Indian lore calls truth or God.

Upanishads are more than thousand in number of which only some have become popular, thanks to the commentaries by thinkers like Gaudapada, Sankara and Ramanuja. The Muktika Upanishad refers to hundred and eight Upanishads. The first ten Upanishads mentioned in the Muktika, along with a few other ones are regarded as principal Upanishads. They are *Īśāvāsya, Taittirīya, Aitaréya, Chhandōgya, Brihadāraṇyaka, Kaṭha, Kéna, Praśna, Mundaka, Māndūkya, Śvétāśwatāra* and *Kauśitaki.*

Īśāvāsya Upanishad, a part of *Śukla Yajur Véda samhita,* contains eighteen highly spiritual mantras. With its first *slōka* alone explaining the secret of *Védānta* it occupies a superior position in Upanishadic hierarchy. This *Upanishad* derived its name from the first word of its first line which has it that everything abides in God (*īśāvāsyamidam sarvam*). While the first mantra emphasizes renunciation resulting from attainment of the highest knowledge as means to realize God, the second mantra recommends the path of *karma* or action for those who lead mundane life. The third verse speaks of those who, failing to follow either of these paths, fall into the world of darkness. Hymns four to eight describe the all inclusive, all embracing and unattached nature of soul which is beyond good and evil. The ninth to the fourteenth describe the imperfection involved in following only one of the paths of *karma* and *upāsana* (or devotion) without harmonizing the both. Hence the Upanishadic injunction to reconcile *karma* and *upāsana.* The last four verses are prayers chanted during the end of life intended to free the soul from cycles of birth and death so that it could attain eternal beatitude. The *Īśa Upanishad* thus points to the need of a desirable reconciliation of the paths of knowledge (*jñāna*), action (*karma*) and devotion (*upāsana*).

Kéna Upanishad, a part of *Sāma Véda* consists four chapters with thirty four *mantras. Kénéshitam patati préshitam manaḥ* is the first mantra or hymn of this *Upanishad* and hence the name *kéna* which means 'by whom". This *Upanishad* is a dialogue between a teacher and his disciple who enquires into the ultimate energy that vitalizes sense organs, mind and life of man. The teacher explains the self or *atman* as all pervading which is beyond everything. It is not controlled but controls sense organs, mind and life. This *Upanishad* elucidates that the nature of *atman* is highly secret that even he who is believed to have known does not really know it. Thus it says:

"It is conceived of by him by whom It is not conceived of.
He by whom It is conceived of, knows It not.
It is not understood by those who (say they) understand It.
It is understood by those who (say they) understand It not.[29]"

Third and forth chapters narrate a story to explain the all inclusive, absolute and the unknowable Brahman. *Kéna Upanishad* has it that individual soul enmeshed by senses, mind and ego gets vision of the absolute only through guidance of the ultimate and not through anything else. This *Upanishad* also recommends ethical disciplines and *upāsanas* or devotion to attain knowledge of Brahman.

Kaṭhopanishad found in *Krishna Yajur Véda* occupies an important place among the Upanishads. It deals with the mind boggling problems of eternal and the ephemeral which it elucidates through the story of Yama-Nachiketa dialogue. This conversation unfolds the supreme knowledge that helps one know Brahman and get free from attachment and cycles of birth and death.

Praśnōpanishad and *Mundakōpanishad*, the two complimentary Upanishads appear in *Aṭharva Véda. Praśna Upanishad* deals with *para* and *apara* or mundane and transcendental knowledge. This *Upanishad*, given in question-answer form, contains the story of six students who approached the teacher, sage Pippalada with spiritual questions. Here the teacher tested the seekers' interest for knowledge, fixing one year *brahmaçharya* or celibacy for them prior to answering each question. The first question dealt with the problem of the origin of living things and the second with the existence of gross body. The answers threw light on the element of *prāṇa* which enlivens sense organs and mind and enkindles the spirit within. Answer to the third question disclosed the origin of *prāṇa* as *atman* and the secret of work or karma as determinant of the whole process. As to the fourth question regarding the state of *sushupti* or deep sleep these Upanishads detail on the four states of soul : *jāgarita, swapna, sushupti* and *turīya.* Answer to the fifth question focuses on *ōmkāra upāsana* for the concentration of mind, the most necessary aspect of self realization. A very detailed description of *ātman* is given through the sixth question and its answer.

The *Muṇḍakōpanishad* is in the form of teacher-taught dialogue the kind found in the *Praśna.* The word *muṇḍaka* means one who has shaven his head as a disciplined *brahmachāri* or seeker of knowledge. It also means knife, which chops off the chords of ignorance and desire. This *Upanishad* comprising 65 mantras is divided into three *muṇḍakas* or portions, each *muṇḍaka* consisting two paragraphs or *khaṇḍas.* This *Upanishad* consisting of Angiras' instruction to his disciple Saunaka explains the superiority of *ātmavidya* or spiritual knowledge over the material. Human soul is described as the enjoyer of the mundane and the pure soul of the eternal bliss. This is symbolically presented through the two birds on the branch of a tree, one eating the fruit and the other still and silent, enjoying the supreme bliss. One is *jīvātman* or individual soul and the other *parmātman* or indwelling supreme spirit, both residing in the same body. While one is attached to the world, the other is free. When a man sees the Universal Ruler in himself, then the distinction between Good and Evil ceases and he is freed from passions and becomes one with universal spirit.

Māndūkya Upanishad, though smallest among the Upanishads is the gem. Its importance is so much that according to *Muktikōpanishad* a study of *Māndūkya* alone suffices a seeker of *mōksha* or salvation (*mumukshu*) to attain *ātmajñāna* or self-knowledge. The profound spiritual knowledge is so condensed in it that it is beyond the ken of ordinary perception. This *Upanishad* would have remained obscure but for the interpretations by later scholars like Gaudapada, the author of *Māndūkyakārika. Māṇḍūkya* leads in interpreting and explaining the *saguṇa* and *nirguṇa* aspects of Brahman. It speaks of *ōmkāra* as the symbol of Brahman which could be meditated on to attain the undifferentiated consciousness.

Taittarīyōpanishad is found in the eighth and ninth chapters of the *Krishna Yajur Veda.* Sankara has classified its *sḷōkas* or verses into *vallis* like *Siksha Valli, Brahmānanda Valli,* and *Brighu valli. Siksha valli* comprises of *sḷōkas* which aim at generating interest towards *brahma jñānānanda* or the bliss deriving from the knowledge of Brahman and preparing seekers for attaining higher wisdom. *Védānta valli* gives an exhaustive description of the nature of *brahman* and *védāntic* knowledge. *Brigu valli* articulates methods to attain *brahmajñāna.* Description of the *kōśas* or layers which cover up the soul is found in this *Upanishad* which ends with a description of the state of realization by one who has attained it.

Aitaréya Upanishad, a part of *Aitaréya Āranyaka* of *Ṛk Véda* has five Aranyakas in it. The subject matter of this *Upanishad* is the destruction of *avidya* which is the cause of *kāma karmas* or desirous actions that bind human being to mundane activities. This *Upanishad* in its wider aspect therefore explains the ways to enlighten the seeker with the streaming effulgence of *vidya* or knowledge to help him realize *Brahman*. Like *Īśa Upanishad*, *Aitaréya* also starts with the declaration that world is the expression of *ātman* itself (*ātmī vā idaméka evāgra āsīt*). The *mahāvākya* or the great saying of *Ṛk Véda*, *prajñānam brahmam* is mentioned in the last *mantra* and ends with description on state of immortality attained through self-realization. The *Upanishad* elaborates on *ātma-brahma* relation or relation between human soul and supreme soul.

Chhāndōgya Upanishad is a part of *Sāma Véda*. This *Upanishad* deriving its name from the word *Chhāndōga* meaning *sāma gāyaka* deals with a wide range of about 110 subjects and bristles with apothegms, all revealing the nature of *Brahman*. One of the gems of Indian spiritual literature, it also mirrors the socio-cultural life including systems of education of the period it was composed. A laudable manual for ethical and virtuous life, both individual and social, *Chhāndōgya* consists of five chapters dealing with different types of *sādhanas* or preparations for the attainment of *Brahman*. It highlights *upāsana* or worship of *ōmkara*, *āditya*, *prāṇa*, etc., all aiming to help the seeker prepare his mind to transcend the world of *karma* to attain *jñāna*. According to this *Upanishad* it is *upāsana* or total surrender of mind to a deity that helps one get concentration, and steady the mind (*amanībhāva*). The most famous saying *tat tvam asi* which is derivative of the spiritual discourse Uddalaka Aruni delivered to his son Swetaketu, the dialogue between Narada and Sanakkumara, emphasizing the importance of the knowledge of *brahman* to attain solace and serenity in life and the story of Indra and the Démon king Virōcana approaching Prajapati for self-knowledge are the highlights of this *Upanishad*. *Chhāndōgya* thus upholds the importance of self-knowledge, establishes the Atman-Brahman identity and discourses on various means for attaining it through different examples.

The word *Bṛhad* which means 'vast and expanding' itself shows the loftiness and depth of *Brhadāraṇyaka Upanishad* which is a part of *Śatapatḥa Brāhmaṇa* of *Śukḷa Yajur Véda*. Like *Chhāndōgya*, *Brhadāraṇyaka,* too, explains its message through stories and anecdotes. *Chhāndōgya* is divided into three *kāndas* or cantos, *Madhu Kānda*,

Yājñāvalkya kānda or *Muni Kānda* and *Khila Kānda*, each consisting two chapters. The first chapter explains the symbolic meaning underlying the Vedic rituals like *aśwamédḥa* wherein sacrificial horse or *médḥyāśwa* symbolizes the all pervading reality of the world. Here the *Upanishad* aims to uplift the seeker's mind from the mere materialism and ritualism to pure spirituality as found in the six *Brahmanas* of its first chapter. In the second chapter king Ajatasatru teaches Brahmin Balaki on self-knowledge and eternity of Brahman. The famous discourse between Yajnjavalkya and Maiteryi that differentiates between the eternal nature of Brahman and the ephemeral nature of worldly riches, too, takes place in this chapter. The third and fourth chapters are of great importance. While the third chapter introduces Yajnjavalkya, the doyen of spiritual knowledge who elucidates lofty ideas about Brahman at a metaphysical tournament at the court of King Janaka of Mithila where a scholarly audience engaged him with a number of hairsplitting questions related to spirituality, the fourth contains spiritual dialogue between Janaka and Yajnjavalkya which zeroes in elaborately on the theory of rebirth of *jīva* or soul. The fifth and the sixth chapters constitute the Khila Kānda which is only an *anubandḥa* or appendix to the *Upanishad* explaining some *upāsanas* or modes of worship for the gradual liberation of soul. The sixth chapter contains the story in which Prajapati explains the superiority of *prāṇa* over physical organs. Here the sense organs meet Prajapati with the question, which among them is more important than the other. Prajapati's reply that the one whose withdrawal leads a person to inactivity is the most important, reveals to the sense organs that without *prāṇa* no life is possible, and hence the superiority of *prāṇa*. The last portion deals with rituals and their procedures for material prosperity like the birth of a noble son, etc. Thus *Bṛhadāraṇyaka*, as its name reveals, is a jungle of knowledge ranging over a wide spectrum of subjects.

The central message of Upanishads or *Védānta* is the idea of unity according to which everything in universe is the expression of one non-dual reality. To help one realize this fundamental non-dual reality Upanishads make use of many ideal paths of understanding and methods of explanations. Being a part of the world which is the expression of this non-dual energy or pure consciousness (*prajñānam brahmam*), the attainment of this monistic unity becomes the ideal.[30] When this Brahman is enveloped by adjuncts of mind, body, life etc., it appears as individual self but when one understands the ultimate truth as the one indwelling spirit of everything the idea of unity becomes reality to the seeker.

The *Bhagavad-Gita* speaks of itself as the nectar churned out from the milk of enlightenment drawn from the cows that are the Upanishads (*sarvōpanishadō gāvō dōgdhạ*).[31] That *Gita*, the gem of philosophy itself is an outcome of Upanishadic thought alone would suffice to proclaim the supreme metaphysical importance of the Upanishads.

Upanishads refer to the macrocosmic and microcosmic character of "that great unborn Soul" which is indestructible, deathless, immortal, fearless... Brahman."[32] Soul according to Upanishads is of indefinable nature. Incomprehensible, it assumes manifold appearances. Unimaginable are its capabilities and unfathomable its potential.

Thus says the *Mundaka Upanishad*:

"Vast, heavenly, of unthinkable form;
And minute than the minute, It shines forth.
It is farther than the far, yet here near at hand;
Set down in the secret place (of the heart);
Even here among those who behold (It)[33]."

The omnipresent, omnipotent and omniscient nature of Soul is thus well explained in Bhagavad-Gita as follows:

It is without and within all beings;
It is moving and unmoving, being subtle;
It is incomprehensible; it is far, yet near.

It is undivided in beings
And yet remains as if divided;
It is the sustainer of beings
As also the destroyer and creator.

It is the light of lights, and is said to be
Knowledge which is beyond all darkness;
It is knowable and accessible through knowledge;
And is implanted in the heart of all beings[34].

The lore speaks about Atman as the very part of Brahman. A purified *ātman* is *brahman* in miniature. The word Brahman which connotes the ultimate reality of universe originally meant reality which grows or swells. Originated from the root *br* which means 'expands', Brahman may be translated into 'the ever expanding one' or the one which tends to expand (*bruhad*). The gross and subtle as well as the infinite energy, Brahman is the all encompassing everything or the basic essence of this universe and all the universes, if any. It is in everything and above everything, the primordial and final reality.

The word *brahman* could thus meticulously be interpreted as that which grows or expands. *Brahman* is the central energy the universe evolves out from and recedes to or expands ever from and contracts to. Upanishads affirm that Brahman is the all inclusive source of everything, the ultimate reality (*sat*). Swami Vivekananda clarifies this idea as follows:

> What is the most evolved notion that man has of this universe. It is intelligence, the adjustment of part to part, the display of intelligence, of which the ancient design theory was an attempt at expression. The beginning was, therefore, intelligence. At the beginning that intelligence becomes involved, and in the end that intelligence gets evolved. The sum total of the intelligence displayed in the universe must, therefore, be the involved universal intelligence unfolding itself. This universal intelligence is what we call God. Call it by any other name, it is absolutely certain that in the beginning there is that Infinite cosmic intelligence. This cosmic intelligence gets involved, and it manifests, evolves itself, until it becomes the perfect man, the "Christ-man," the "Buddha-man." Then it goes back to its own source.[35]

Upanishadic Seers, who sought after this idea of unity explain it as Absolute, One without a second, encompassing all, devoid of qualities and dwells in each entity of the world as consciousness. They name it as Brahman and "bring out in several fanciful and mythological accounts of creation the great truth of the oneness of the world"[36]. Suffice it to say, the ultimate cosmic principle is the Brahman which is the soul in all things. *Maitri Upanishad* explains Brahman as the cosmic intelligence. It says:

> "Verily, in the beginning this world was Brahma, the limitless One : limitless to the east, limitless to the west, limitless to the north, and above and below, limitless in every direction. Truly, for him east and the other directions exist not, nor across, nor below, nor above.
>
> Incomprehensible is that supreme Soul (*ātman*), unlimited, unborn, not to be reasoned about, unthinkable. He whose soul is space (*ākāśātman*)! In the dissolution of the world He alone remains awake. From that space He assuredly awakes this world, which is a mass of thought. It is thought by Him, and in Him it disappears.[37]"

These lines bring out the monistic idea regarding Brahman. Sankara's finding *Brahma satyam jaganmithya jīvō brahmaiva nāpara* or Brahman alone is the reality since *jīva* is nothing other than Brahman is of much significance. *Jagath* which means 'ever moving' is indeed the reflection of the very Brahman itself which, too, is ever expanding, dynamic and vibrant. Brahman is not god conceived in ordinary sense of the term. It is not a concept which serves the purpose of religion, sociology or theology. It is the primordial energy or undifferentiated consciousness and the ultimate one which is all-comprehending.

Cosmology of ancient India as discoursed by Yajnjavalkya in *Bṛahadāraṇyaka Upanishad* views space as only one of the derivative of Brahman. (*Brahadāraṇyaka*, 38-9) Space does not have absolute nature but is only relative to the degree of enlightenment attained by mind which is the locus of *māya* or hallucination. Brahman is postulated as manifest in a person's psychic activities playing with *karaṇa* and *anthakkaraṇa* (sense organs and the mind). The more the mind is steadied the brighter the eternity or infinitude shines. Out-stepping the confines of time and space, one becomes the very part of eternity itself. According to *Gita*, space and time stretch in their infinitude before one with steadied wisdom or *sthitaprajña.* He sees the far as he sees the near. He sees the future as he sees the present. Hence his capability to speak about what happens far away and what is stored in the future, one of the *ashtaiśwaryasiddhis* or rare potentials attained by supermen. Sri Aurobindo describes it as follows:

> "Even in Its universal being Brahman exceeds the Movement. Exceeding Time, it contains in Itself past, present and future simultaneously and has not to run to the end of conceivable Time. Exceeding Space, It contains all formations in Itself coincidently and has not to run to the end of conceivable Space. Exceeding Causality, It contains freely in Itself all eventualities as well as all potentialities without being bound by the apparent chain of causality by which they are linked in the universe. Everything is already realized by It as the Lord before it can be accomplished by the separated personalities in the movement.[38]"

When the infinite consciousness or primordial energy wills to evolve itself into appearance, the first derivative, *chit-śakti* or *māya* emanates. *Māya* is the Brahman's manifesting power causing the appearance of world with its name and form, differences and diversities, time and space and all that are governed by the principle of causality. Brahman manifests with the same care and accuracy in minutest as well as the biggest entities, maintaining the natural law of energy conservation, transforming itself from one state to another without any change in the sum total of energy. The *māya* thus works in different ways to cause the appearance of the world of differences and diversities simultaneous with its maintaining the totality of energy through its dynamics of evolution and manifestation. According to Sri Aurobindo:

> Science reveals to us how minute is the care, how cunning the device, how intense the absorption it bestows upon the smallest of its works even as on the largest. This mighty energy is an equal and impartial mother, *samam brahma,* in the great term of the Gita, and its intensity and force of movement is the same in the formation and upholding of a system of suns and the organization of the life of an ant-hill.[39]

The power and the 'Absolute' co-exist in their potential phase in a universal homogeneity. Force which is the derivative of the undifferentiated is not an unintelligent energy but has consciousness or *bōdḥa* inherent in it.

The cosmic rest of Brahman between the two cycles of manifestations is symbolically presented by the lore through the 'Cosmic Sleep' of Vishnu on the infinity again represented through the serpent *Ananta* meaning the infinite, all amidst the infinite water sheet. It is the state to which Brahman withdraws after manifestation to prepare itself for the next cycle of creation in its eternal recurrence. This phase in which universe exists only in a potential form, just as the future tree exists in the seed, is the state of *praḷaya* or absorption. The first fluttering, waving, thought (*prathama spanda*) turns the 'Being' into the 'Become' or the unmanifest into the manifest. Out of the blissful infinite which is in perfect equilibrium the form arises. Brahman is the lord of consciousness force which through expanding and contracting processes or manifestation and withdrawal gets transformed into material world of differences and diversities. Sri Aurobindo thus explains it:

> "Matter is the presentation of force which is most easily intelligible to our intelligence, molded as it is by contacts in Matter to which a mind involved in material brain gives the

> response. The elementary state of material Force is, in the view of the old Indian physicists, a condition of purer material extension in Space of which the peculiar property is vibration typified to us by the phenomenon of sound. But vibration in this state of ether is not sufficient to create forms. There must first be some obstruction in the flow of the Force ocean, some contraction and expansion, some interplay of vibrations, some impinging of force upon force so as to create a beginning of fixed relation and mutual effects. Material Force modifying its first ethereal status assumes a second, called in the old language the aerial, of which the special property is contact between force and force, contact that is the basis of all material relations. Still we have not as yet real forms but only varying forces. A sustaining principle is needed. This is provided by a third self-modification of the primitive Force of which the principle of light, electricity, fire and heat is for us the characteristic manifestation. Even then, we can have forms of force preserving their own character and peculiar action, but not stable forms of Matter. A fourth state characterized by diffusion and a first medium of permanent attractions and repulsions, termed picturesquely water or the liquid state, and a fifth of cohesion, termed earth or the solid state, complete the necessary elements.[40]"

The Brahman has thus two aspects. It is the ultimate, undifferentiated, homogenous reality in which everything exists in a potential state which is indeterminate with no qualitative difference. This is *nirguṇabrahman* which is *śivam* or bliss. *Taittirīya Upanishad* refers to Brahman as *ānanda* and everything as born of the bliss (*ānandam brahma, ānandādhyeva khlvimāni bhutāni jāyante*). It is *Vishnu* or the one with expanding and all pervading nature. When *nirguṇabrahman* through its own deliberate thought separates its power or force, the world with its manifoldness arises. *Māya* or *chit-śakti* is that which projects the world out of *Brahman.*

> Sacred poetry (*chhandas*), the sacrifices, the ceremonies, the ordinances, the past, the future, and what the Vedas declare this whole world, the illusion-maker (*māyin*) projects out of this [*Brahma*] and in it by illusion.[41]

According to *Ṛk Véda* in the beginning there was neither nothingness nor differentiated substances (*nasadāsinnō sadāsīt*) but only eternal, undifferentiated pure consciousness. *Taittirīya* has it that the *Barhman* desired thus:

> "Would that I were many! Let me procreate myself! Having performed austerity He created this whole world, whatever there is here. Having created it, into it, indeed, He entered. Having entered it, He became both the actual (*sat*) and the yon (*tya*), both the defined (*nirukta*) and the undefined, both the based and the non-based, both the consciousness (vijñāna) and the unconscious, both the real (*satya*) and the false (*anṛta*). As the real, He became whatever there is here.[42]"

In *Kaṭha Upanishad* Brahman is explained as the life source (*prāṇa*) which controls every worldly occurrence. Swami Vivekananda explains *Brahman* as *Prāṇa* or the life that infuses *spanda* or vibration into the cosmos. According to him,

> ... all the forces, whether you call them gravitation, or attraction, or repulsion, whether expressing themselves as heat, or electricity, or magnetism, are nothing but the variations of that unit energy. Whether they express themselves as thought, reflected from *antahkarana*, the inner organs of man, or as action from an external organ, the unit from which they spring is what is called *prāṇa*. Again, what is *prāṇa; prāṇa* is *spandana* or vibration. When all this universe shall have resolved back into its primal state, what becomes of this infinite force. Do they think that it becomes extinct. Of course no. If it became extinct, what would be the cause of the next wave, because the motion is going in wave forms, rising, falling, rising again, falling again. Here is the word *srushti*, which expresses the universe... It is *srushti*, projection. At the end of a cycle, every thing becomes finer and finer and is resolved back into the primal state from which it sprang, and therefore it remains for a time quiescent, to spring forth again. That is *srushti*, Projection. And what becomes of all these forces, the *prānas* They are resolved back into the primal *prāṇa*, and this *prāna* becomes almost motionless - not entirely motionless; and

> that is what is described in the Vedic *Sūkta*: "It vibrated without vibrations" - *ānidavātam...* And what becomes of what you call matter The forces permeate all matter; they all dissolve into *ākāśa* from which they again come out; this *akasha* is the primal matter. Whether you translate it as ether or anything else, the idea is that this *ākāśa* is the primal form of matter. This *ākāśa* vibrates under the action of *prāṇ a*, and when the next *srushṭi* is coming up, as the vibrations become quicker, the *ākāśa* is lashed into all these wave forms which we call suns, moons and systems[43]."

There is no primordial substance employed in the creation of cosmos like clay used by the potter to mould pot. Hence the Upanishadic comparison of mundane life with dream to give a fitting explanation for the universe. In dream or *swapna* which is a virtual reality one experiences as in an awakened mood. But the difference here is that in dream with no physical involvement, mind alone becomes the enjoyer, the enjoyed and enjoyment, a process where the three combine to experience evanescence. But in dream none realizes that what is experienced is only ephemeral. That it was dream itself is realized only with the dream giving way to awakened state. Quiet similar is the awakened mood or *jāgrat*. The occurrence of the world, the Upanishads say, is like a dream. World is the differentiated consciousness which comes from undifferentiated consciousness. Just like one falls into dream from awakened mood to which mind gets back after sleep individuals and things evolve from the undifferentiated and attain differentiated state of entities with separate identities. And after a span just as the mind returns from dream to wakened state the differentiated entity returns to the undifferentiated. This is the *māyāvāda* which is the basis of *advaita vēdānta*. According to this explanation Brahman remains in both unmanifest and manifest forms simultaneously. Even when Brahman manifests into the multitude of appearances it remains unchanged, say the Upanishads. It thus with its total content and state unchanging, produces everything from it and draws them back. This is like magician conjuring up and away the magical world. The world thus appears like an enlarged dream, a big magic or *māya* created by Brahman. Hence the word *māyin* to describe Brahman. *Māya* is inherent in the very *māyin* like the magical power in the magician. According to Upanishad *māya* is the power of *māyin*, the powerful. *Maya* creates an infinite variety out of the undifferentiated oneness. Being the one doing important (*prakrushta*) works (*kruti*) *māya* is also called *prakruti. Prakruti* according to the *Sānkhya* is the undifferentiated whole which is the 'being', the 'becoming' as well as the will that causes the 'being' to 'become'. It is the Brahman that causes, fills and out-steps itself. World is thus Brahman in both its manifest and unmanifest forms. But this duality is only on the outer surface which vanishes at the awakening of consciousness which is within oneself as well as in the entirety, the *Brahman.* When one realizes that world is only a manifestation of *Brahman* which is the embodiment of *bōdḥa* or consciousness he attains the state of consciousness or *bōdḥa* or Buddhahood. Hence the call of Gita to attain *bōdḥa* or supreme consciousness (*buddḥau śaraṇamanviścha*) or the later prayer of Gautama Buddha for seeking refuge in *bodha* (*Buddham śaraṇam gachhāmi*). What is supreme is the *bōdha* or consciousness because it is the very *Brahman.* Everything emanates from *bōdha* or pure consciousness and returns to it.

But how could one know that world is only a manifestation of Brahman or how to explain that it is consciousness that manifests as visible cosmos are problems that confront an Indian cosmologist. When the world of matter is analyzed into simple constituents one comes to the idea of self or consciousness. Every stage of analysis proves that all that are analyzed are not realities but consciousness that realizes the ephemeral nature of the mundane. Hence a Vedantin's refutation, 'this is not' (*néti*) the reality but consciousness that helps one know the unreality. This is the most convincing demonstration of the existence of omnipresent consciousness. It is necessary to explain how consciousness appears as things and events. Upanishads point to mind as pure consciousness possessed by *māya* or force. They like modern science opine that force or motion is the cause of appearances. Analyzing a complex unit to the last, cloth for instance, one comes across thread, cotton, atom and finally sub-atomic particles which are in motion giving visibility to the particle. This force of motion is the cause of visible universe according to Upanishads. World is called *jagat* or the ever moving that results in *lōka* or the visible. *lōkyaté iti lōkaḥ* or what is subject to eye - *lōchana* - is *lōka* or world. Movement or speed brings in visibility and if movement stops visibility ceases and with it the cosmos, too. That velocity results in mass is thus the finding Vedanta and modern physics agree alike. All what are visible are thus unrealities or mere appearances due to superimposition (*adhyārōpa*) which is a play of *māya* with mind as its locus. Citing the example of the rope-snake confusion, Upanishads say that visible world is superimposed on Brahman just as the snake on the rope. One may take the rope for a snake till he sees the reality that it is no snake but rope.

According to *Sānkhya*, Brahman contains the qualities *sattva*, *rajas* and *tamas* (*salila*) in perfect equilibrium. When this equilibrium is disturbed by the force of *prakruti* the *sattva* is transformed into *rajas* and *rajas* into *tamas* and materialization takes place. When momentum of force increases *sattva* becomes faint and *rajas* dominates and when momentum reaches the maximum *tamas* dominates and results in materialization. Solidity and mass are thus results of motion. Experiments by high speed particle accelerators have shown that particles come out of nothing. An examination of the structure of an atom, especially its planetary model makes this clear. An atom consists mostly of empty space with nucleus at the centre which contains almost the whole weight of an atom. Electrons revolving around the nucleus have only negligible weight. This weight difference is due to the speed of particles. The speed of particles in the nucleus is 40,000 miles per second whereas the speed of the electrons is 600 miles per second. It is the speed of particle which appears as mass. Atom which is mostly of empty space appears as matter due to high velocity of its particles that cover up the empty space giving the appearance of a solid matter. This high speed mobility or motion is thus the reason of visibility. When motion ceases, visibility, too, ceases with matter vanishing into disappearance. When the world is no more *jagat* or moving, it is no more *lōka* or visible. With movement or *spanda* stopping the world as one sees also ceases to exist. To explain this *Vēdānta* uses the example of *alāta barmaṇa* or swirling of torch that causes the appearance of circle filled with fire.

> *riju vakrādikābhāsa*
> *malātaspanditam yathā*
> *grahaṇagrāhakābhāsam*
> *vijñānaspanditam tathā*
>
> "Just like the speedy movement of fire at the end of the faggot band appears straight and curved, so is the *vijñāna* or the unreal knowledge which appears the way one perceives it.
>
> *aspandamānamalāta*
> *manābhāsamajam yathā*
> *aspandamānam vijñāna*
> *manābhāsamajam tathā*[44]

"Just as there is no straight or curved line of fire when the fire at the end of the faggot band remains still, so is the absence of differences when *vijñāna* or the unreal knowledge ceases to work (*Jñāna* or the real knowledge dawns when the *vijñāna* or the unreal knowledge ceases.)

Revolving a burning faggot gives the appearance of a fire-circle which ceases to exist when revolving stops. Here it is clear that the fire-circle comes from the act of revolving the fire. Consequently when revolving stops the circle of fire vanishes like an illusion. Likewise the world of experience is only a fanciful creation resulting from movement or force of magic wand of the great magician, the Brahman or the undifferentiated consciousness.

"The many in the universe are sometimes called parts of the universal Brahman as the waves are parts of the sea. But, in truth, these waves are each of them that sea, their diversities being those of frontal or superficial appearances caused by the sea's motion. As each object in the universe is really the whole universe in a different frontal appearance, so each individual soul is all Brahman regarding itself and world from a centre of cosmic consciousness[45].

When this movement is no more, there is no mind and also no world. The permanent union with the Absolute is possible only in *samādhi.*

manōdriśyamidam dvaitam
yatkinchil sacharācharam
manasōhyamanībhāvé
dvaitam naivōpalabhyaté

"The duality seen in all the moving
and unmoving is the mind-born,
when the mind vanishes, with it
would vanish all the dualities.[46]

Diversity thus disappears before a coherent mind. Gaudapada even carried his views to the extreme of the non-creation of the world or *ajātavāda.* To quote him:

"Some people regard the universe as the greatness of God, others as his creation, others as a dream, others as an illusion, others think of the world as an accidental product of time. Others regard it merely as the will of the God... still others the object of His enjoyment, some people call it a play of God, and yet others regard it as God's nature[47]."

But Gaudapada's view of non-creation would dawn only to one who has control over his mind to the extent of realizing world as a mirage. Having crossed the world of dualities affected by happiness and sorrows, he experiences perfect bliss. Sankara's theory of *māya* should be studied in this light. He does not completely negate the existence of world but states that the world disappears for a person who realizes the highest reality or *paramārthikasatta* like the hallucination of snake in the rope ceases when the rope is apprehended.

Seekers of *mōksha* or liberation used to mistake material world as an obstacle in their attaining it and tended to negate the reality of matter. But Upanishads remove this ignorance, explaining material world as manifestations of Brahman or the Absolute indwelling spirit of individual soul. This Upanishadic view is thus explained by Sri Aurobindo:

> "There are always two possible views of the universe. The one supposes, with modern Science, Matter to be the beginning of things and studies everything as an evolution from Matter; or, if not Matter, then, with the Sankhya philosophy, an indeterminate inconscient, active Force or *prakruti* of which even mind and reason are mechanical operations, the conscious soul, if any exist, being a quite different and, although conscient, yet inactive entity. The other supposes the conscious soul, the *purusha*, to be the material as well as the cause of the universe and *prakruti* to be only its *śakti* or the material of forms. The latter is the view of the Upanishads.[48]"

Mundaka Upanishad, too, endorses the view that material world with its diverse experiences forms an arena to practice renunciation and spiritual life. To develop renunciation there must be a world to renounce. Brahman is the paternal aspect and material world the maternal which foster creative unity i.e., spiritual realization. Modern scientific discovery that mass is a form of energy established that there is a fundamental hidden reality, compassing towards a spiritual something. The seers of Upanishads intuitively experienced this 'spiritual' and realized that consciousness is the ultimate reality which manifests as material world.

> For in that higher and less hampered existence we perceive that consciousness and being are not different from each

> other, but all being is a supreme consciousness, all consciousness is self-existence, eternal in itself, real in its works and neither a dream nor an evolution. The world is real precisely because it exists only in consciousness; for it is a Conscious Energy, one with Being that creates it. It is the existence of material form in its own right apart from the self-illumined energy which assumes the form ...[49]

Human body, considered a hindrance to self-realization, is in fact manifestation of the ultimate reality. The sense organs and mind combine into physical form; mind-consciousness combine makes life. The world as matter is not the creation of mind. That matter ever existed, exists and will exist as the seat of energy is scientifically proved. Brahman the ultimate, involutes into world and resides in everything material, remaining transcendent, too. Material world thus becomes the manifestation of ultimate consciousness, Brahman. Mind is only a higher expression of Absolute consciousness through which one can experience material world. Sense organs and mind (*karaṇa* and *antakkaraṇa*) help one experience the external world. Of these mind is superior, coordinating and assimilating the sensations produced by the work of force. It is thus through sense organs and mind the force or *māya* makes itself felt. This spiritual relevance of material body or material world is thus well summed up:

> In other words, if Brahman has entered into form and represented Its being in material substance, it can only be to enjoy self-manifestation in the figures of relative and phenomenal consciousness. Brahman is in this world to represent Itself in the values of Life. Life exists in Brahman in order to discover Brahman in itself. Therefore man's importance in the world is that he gives to it that development of consciousness in which its transfiguration by a perfect self-discovery becomes possible. To fulfill god in life is man's manhood. He starts from the animal vitality and its activities, but a divine existence is its objective.[50]

Existence in primal stage is subtle. Subtlety is the nature of Brahman. But passing trough different levels of manifestation it becomes complex and gross at different levels of material or physical plain. Physical plain is a reality in its gross manifested form which is both universal and particular. The different parts, for instance, the mineral world, plant life, animal kingdom, and human society are related to the highest not in an abstract or mechanical way but as the very parts of the universal. All parts in universe share the light of this universal spirit and possess specific features on account of special duties assigned to them.[51] It is *Brahman* or consciousness that manifests as particles. *Chitśakti* or consciousness manifests as *chétanāśakti* or life force and finally as *jaṭhaśakti* or material particles. (*laḷitāsahasranāma* explains both spirit or *chitśakti* and matter or *jaṭhaśakti* as the manifestations of the Brahman - *chitśakti chétanārūpā jaṭhaśakti jaṭhātmikā*). It is relevant to ponder over what Sri Aurobindo writes:

> "Is the material state an emptiness of consciousness - even though from the point of view of evolution an original and not an intermediate sleep. And by sleep the human example teaches us that we mean not a suspension of consciousness, but its gathering inward away from conscious physical response to the impacts of external things. And is not this what all existence is that has not yet developed means of outward communication with the external physical world. Is there not a conscious Soul, a *Purusha* who wakes for ever even in all that sleeps.

To this *Brhadāraṇyaka Upanishad* answers that everything in this world is Brahman which is *sat* or pure intelligence. In sleep with the mind and body withdrawing from activity the *Atman* finds itself in perfect union with *Brahman*. This is the state of *sushupti* wherein human soul, becoming free of sense organs and mind, enjoys bliss in perfect union with the Absolute. In *Chhāndōgya* Upanishad Uddalaka Aruni thus explains to Swetaketu on sleep:

"Understand from me, my dear, the condition of sleep. When a person here sleeps *(svapiti)*, as it is called, then, my dear, he has reached Being, he has gone to his own (*svamāpita*). Therefore they say of him "he sleeps"; for he has gone to his own.[52]

Description of four states of the self, waking (*jāgarita sthāna*), dreaming (*svapana sthāna*), deep sleep (*sushupta*) and the final stage of bliss (*turīya*) is found in Upanishads. In *Māndūkya Upanishad* the states of soul are explained by comparing it with the syllable AUM. The first three states are represented by syllables (*mātras*) - 'A-U-M' and *turīya* is the fourth syllable-less state. *Turīya* is the state of perfect bliss enjoyed through the union with the ultimate. Still in *sushupti* one attains only a temporary union with the self.[53]

To bring the primary energy content in oneself into communion with universal energy was the much sought after goal of ancient sages.

In fact they were the seekers of unity, the state wherein there is no *dvaita* or duality and everything dwells in the bliss of non-duality or *advaita*. They enjoyed the nectar of the ultimate harmony or a creative unity.

Ancient sages prescribe the ways, too, to realize it. It is *Yōga*, the preparation that helps one communion with the universal spirit or if to quote Einstein that "super-personal content" whose "overpowering meaningfulness" is most important. Its two steps *dhyāna* and *dhāraṇa* bring the *dhi* or intellect into the balanced state or *samādḥi*. This state wherein intellect, mind and consciousness become balanced is the *samadḥiprajña*, the end of *dḥyāna*. Here *dḥyāta* or the seeker, *dḥyēya*, the sought after and *dḥyāna*, the process of seeking, compared to three petals or *tripuṭi*, fuse together and what remains is only the eternal, pure light or consciousness which is undivided (*akhanḍa*). When *tripuṭi* or the three petals of *dhyāna* whither, there emerges pure enlightenment, *akhanḍabōdḥasatta* or undifferentiated consciousness that encompasses everything including time and space with all their infinity as parts of an undifferentiated whole. This is the state of Unity where individual consciousness gets itself in total identity with universal or cosmic consciousness, i.e. *Brahman* or in which *atman* realizes itself as *brahman*. This state is variously described as *purusha*, *brahman*, *chaitanyam*, *chit*, *samvit*, *ātman* etc. *Samādḥi* is thus the state in which mind becomes one with pure soul or *ātman* or mind ceases to exist for the *māya* to influence. Here philosophy comes almost in agreement with modern science both in means and end. It is interesting to note that modern science instead of using the term 'observation' uses 'participation' because it says that to know the secret of any universal phenomenon one should be a participant rather than observer of it. However both could still not be equated due to some fundamental differences. Upanishads say that when mind attains complete equanimity the supreme self pervades the mind and the individual soul gets into unity with the supreme. Thus says *Kaṭha Upanishad*:

> "The journey of life can be safely completed, and the Supreme world of Vishnu [*Vishnu* is one which expands, one with *vishalībhāva* or tendency to expand and grow, another term used to denote *brahman*] reached only if one keeps a watchful control over the senses. The body is like a chariot to which the senses are yoked like horses. The mind is like the reins, which enable the charioteer, viz., the understanding, to hold the horses, i.e., the senses in check.

The Soul rides on the chariot, and the road is the world of objects over the senses move. If the reins are not held firmly and wisely, the senses, like vicious horses, will get out of control, and the chariot will not reach the goal, but will go round and round in births and re-births. If the man is wise, and controls his mind, his senses will be like good horses driven by a good driver.[54]"

Thus for realizing the Brahman, Upanishads recommend certain ethical disciplines like truthfulness, ascetic life, right insight etc. They are considered essential prerequisites of *upāsana*, the means for realizing Brahman. Only through *upāsana* or meditation one can realize the essential identity with the universal self. Among the different types of *upāsana* to attain Brahman, *ōmkāra upāsana* is mostly recommended. *Ōm* is referred as the symbol of Brahman. *Māndūkya Upanishad* calls the self itself *ōm.*

hari ōm. ōmityétadaksharam idam sarvam
tasyōpavyākhyānam bhūtam bhavad bhavishyaditi
sarvamōmkāra éva. yacchanyāt
trikālātitam tadapyōmkāra évacha

"Everything is the letter *ōm.* Its clear explanation is that past, present and future are all *ōmkara.* Even what out-step these three i.e. the past-present-future continuum are all *ōmkara.*[55]

Verily everything, the Upanishads say, is encompassed by *ōmkara*, the infinity. It is both *ātman* and *brahman*, calm, blissful and the undivided whole that sheds one's mundane dualistic feeling. Meditating on *ōm*, one crosses the world of divisions, dualities and dimensions and gets into that of perfect unity and wholesomeness. It is the beginning, the middle and the end, all fusing together into an infinite whole.

This atman resides in the three-phased syllable *ōm.* These three phases are *akāra*, *ukāra* and *makāra.*[56]

These three letters *a*, *u* and *ma* (A U M) pronounced in combination as *ōm* is the generalized symbol of all *nāma* and *rūpa* or sounds and forms. The first sound A represents the beginning, U the middle and M the end. According to *Māndūkya Upanishad*, A or *akāra* is the fully awakened consciousness and light (*jāgaritasthānō vaiśvānarō akāra prathama mātra*).[57] "The letter A is the least differentiated of all sounds. Therefore Krishna says in the Gita *aksharāṇām akārōsmi* - I am A among the letters."[58] He who realizes *akāra* as *ādimatwa* (being first) obtains verily all desires.

Besides, all articulate sounds produced manifest as *ōm,* i.e. AUM which begins with the root of tongue and ending in lips. "Throat sound is A, and M is the last lips sound and the U represents the rolling forward of the impulse which begins at the root of the tongue till it ends in the lips."[59] *Ōm* thus represents the whole phenomenon of sound manifestation and is the fittest symbol of Brahman or truly symbolic of God. It is *brahman,* the *akhaṇḍa-satchidānanda,* the undivided Existence-Knowledge-Bliss *ōm* represents. *Upāsana* or meditation on *ōm* helps the seeker gets one with Brahman.

The effect of *ōmkara-upāsana* is explained in the *Praśna Upanishad* where Satyakama's teacher tells him that

> just as a snake is relieved of its slough, similarly is the man who meditates on *ōm* relieved of his sins, and, by the power of his chants, is lifted to the highest world where he beholds the person who informs the body, and who stands supreme above any living complex whatsoever.[60]

Śvétāśwatāra Upanishad also recommends practice of *yōga* for realizing unity. *Yōga* helps one shed all egos and separate identity, come into communion with the entirety and see oneself in everything and everything in oneself. All the infinity, both of time and space is in him; he is the entirety condensed. *Māndūkyakārika* of Gaudapada speaks of the complete annihilation of mind through *yōga. Ōmkāra upāsana* as well as *yōga* thus help one to get into communion with the ultimate reality which is the beginning and end combined in one, i.e. the infinite differently called in Upanishads as *brahman, bōdha, ānanda, chaitanya,* etc.

> *chaitanyādāgatam sthūla-*
> *sūkshmātmakamidam jagat.*[61]
>
> "Universe, both subtle and gross, sources off the undifferentiated consciousness.
>
> *manasaivānudrushṭhavyam*
> *nēha nānāsti kinchana*
> *mrutyōḥ sa mrutyumāpnōti*
> *yā iha nānēti paśyati.*[62]
>
> "That there is nothing as differences should be understood. One who, missing the sight of unity, sees only differences would whirl through the cycles of death, i.e. from death to death.

Brahman or *ānanda* or the ultimate bliss is thus the starting and finishing point of all the universal entities- *Ānandam brahma*. *Ānanda* is *brahman* or ultimate truth which is the supreme bliss, says *Taittirīya Upanishad.* Therefore the Upanishad says:

ānandādhyēva khalvimāni bhūtāni
jāyatē, ānandēna jātāni jīvanti
ānandam prayantyabhisamviśanti.[63]

Or

Everything is born of *ānanda*
Everything abides in *ānanda*
Everything returns to *ānanda.*

Hence the call of Upanishads to know and experience this *ananda* or bliss wherein one feels oneself as the universal whole, wherein there is no difference, where all the seeming differences drop off to experience an unbearable ecstasy in a creative unity.

Vedic India thus presents the picture of a highly educated people. Though it is commonly believed that Vedic people generally practised chanting the *Vedas* rather than writing them so as to avoid phonetic error it would be equally foolish to conclude that a people who were well versed with the use of syllables, meter and all the rules related to the use of letters, themselves divided into vowels and consonants, were ill at home in the art of writing. It is another fallacy born of the European Indologists' ignorance of Indian culture or attempt at deliberate distortion of it that made some of them conclude that Vedic Aryans did not know the art of writing. In fact Vedic literature gives the picture of a literate people who knew the art of writing. The fact that *Vedic Manthras* were not put to writing does not mean that writing alone was not practised while the other branches of learning were put to practical experimentation. Our ignorance about whether the Vedic people wrote or not, is no evidence to conclude that they didn't know the art of writing.

References

1. *Mahabharata*, 2. 37. 34 & 7. 135. 31.
2. Anantalal Thakur, 'Gautama', in VS Raghavan (Ed), *Founders of Philosophy*, Delhi, 1981, p. 46).
3. Surendranath Dasgupta, *A History of Indian Philosophy*, Delhi, 1988, Vol. I, p. 285.

4. Albert Einstein, 'Science, Philosophy and Religion', A Symposium, published by the *Conference of Science, Philosophy and Religion in their relation to the Democratic ways of Life*, Inc., New York, 1941.
5. Surendranath Dasgupta, *Op. Cit*, p. 287.
6. *Gita.* X. 26.
7. Sri Aurobindo, *The Synthesis of Yoga*, Pondicherry, 1984, p. 1.
8. *Gita*, II. 28.
9. It is interesting to have a passing reference to the world view brought in by modern physics. The following are the words of David Bohm, one of the interpreters of Quantum theory:

    One is led to a new notion of unbroken wholeness which denies the classical idea of analyzability of the world into separately and independently existing parts... We have reversed the usual classical notion that the independent "elementary parts" of the world are the fundamental reality, and that the various systems are merely particular contingent forms and arrangements of these parts. Rather, we say that inseparable quantum interconnectedness of the whole universe is the fundamental reality, and that relatively independently behaving parts are mere particular and contingent forms within this whole.

    See D. Bohm & B. Hiley, "On the Intuitive Understanding of Non-locality as Implied by Quantum Theory," *Foundations of Physics*, Vol. 5, New York, 1975, pp. 92, 102.

    According to Fritjof Capra who makes comparative study between the world views expounded by eastern mysticism and modern physics:

    The Quantum Theory forces us to see the universe not as a collection of physical objects , but rather as a complicated web of relations between the various parts of a unified whole. Fritjof Capra, *The Tao of Physics*, Colorado, 1984, p. 124.

    Heisenberg further confirms this when he says that the world appears as a complicated tissue of events, in which connections of different kinds alternate or overlap or combine and thereby determine the texture of the whole. W. Heisenberg, *Physics and Philosophy*, New York, 1958, p. 107.
10. Sri Aurobindo, *The Life Divine*, Pondicherry, 1982, p. 78.
11. Sri Aurobindo, *See Sri Aurobindo Library Centenary Edition*, Vol. 15, p. 6.
12. Aswini Kumar Lal, 'Big-Bang: A Critical Review', *Journal of Cosmology*, 2010, Vol. 6, 1533-1547, January 30, 2010.
13. Gita. XI. 12.
14. *Taitiriyopanishad.* 6.
15. *Aitareyopanishad.* I. 1.

16. *Swetasvatara Upanishad.* II. 8.
17. *Ibid,* II. 4, 5.
18. *Ibid,* II. 12, 15.
19. R.D. Ranade, *A Constructive Survey of Upanishadic Philosophy,* Bombay, 1986, pp. 137-138.
20. *Katha Upanishad,* III. 11.
21. R.D. Ranade, *Op. Cit,* p. 138.
22. *Gita,* II. 62-63.
23. *Ibid,* II. 48.
24. *Ibid,* II. 49. One may study this in the light of Gautama Buddha's call *Buddham saranam gachhami.* See Appendix III.
25. *Ibid,* II. 55, 56, 57.
26. *Ibid,* II. 61.
27. *Ibid,* II. 71.
28. Sri Aurobindo, *The Synthesis of Yoga,* Pondicherry, 1984, p. 353.
29. *Kena Upanishad,* 1-11.
30. *Aitareya Upanishad,* 5.3.
31. Dhyanasloka, *Gita.*
32. *Brahadaranyaka Upanishad,* 4. 4. 25.
33. *Mundaka Upanishad,* 3.3.7, Robert Earnest Hume, *Thirteen Principal Upanishads,* p. 375.
34. *Gita.* XIII, 13-17.
35. Swami Vivekananda, *Complete Works,* Volume II, Kolkata, 2009, pp. 209-210.
36. S. Radhakrishnan, *Indian Philosophy,* Vol. I, p.146.
37. *Maitri Upanishad,* 6.17, Robert Earnest Hume, *Op. Cit,* p. 435.
38. Sri Aurobindo, *The Upanishads,* p. 39.
39. Sri Aurobindo, Life Divine, pp. 71-72.
40. *Ibid,* pp. 80-81.
41. Robert Ernest Hume, *Op. Cit,* p. 404.
42. Ibid, p. 287.
43. Swami Vivekananda, *Complete Works,* Vol. III, pp. 399-400.
44. *Mandukyakarika,* 162-163.
45. Sri Aurobindo, *The Upanishads,* p. 36.
46. *Mandukyakarika,* 98; Swami Jnananandasaraswati, *mandu-kyopanishattum-Gaudapadakarikayum* (Malayalam), Ananda-kutiram, Kanyakumari, 1995, p.122.
47. *Mandukyakarika.* 7, 8, 9.

48. Sri Aurobindo, *The Upanishads*, p. 131.
49. Sri Aurobindo, *Life Divine*, p. 22.
50. *Ibid*, p. 36.
51. S. Radhakrishnan, *Indian Philosophy*, Vol. I, London, 2010, P. 131.
52. *Chhandogya Upanishad*, 6.8.1; Robert Ernest Hume, *Op. Cit*, p. 244.
53, *Mandukya Upanishad*. 8.
54. *Katha Upanishad*, 3. 3,4,5,9; C.Rajagopalachari, *Upanishads*, Bharatiya Vidya Bhavan, Bombay, 1982, p. 13 .
55. *Mandukya Upanishad*, 1.
56. *Ibid*, 8.
57. *Ibid*, 9.
58. Swami Vivekananda, *Complete Works*, Vol. III, p. 58.
59. *Ibid*.
60. *Prasana Upanishad 5. 1-5*; Ranade, *Op. Cit*, p. 245.
61. Sree Narayana Guru, *Darsanamala*, 2.1.
62. *Bṛuhadaṛanyaka Upanishad*. 4. 4. 19.
63. *Taittiriya Upanishad*, 3. 6.

8

Position of Woman in Vedic Society

The status of woman in ancient India has been a topic of dispute. It is generally said that the birth of a daughter was not much welcomed in early societies. But India presented a different picture. Though the birth of a daughter would entail many burdens to the family, pertaining to her upbringing, education and marriage, the Vedic society was desirous of getting a daughter. We find one of the early *Upanishads* recommending certain rituals to the householder for ensuring the birth of a scholarly daughter (*duhitāmé panḍitā jāyaté*).[1] According to A S Altekar, the birth of a daughter was much desired in cultured families in ancient India. And once born, she was treated with all the honours at par with the boys.

The lore has it that the society had taken much care in educating its girls. *Atḥarva Véda* observes that a maiden can succeed in her married life only if she is properly trained during studentship (*brahmacharyéṇa kanyām yuvāvindatépatīm*). According to Manu "women who are destitute of the knowledge of the Vedic texts are as impure as falsehood itself. That is the fixed rule".[2] Though Manu is silent about the type of education and the way it was to be imparted, it is evident that the Vedic teacher was so particular about female education as to get woman trained in all walks of life, including education and upbringing of children. And it is not a surprise if ancient Indian society produced a host of highly educated ladies and scholars. The *Ramayana* says that Sita was educated in Vedas, and refers to her as hurrying to the riverbank for her evening prayer in accompaniment of Vedic chants. Vedic women, as presented by the lore, were educated in all branches of knowledge. We come to hear of the women authors of Vedic hymns like Viswavara, Lopamudra, etc. They were also well versed in many arts including the performing ones. Lore refers to the lady dancers like Urvasi and Menaka. Also *Mahabharata* refers to the lotus-faced girls of the harem of king Nala of whom the swan introduces himself as the dance tutor at his maiden meeting with Damayanthi, the princess of Ayodhya. The science and art of developing portrait of human faces out of character-sketch seems to have been familiar to girls as evident from the story of Usha and Aniruddha wherein Chitralekha, having heard the characteristics of the youth Usha met in her dream, stroked with her brush up to the picture of Aniruddha through successive portrayal of the faces of Yadu family. Women received training in arms and guard duties. Ramayana speaks about the 'sthridhyakshas' or women chiefs who guarded the entrance and harems:

thatra kāshayinō vriddhān vétrapāṇin svalankritān
dadarśa vishṭitān dvāri strīdhyakshān susamāhitān.[3]

Even ordinary ladies who served in the palace, Ramayana says, were endowed with a high sense of political consciousness. These women, the epic says, opined that "Rama is not hot tempered though amidst mental strains, he renounces anger and pleases those in anger and agony"[4]. That patience is the foremost of the qualities a king calls for was known to these ones. And they condemned king Dasaratha's sending Rama to forest as an act as foolish (*abuddhir*) as leaving all beings (*sarvabhūtānām*) to trouble. Women excelled in spiritual knowledge, too. Ladies were of great regard in the field of Vedic knowledge. *Atharva Veda* hails Pavamani as the mother of Vedas:

stutā mayā varadā védamātā
prachōdayantām pavamāni dvijānām[5].

Again it is equally interesting to note that Vedic thinkers identified knowledge itself with female energy by placing Saraswati, a Goddess as the deity of learning. They gave a female attribute to whatever was found good and noble. Sri Aurobindo points out that the female deity Usha the Vedic forefathers worshiped was a symbolic representation of ever widening mental and intellectual awakening. Everywhere the lore speaks about the supremacy of female energy without which the superman or God cannot work out his cosmic web.

There were *Brahmavādins* who aimed at high excellence in scholarship; and the lady scholars, specialized in *mīmāmsa* were called *kāsakritsnas.*[6] Girls were given enough freedom to choose the period of their education. *Smrutis* mention two types of girl students in ancient Indian society. The life long students of sacred texts were called *brahmavādinis* and those girls who opted to study till their marriage were called *sadyōvadhus.* While Brahmavadinis with their austere spiritual disciplines catered to the spiritual well being of society, Sadyovadhus dedicated themselves to the welfare of their families, performing routine domestic duties. But the both continued to enjoy the same status in society even after centuries as evident from the writings of Panini who calls the *brahmāvidinis* as *upādhyāya, upādhyāyi* and *āchārya* and *sadyōvadhus* as *upādhyāyini* and *āchāryāni.*[7]

There are good examples of women considering spiritual knowledge as more enduring than any material possession. *Bṛuhadāraṇyaka Upanishad* mentions an interesting story of a woman asking her husband to give her spiritual knowledge instead of the mundane treasure. The story has it that Yajnavalkya, the metaphysicist at the court of king Janaka Videha of Mithila, prior to his leaving for ascetic life asked his wife Maitreyi what part of the material property she wanted from him. He wanted to divide his material possessions between his two wives - Maitreyi and Katyayani. Maitreyi, his first wife, refused to accept his property and asked him to grant her everlasting wealth of knowledge or *ātmajñāna.* She asked, "What alone is the ultimate knowledge teach me that alone" (*yadéva bhagavan vēda tadévamé brūhiti*)[8]. Gargi Vachakhnavi even challenged, Yajnavalkya the doyen of spiritual knowledge, engaging him in a hairsplitting metaphysical tournament at the court of Mithila.[9] Her arguments with Yajnjavalkya which constitute India's early knowledge on cosmology were noted for their high scholarship both in spirituality and science of logic. Honoured to be the spokesperson of the distinguished philosophers of the royal court of the illustrious Janaka who graced many ascetics of the time with *brahmajñāna,* Gargi with her erudition and ruthless logic put many heavy weights of knowledge in puzzle. Gargi grilled Yajnjavalkya, the one who made *yajnja* or highest disciplines of spiritual life his mantle with questions on ultimate realities regarding the origin and evolution of universe. To Yajnjavalkya who said that on the eve of creation there was *apa* or water as the warp and weft Gargi asked about the origin of water because for everything there must be a cause behind or a source of origin.

yadidam sarvmapsu ōtam cha prōtam cha
kasminnu khalvāpa ōtaścha prōtaschéti.

"If in water was laid the warp and woof of everything,
Wherein was the warp and weft of water laid.

Thus one after the other she dragged Yajnjavalkya through many scientific speculations and perceptions until the latter spoke about the ultimate reality which can't be subjected to scientific experimentation but something divine to be experienced. Only after having heard that the problem she asked is the divine itself which is beyond speculation and no subject to be put to a mere analysis of mundane science and logic and that, it is to be known through *āgama* or experience that Gargi left. Literature mentions a number of other woman scholars like Atreyi, a student of Vedanta who was reading under sages like Valmiki and Agastya. We could therefore believe that at least a considerable number of women were educated.

The parents' anxiety to see the daughter married in time and well settled may be noticed all throughout the ancient literatures. Ramayana tells that when Sita attained the marriageable age the anxiety of her father, King Janaka became as intense as that of a poor man who loses all his money.[10] Because girls remaining in the house after marriageable age was rather humiliating. Thus says Ramayana:

"The father may be equal to Indra [God of the celestials] in every respect, position, power, wealth, honour. Nevertheless if he has a daughter not yet married, from his equal and from his inferior he gets humiliation, censure of the worst kind.[11]

To get the daughter married in time parents neglected even caste and custom. This is what we learn when *Mahabharata* says that with Kshatriyas having failed the test arranged to win the hands of Draupati it was thrown open to Brahmins also. King Drupata was so much anxious to send his daughter in marriage at the earliest. According to Vedic tradition, a girl remaining unmarried after marriageable age is sinful. Vasishta says, "if she stays in the house after her marriageable age, sin falls on the father"[12]. *Smrutis* thus make it obligatory on the parents to get the daughters married at the appropriate age, which varied in different smrutis.

Ṛk Véda has it that girls were to be married only at the matured age.[13] But once at the threshold of youth women had the right to choose their life partners with the consent of their parents. However majority of literatures seem to have insisted on a right choice since Dharmasastras made it obligatory on society to send them in marriage only with suitable husbands. This may well be vouched from that Manu had permitted fathers to keep their daughters unmarried even to the end of their life, if she did not get any suitable alliance.

kāmamāmaranāt tishṭhédgruhé kanyartumatyapi
na chaivaināṁ prayachhéttu guṇahīnāya karhichit.[14]

"Even if the girl after attaining puberty remains unmarried till her death,
She should not be sent in marriage to one devoid of qualities."

Quiet often the role of parents was reduced to the level of mere facilitators since the society made it obligatory on them to have all necessary arrangements done for the daughters' marriage with the grooms they selected. This system was accepted among the elites of society, especially the ruling class which followed the system of *swayamvara* or self-choice wherein girls of princely houses set out to select their grooms. Here they were permitted to marry the most qualified from a long list or array eagerly awaiting the bridal garland. *Ṛk Véda* refers to the beautiful brides selecting their life partners.[15] The story of Savitri given in *Mahabharata* proves an interesting example. The groom she selected was the scion of an ousted dynasty with his days numbered according to astrological predictions notwithstanding, the desire of Savitri prevailed. It was her adamant stand that compelled her father Aswapati to send her in marriage with Satyavan whom fate compelled to be a forest dweller. Competence was always hailed in the masculine eligibility as is revealed from the *swayamvara* of Sita which her father Janaka declared would only be with a groom capable of breaking the weighty bow dedicated to Lord Siva. Not different is the case of Draupati's marriage. She would not be sent in marriage with those who failed to dart at the goal through the narrow hole of a fast revolving disc. Interestingly King Drupata threw open the contest to non-princely contesters, too, when he saw all the Kshatriyas failing to win the hands of Draupati and it was only at this juncture that Arjuna, disguised as Brahmin, turned up for contest and won Draupati's hand. The case was more or less the same among the princely class. Likewise was the case of lovers, who without any fear of social ostracism, carried on their affair and got married either with or without getting permission of kith and kin. In many cases one could see girls eloping with their loved ones braving all social and family odds. The Mahabharata story of Subhadra eloping with Arjuna or the Puranic incident of Srikrishna taking away princess Rukmini braving the might of her kith and kin prove fitting examples. According to certain versions of Ramayana Sita had developed pleasant feelings about Rama at her first glance of his handsome figure as he trod the street of Mithila in company of sage Viswamitra to attend the sacrificial ceremony there. The pairs falling in love and getting married were thus not unoften. The freedom the society gave the girl went much beyond. For instance, in cases wherein bride lost her male guardian lore permits her to arrange everything for her marriage with the help of elder members of the family and society.

Marriage being an important factor that determined the status and position of women as well as the entire family and society, ancient Indian law-givers accorded it as much sublimity as possible and took much caution to see to it that once performed, it would last for good. Marriage according to the land's belief was the reunion of couples of previous births. The greatest prayer between man and wife, it was symbolic of the perfect union between male and female energies, yet another instance of the idea of ultimate unity. It was for the working out of *Dharma* or cosmic order. Hence the terms *sahadharma* and *sahadharmiṇi* or the divine duties the tradition expects of the couples and the wife who performs all such duties in company of her man. They are expected to be the instruments through which the divine will executes its cosmic principles or the *Rita*. Marriage was therefore to the Hindus the greatest sacrament. Naturally the cultural background of womanhood was something to be greatly emphasized according to *Smruti* writers who believed that "home and family constitute the bedrock of society and women is that figure on whom the stability and sanctity of the home and household life depend."[16]

Abovc mentioned types of marriages apart, literary works speak of the regularly practised eight kinds of marriages. They werc *brahma, daiva, prājapatya*, and *ārsha* forms which were approved by all ancient scriptures and *paiśācha, rākshasa, āsura* and *gāndharva* which the ancient law givers proscribed for the Brahmins.[17] The *Smrutis* give detailed account of the different types of marriages to be performed by men of different levels.

Manu thus prescribes the first four marriages as desirable to Brahmanas (*chaturō brāhmaṇāsyādyān praśāstān kavayō viduḥ*) and condemns the rest as fitting only to other segments.[18] The marriage wherein bride's father invites the groom who is educated in Vedas and of noble conduct and character and gives him the daughter spruced up in costly garment and gold ornaments is called *Brahma* rite.[19] The gift of a daughter decked in gold ornaments to a priest who duly officiates at a sacrifice during the course of its performance is *Daiva* rite.[20] *Ārsha* type of marriage, with the groom paying the bride's price (*kanyāśulka*) in the form of a cow and a bull or two pairs (*gōmidḥuna*) appears to be queerer than the other ones and has evoked criticisms as well as admiration. Scholars of indology, commenting on this system often had it that in ancient India girl was a much priced one and the system was symbolic of socio-cultural value she held in ancient tradition. Though it has also been negatively criticized as 'purchase' of girl any sensible thought could never construe that a bride with all her costly dowry and ornaments would be as cheap as to be compared in value with a cow and bull. Perhaps the *gōmidḥuna* betokened the high socio-economic value the bride possessed or symbolic of the pair (*midḥuna*) getting perfect union. It might also be indicative of the hope the groom offered to bride's father that their married life would be a perfect harmony which the in-laws naturally expects of a son-in-law. Again the Smruti itself warns the father against taking even the smallest gratuity for his daughter since social laws of the time would disparage such a man as the seller of his offspring. The *kanyāśulka* ceremony could thus be taken as a token of respect and kindness towards the maidens and in-laws.[21] Hence the untenability of the negative view that it was bride-purchase. Fourth one is *prajāpatya* marriage. According to this system bride's father invites the groom and after honouring him gives his daughter as a gift asking the couple, "may both of you perform together your duties" (*sahōbhau charatam dharmamiti*).[22] Since these types of marriages are graced with the touch of nobility and cultural aristocracy becoming of pious and the learned, law givers of ancient India prescribed them for the learned i.e. Brahmins. Performed in accompaniment of Vedic chants and religious rites, they were hailed noble.

The lore also refers to other four systems of marriage which it did not seem to have recommended for the noblest group. They were *gāndharva*, *paiśācha*, *rākshasa* and *āsura* in which bride had to suffer both mental and physical pain from the bridegroom who noosed the bride into the nuptial knot through cruel and crooked means. True, the *gāndharva* and *rākshasa* types of marriage were approved by some scriptures including Manu though they did not favour it because of the arbitrariness involved as well as the lack of spiritual serenity.

> The voluntary union of a maiden and her lover one must know (to be) the *gandharva* rite, which springs from desire and has sexual intercourse for its purpose.[23]
>
> The forcible abduction of a maiden from her home, while she cries out and weeps, after (her kinsmen) have been slain or wounded and (their houses) broken open, is called the Rakshasa rite.[24]

But Smruti writers proscribe the last two, *paiśācha* and *āsura*, they being heinous of all. The undesirability involved in them is clear when *Dharmaśāstras* condemn their barbaric nature.

> When the bridegroom receives a maiden, after having given as much wealth as he can afford, to the kinsmen and to the bride herself, according to his own will, that is called the *āsura* rite.[25]

Here the statement 'according to his own will' is to be specially noticed because it is not the one performed in line with injunctions of laws or socially accepted norms. Indeed this system never got the social or scriptural imprimatur. It is to be noted that this was the general attitude of the society as well as Dharmasastras as inferred from the writings of Medhatiti, Narada and Kullukabhatta.

> When (a man) by stealth seduces a girl who is sleeping, intoxicated or disordered in intellect, that is the eight, the most base and sinful rite of *paiśācha*.[26]

These are indeed systems which even the most modern societies with people addicted to consumerism and colonial mindset whom one may call civilized barbarians would abhor, leave alone the ancient Indian society adhered to spiritual and ethical culture. It is thus clear that ancient Indian society had some noble ideas regarding marriage. Deemed the most sublime of all social institutions, it was to be performed like any other sacrament of life. The greatest prayer between man and wife for the observance of *dharma* or the sacred law required to maintain *rita* or the social as well as the eternal order, marriage in ancient India was not merely personal but social, too. Performed for the upkeep and progress of culture, it was a social institution which formed one of the corner stones of human civilization. Marriage was indeed *dharma* itself, as may be noted from *sahadharmiṇi* another word for wife, i.e. one who is partner to man in all the observance of his *dharma* or duties of life. It was expected to spiritually disciplined man, to turn the *gruhastḥa* or the householder into an *āsrami* or a man of discipline, and hence the word *gruhasthāsrama* for the household life.

Marriage being the ceremony to ensure safety and welfare of the fair sex and to maintain social harmony and equilibrium, the law givers prescribe it from the same caste. Thus says Manu, "... a twice-born man shall marry wife of equal caste who is endowed with auspicious bodily marks".[27] But in exceptional cases marriage from other castes were also permitted. Manu having fixed the standard and duties of each *varṇa* would not support the degrading of a high-born by marrying a low-born. One may note the opinion of Indian thinkers including Srikrishna that the four *varnas* are created according to the tastes and duties of a person (*guṇakarma vibhāgaśa*). Therefore deteriorating in *guṇa* and *karma* by marrying the low born was something inadmissible to them. Hence their becoming averse to *anulōma* marriage wherein the high born marries a base born woman. Yet the very same society seems to have often crossed caste barriers, and inter-caste marriages had been in vogue for a long time as found in the literature of the time. After all this is a question to be discussed in connection with the caste scenario of ancient India wherein people crossed caste barriers on many occasions giving importance to capabilities. The caste itself having thus proved a mere phantom on many occasions, inter-caste marriages took place. Parasara marrying Matsyagandhi, the king of Panchala as mentioned already readying to send her daughter in marriage with groom of other communities when the Kshatriyas seemed to have lost their chance in the archery test are good examples. Naturally in a society whcrein people often threw the caste laws to wind dictates against the *Anulōma* marriage, too, must have certainly been a thing of unimportance. Yet it is again to be noticed that Manu was dead against the *pratilōma* marriage in which the highborn maiden was married to a lowborn groom. *anulōma* is in any way better than *pratilōma*, Manu seems to have believed. The *pratilōma* marriage might not elevate the mental and temporal status of girls except in her plummeting in standards. But the girl married to a highborn man who is above her in mental faculties and material planes would get the chance to be elevated to the standards of her husband. Manu must have believed that it is the husband who influences the life of the wife rather than vice-versa and sets her standards. Probably this is why he prescribes *anulōma* marriage instead of *pratilōma*.

Manu also proscribes blood related marriages. Marrying a *sapiṇḍa* (one belonging to blood relation) is an unpardonable sin, which would entail consequences of grave dimensions, Manu believes.

> "A (damsel) who is neither a *sapiṇḍa* on the mother's side, nor belongs to the same family on the father's side is recommended ... for wedlock and conjugal union.[28]

Along with the physical and physiological problems such marriages are likely to result in Manu takes this as an unnatural relation, too, which is sinful, entailing inordinate social and moral disorders. Therefore he says:

> "He who has approached the daughter of his father's sister, (who is almost equal to) sister, (the daughter) of his mother's sister, or of his mother's full brother...
>
> A ... man (who) takes as his wife any of these three ... sinks low.[29]

Manu was thus dead against blood related marriages or marriages between *sapindas* or relatives, both paternal as well as maternal. Both, he believed would bring in physiological as well as moral disorders to the posterity. Hence his dictate against this barbarous practice which has been universally condemned.

Though the lore makes mention of the wealth women were to legally inherit, it does not allude to the existence of dowry system. With brides themselves having been socially reckoned as an invaluable wealth, the bridegrooms, if to quote an illustrious indologist, "could not have dreamt of demanding a further dowry or donation"[30]. As a matter of fact there are no references either in *Smrutis* or in other Vedic literatures to dowry or any pre-nuptial contract payment made by bride's father with the bridegroom or his guardian.[31] It is true that in affluent families the bride's father voluntarily used to give gifts in the form of cows, horses, elephants and ornaments as a symbol of love and affection towards his son-in-law at the time of marriage. For instance Draupati, Subhadra and Uttara brought to their husbands' houses rich presents of horses, elephants and numerous types of jewels. Sita is mentioned in Ramayana as decked in gold ornaments at the time of marriage.

As usual in ancient Indian society men administered the family property. But the Vedic society never stood against women administering financial matters. In fact the law givers of the time do mention women's property rights. Manu in his Dharmasastra has it that the women in the absence of male members, for instance a girl who has no brother, should take care of the family property and finance. After all, Manu believes that since the daughter is equal to son (*putréṇa duhitā samāḥ*), she could inherit her family property.[32] He believes that woman was created for the continuance and prosperity of the family or *vamśa*. He again says that mother's wealth belongs to the daughter (*mātustu yautakam yatsyāt kumārī bhāga évasa*)[33]. Also it should be noticed that according to the law givers if the girls remain unmarried they had the right to inherit the paternal share. Simply speaking, Manu makes it obligatory on male folk to administer the property of women on their behalf. The legal right he leaves with the women so that she could directly undertake financial management in the absence of male members. Indeed the law givers accept the property right of woman and all her wealth totaled they called *strīdḥana* or the wealth of woman which included her share from the father's and mother's properties, gifts given by parents, ornaments and gifts given by her other relatives and property acquired by her through purchase and earnings from her own labour. Manu says:

> "What was given before the nuptial fire, what was given on the bridal procession, what was given in token of Love, and what was received from her brother, mother or father, that is called the six-fold property of a woman.[34]"

Strīdhana was thus the private property the woman owned. Manu considered it a sin to appropriate the woman's wealth.

> "But those (male) relations who, in their folly, live on a separate property of woman, the beasts of burden, carriages and cloths of woman, commits sin and will sink into hell.[35]"

From this it is clear that in ancient India women enjoyed economic independence like men and that the laws recognized *strīdḥana* or wealth of woman. But it should not be construed that *strīdḥana* of Vedic times could be equated with the horse-trading in connection with the prenuptial financial negotiations between the groom and the girl's father as found in modern times. What she had was her wealth or *strīdḥana* and did not connote anything further. After all in a society wherein woman herself was deemed an invaluable wealth there was little chance of it thinking in terms of money based bargaining. Welfare was to it, wealth and woman was the basis of all the welfare. Woman really betokened welfare and prosperity in ancient Indian society. Naturally even in modern Indian society one can hardly imagine of taking an unchaste and incorrigible bride rich though she is. That wealth would not make woman but woman is the wealth and light of the family is a sublime idea as old as the genesis of Indian culture.

There were also provisions for divorce and remarriage for women in ancient society. But it was always conditional. Divorcing and remarrying at will was not freely allowed. Divorce was permitted to the women in case the husband was impotent, insane or suffering from incurable or contagious diseases. She could remarry on her becoming a widow, or when the husband lives separately from her or remains untraced for a long time or turns an ascetic or even misbehaves. Having been separated from the first husband she could either select a lonely or an ascetic life or remarry and lead a settled life. Early literatures make mention of the system of *niyōga* according to which widow could lead married life with the brother of her husband and beget children. The *niyōga* is mentioned in early literatures, especially Mahabharata. Several heroes of Mahabharata and Puranas were born of *niyōga.* According to Mahabharata, "If a woman loses her husband, she marries the brother-in-law".[36] But this was permitted only to those without an issue from the deceased husband.

> "On failure of issue (by her husband) a woman who has been authorized, may obtain, (in the) proper (manner prescribed), the desired offspring by (cohabitation with) a brother-in-law or (with some other) Sapinda (of the husband).[37]"

But a woman with issue was not permitted to have recourse to *niyōga.* Baudhayana strongly comes out against a woman with children taking to this practice.[38] Similarly it should be noticed that recourse to *niyōga* depended fully on the likes and dislikes of the widow, and if she was unwilling she could not be coaxed and compelled to submit to *niyōga.* Here woman's freedom was fully recognized by the law makers. But that *niyōga* was only for begetting children and not for fulfillment of any financial or carnal pleasure is well attested by laws which prohibit the parties to continue it after conception takes place.[39] While Narada is very much particular about this, Manu enforces even physical austerity, too.

> "He (who is) appointed to (cohabit with) the widow shall (approach her) at night anointed with clarified butter and silent, (and) beget one son, by no means a second.[40]"

But this should be only after the elapse of one year after the husband's death. *Niyōga* however was not wholeheartedly entertained even by the very law givers who set the required regulations for it. Even

Manu condemned it as a beastly arrangement, something "fit for cattle" (*paśudharma*) which was started during the reign of an immoral and heinous king called Vena, and no longer permissible to be followed.[41] Along with *niyōga* remarriage, too, seems to have prevailed though not on a large scale. *Athạrva Véda* for instance refers to a woman getting remarried, and "lays down a ritual to secure the union of the new couple in heaven".[42] But these are only a few instances of widow remarriage and do not seem to have been commonplace. However the remarried women whether of *niyōga* or usual category, never felt any social ostracism. On the other hand they enjoyed all kinds of freedom just as in the case of other widows who were sole controllers of the estates of their deceased husbands as well as of their children.

Literature has it that woman had enjoyed great freedom, receiving respect from all members of her husband's family. Regarded as the symbol of economic, moral and spiritual prosperity within the home, she exercised considerable sway in household management.[43] *Smrutis* turn highly favourable to woman when it allows even physical union only when desired by the wife. Following verses of *Manu Smruti* infer us on the purity and nobility of man and wife relation.

> "The husband, who wedded her with sacred texts, always gives happiness to his wife, both in season and out of season, in this world and in the next.[44]"
>
> "Though destitute of virtue, or seeking pleasure (elsewhere), or devoid of good qualities, (yet) a husband must be constantly worshipped as a god by a faithful wife.[45]"
>
> "A faithful wife, who desires to dwell (after death) with her husband, must never do anything that might displease him who took her hand, whether he be alive or dead.[46]"
>
> "(At her pleasure let her emaciate her body by (living on) pure flowers, roots and fruit; but she must never even mention the name of another man after her husband has died.[47]"
>
> "Until death let her be patient (of hardships), self-controlled, and chaste and strive (to fulfill) that most excellent duty which (is prescribed) for wives who have one husband only.[48]"

Manu's advise to woman to be faithful to her husband even if he is "destitute of virtue, or seeking pleasure (elsewhere), or devoid of good qualities" may not however be taken as licence for the husband to indulge in immoralities since he makes it obligatory on him "who wedded her with sacred texts" to give her happiness always, "both in season and out of season, in this world and in the next". It is also to be noticed that Manu always preferred a life of chastity for the widow to remarriage since man and wife relation is something transcendental, a relation existing "in this world and in the next". It was a spiritual union which Manu wanted to preserve with all the serenity and purity. Of course to have a second husband is a material necessity which the society may not oppose just because woman's life without male help would be a hell. It is true that literatures including the spiritual, mention the systems of *niyōga* or any other type of second marriage. But taking the lofty ideal regarding man and wife relation which they deemed a great prayer for the fulfillment of ultimate *dharma* they did not give the final imprimatur to remarriage or polyandry. Consequently all such practices they declined as unlawful and undesirable. It is in this context that one must ponder over the issues of polyandry and polygamy referred to in literature. It is interesting to note that even as various stories are found woven around how such practices came to vogue or how such incidents were justified by the leading figures of the time the law givers openly proscribed them. Mahabharata gives the story of Draupati becoming wife of the five Pandava brothers by chance. That the words of mother though uttered unknowingly could not be anything but true and it was accordingly that Draupati became wife of the five is the apology Swami Vivekananda gives here though the Swami, too, speaks of this as "evidently a glimpse of the past polyandrous life"[49]. Even Vyasa judged it as definitely running in contrast to the then existing laws and disparaged it as *adharma* though to satisfy Drupada he said that it was pre-ordained and narrated how Draupati in her former life prayed Lord Siva for a good husband, repeating the prayer five times and the lord promised her five husbands. Kunti, too, was taken aback when she came to know of how much heinous it would be to see Draupati becoming wife of the five, a system never practised in her tradition. And even when Yudhishtira tried to justify polyandry, illustrating the marriage of Jatila with seven rishis and citing it as a part of the Pandu tradition, the system was still widely condemned. It is again interesting that this tradition, even if there was such a one, was widely condemned. According to Mahabharata, King Drupada opposed it though he finally heeded to circumstance. Protest against polyandry came from

Karna, too. Again Vyasa himself disparages the country of Madra with which Pandu had matrimonial alliance, as a land of matrilineal descend and loose sexual relations.[50] The Epic writer thus definitely condemned this tradition of the Pandu which Yudhishtira cited to justify polyandry. However, it is also to be noticed that literature gives only a few examples to polyandry which cannot be generalized and be taken as a commonly practised system. But Polygamy, unlike polyandry, was widely practised as seen from many stories of *Itihasas* as well as *Puranas.* But this, too, was never the social ideal and was always condemned by the law givers of ancient India. The ideal regarding *pativrata* was highly hailed and the authors of the *Itihasas* come waxing eloquent when they pass by such aspects. Manu certainly opposes both Polyandry and polygamy when he upholds the spiritual character of man and wife relation which according to him, as already pointed out, was the bond that bound them together through the cycles of birth and death. *Ékapatnīvrata* was the highest ideal in married life. Ramayana, though speaks about many stories related to polygamy never admires the system as ideal. But he eulogizes Sri Rama as the symbol of morality. The Epic writer designates Rama alone as gem of all social morals, the *maryādāpurushōttama.* Rama had only one wife and even after his having banished her to forest he would not recourse to a second wife. His life still belonged to Sita, this gem of Indian manhood firmly believed. Thus among all characters of Ramayana only Rama with his *ékapatnīvrata* or having only one wife proved to be the ideal man in the narrations of the epic bard. Certainly he was the ideal man of ancient Indian tradition who satisfied all the required criteria. It is thus clear that whatever systems people might have practised, the laws never allowed unvirtuous practises because the ideal they upheld was lofty.

It is always thus an ideal woman the laws of ancient India envisioned. It is interesting to note that though *Itihasas* of India bristle with woman characters, all noted for their aristocracy in their birth as well as character, it is always the women of chastity who got plaudits of Valmiki and Vyasa. Naturally, Sita and Savitri of high chastity proved to be the gems of Indian womanhood.

Indian literature is always eloquent on the principle of chastity and only chaste ones were hailed as the gems of womanhood. Indian tradition deemed woman as the very bedrock of the society's cultural progress and as such expected more from her than man. Forbearance and tolerance were the hallmarks of Indian woman and she was expected to tolerate up to the hilt to maintain the traditions and social values unbroken. With multifarious roles as wife, mother, sister, daughter etc., she was to light up the entire family which was the potential unit of society which in turn makes, a nation or people. She was the mother or preserver of moral values and hence the mother of the entire society. In ancient India she was a great corrective force in many respects.

All the *Puranas*, *Itihasas* and *Smrutis* wax eloquent on the role of Indian woman as wife who is the eternal companion of her husband and the *sahadharmiṇi*, or his spiritual companion in his pilgrimage to Dharma or the ultimate truth.[51] The author of Ramayana highlights this aspect with Sita telling the following to Rama who was about to leave the palace for the forest

> "A woman given by her father with holy water into the hands of the bridegroom belongs to him and cannot be separated from him in this world or in the other. I am not going to leave you knowing this *dharma*. Even after death, she is his... I am yours, to share your joys and your sorrows...[52]"

The role woman played in the life of man and her duties to him as given in Ramayana are further illustrated by a modern Indian thinker putting the following on the lips of Sita who stood her ground against Rama's standpoint to douse her longing to accompany him to forest.

> "A fine speech you have made, O knower of *Dharma*. It is to me a strange doctrine that a wife is diverse from her husband and that his duty is not hers, and that she has no right to share in it. I can never accept it. I hold that your fortunes are mine, and if Rama has to go to the forest, the command includes Sita also, who is part of him. I shall walk in front of you in the forest ways and tread the thorns and the hard ground to make them smooth for your feet. Do not think me obstinate. My father and mother have instructed me in *Dharma*."
>
> "To go with you wherever you go □ that is my only course. If you must go to the forest today, then today I go with you. There is no room for any discussion. Do not think that I cannot bear forest life. With you by my side it will be a joyous holiday. I shall not be a source of trouble to you. I shall eat fruit and roots like you and I shall not lag behind as we walk.[53]"

Firm in her becoming the very second self of her lord, Sita said, "Separated from thee, I should not wish to dwell even in heaven." That wherever the husband is, is to wife her real heaven, was what this doyen of Indian women firmly believed. Even to the death she would follow him and if possible retrieve him from mortality. This is what Vyasa tells through his story of Savitri whose life was the very example of chastity. Savitri, who practised the eternal law regarding man and wife relationship, the Mahabharata says, retrieved the soul of Satyavan, her husband from God of death. Story has it that when Satyavan died even the emissaries of Yama, the God of death could not reach his body which was resting on the lap of Savitri. And even when Yama came and took away the soul of Satyavan, Savitri followed him in grief. She could not remain a single moment away from him, and to the Yama's question, "Savitri, daughter, why are you following me," she replied, "I am not following thee, Father, but this is also the fate of the woman, she follows where her love takes her, and the eternal law separates not loving man and faithful wife"[54]. And she returned only after Yama gave back the soul of her husband. Thus through the stories of these gems of Indian womanhood authors of the *Itihasas* bring out the role and duties of an ideal woman and her power which went up to the level of helping her husband transcend even death. Chastity, ancient Indians believed, was a spiritual gift that could immortalize the mortals.

The companion through out, wife was a source of man's happiness and relief in pain and a real friend in his life who consoles him in his misfortunes and congratulates him in his victories. She was truly the corrective force in husband's life. How Sita took this role is well narrated in Ramayana when she warned her husband against the constant use of arms, a habit that may naturally make anyone, even a peace-loving man, war-like. She reminds Rama thus:

> "I am not teaching you anything, I only remind you of what you already know (*smarayē tvam na śikshaye*)." Unfortunately in life some circumstances occur and drive some fruitful thoughts away from the mind. They go to the corner as it were, of your mind, and it is necessary to bring them to the centre. I do that service.[55]

The very half of man's life, wife had the entire moral and legal rights in his life, and without her his life would be imperfect. She accompanied him in all religious sacrifices and public functions. Husband should do all religious functions in company of his wife, the Vedas ordained. It is interesting that when Rama was to be anointed as King of Ayodhya the royal priests insisted that Sita be on his side during the ceremony. Wife was thus the companion of man in all walks of life and her absence would lead to all imperfections in his life, India's tradition believed. She was the *ardhāngini* or one half of the husband without whom his life would be incomplete, says *Śatapatha Brāhmaṇa.* Wife was her husband's valued partner whose co-operation was indispensable for happiness and success in family life and was the source of inspiration for husband in all material and moral pursuits of life.

> *āpatyam dharmakaryāṇi śusrūshā ratiruttamā*
> *dārādhīnastathā svargaḥ pitruṇāmātmanaścha ha.*[56]
> "Offspring (due to performance of) religious rites, faithful service, highest conjugal happiness and heavenly bliss for the ancestors and oneself, depends on one's wife alone.[57]"
> Manu again says:
> "In that family, where the husband is pleased with his wife (*santhushṭō bhāryayā bharttā*) and wife with her husband (*bhartrā bhāryā thathaivacha*), happiness will assuredly be lasting (*kalyāṇam tatravai dhruvam*).[58]"

She was also to be a good manager of family affairs including money matters which she should control well.

> "She must always be cheerful, clever in the management of her household affairs, careful in cleaning her utensils, and economical in expenditure (*vyayē chāmuktahastayā*).[59]"

Manu advises the woman who has only one husband to be patient of all hardships until death, self-controlled, and chaste and strive to fulfill that most excellent duty the scripture prescribes for her.[60] Man and wife relation was thus complimentary, both sharing spiritual and material prosperity and was marked with mutual respect and sincerity. It was another expression of the spiritual and moral monism when Manu declares that "the husband is declared to be one with the wife." Family life was thus a *sādhana* or preparation for a higher life transcending the world of mere erotic and material love.

However, in family her greatest role was that of the mother. Suffice it to cite Swami Vivekananda who held Indian womanhood as the divine motherhood. Reflection of the female energy, the half of the cosmic energy, she was considered *parāśakti* or the supreme energy concealed in human form. Naturally it was believed that womanhood would become perfect when only it attains motherhood. Woman was mother to the ancient Indians and was always addressed respectfully with words like *mā* or mother or *bhavati* or respected one. Even to the beggar girl who knocks at the door an ancient or a modern Indian would only say, 'nothing is with me mother, please go'! The culture of the land would not permit an Indian to address even a beggar girl anything but mother. Even the custom of sending woman for begging itself was discouraged and seldom practised. Woman thus mothered the entire family and it is interesting that Indian families were mother ruling ones. She was the supreme teacher. It would be relevant to note how the law giver of ancient India comments on this aspect.

> *upādhyāyān dasāchārya āchāryāṇām śatam pitā*
> *sahasram tu pitrun mātā gauravéṇātirichyaté*[61]
>
> "The teacher is ten times more venerable than a sub-teacher, the father a hundred times more than the teacher, but the mother a thousand times more than the father."

Woman taught her children spiritual and material lessons. She was the educating, intellectualizing and enlightening agent who disciplined young ones. Evidences are enough to prove the role they played as teachers in the all-round uplift of their children. *Itihasas* and *Puranas* mention mothers who trained them in morals and values of life. Indian mothers not only influenced their children and all household affairs, but their grown up sons also to whom their word was law. While studying this long drawn maternal influence one comes across the advice Sumitra gave her son Lakshmana who was to accompany his elder brother Rama and Sita to forest. Her instruction to Lakshmana to look to Sita as mother is indeed the Ramayana culture condensed, repetition and reassertion of the message the lore of India has been carrying down the millennia that elder sister-in-law is equal to mother and that she should be treated with as much respect and reverence as one does to the mother. It would be appropriate to cite the story of Madalasa and her son Vikranta to illustrate the position of Indian woman as mother. According to Markandeya Purana, Madalasa taught Vikranta knowledge of the self as he grew up by ministering to him even in sickness. Caressing the baby crying on her lap, she would say:

> "My child thou art without a name or form, and it is but in fantasy that thou hast been given a name. This thy body,

framed of the five elements, is not thine in sooth, nor art thou of it. Why dost thou weep, or may be, thou weepest not; it is the sound self born that cometh forth from the king's son. In the body dwells another self, and therewith abideth not the thought that 'This is mine', which appertaineth to the flesh. Shame that man is so deceived![62]

Woman was thus mother, teacher and monitor of the house, whose interests and preferences seem not to have been interfered with by anybody including her husband since her doings were always on the right path. Naturally, she turned out to be the most cared wealth of family and society, a potential unit of socio-cultural progress who should be petted, protected and promoted. And it is no surprise that lawgivers of ancient India made it obligatory on men folk to protect the fair sex. Thus ordains Manu:

pitā rakshati kaumāré bhartā rakshati yauvané
rakshanti sthaviré putrā na strī svātantryamarhati.[63]

This text usually comes in for being disparaged. It is used to be translated as follows:

"Her father protects her in childhood, husband in youth and sons in old age, a woman is not fit for independence.[64]"

It may appear surprising that this law giver who accords all kinds of importance, reverence and respects to fair sex bars freedom to them by saying in his manual that *na stri svatantryamarhati* or woman deserves no freedom. Manu emphasizes this aspect repeatedly:

balyé piturvase tishṭét pāṇigrāhasya yauvané
putrāṇām bhartari préta na bhajét stri svatantratām.[65]

"In childhood a female must be subject to her father, in youth to her husband, when her lord is dead to her sons; a woman must never be independent.[66]"

Surely Manu makes it obligatory on men to protect women. It is after all a biological and natural necessity and any kind of unnecessary freedom could only bring in disorders. It is to be noticed that not only in case of woman but for men, too, the *Smrutis* set some disciplines as in the case of students, householders, etc. It cannot be that woman alone should be exempted from limitations of society. The *Smrutis* thus while fixing certain disciplines to each segment of society had extended the same to the fair sex, too. It is illogical to argue that *Smritikāras* of ancient India while disciplining all other sides of social life should have left woman alone to indiscipline. It was thus only a part of common social ethics the law giver applied in its wider aspect. The problem again is with the lack of contextual interpretation. One may notice that word *arhati* bore different contextual meanings in Sanskrit and other languages. It is interesting to note how the word is used by Srikrishna in the 'Sankhyayoga' of *Bhagavad-Gita* where he repeatedly tells Arjuna, *na tvam śōchitumarhasi* or *naivam śōchitumarhasi.*[67] Here discoursing on the immortality and indestructibility of the soul Krishna convinces Arjuna the meaninglessness of the delusions that are birth and death and that it is unnecessary to be grieved at death. Therefore he says, *na tvam śōchitumarhasi* which could very sensibly be translated as "you need not be worried". If to take the word *arhat* for 'deserving' it should be argued that it requires certain criteria or qualification to grieve! Therefore the meaning is simply "you need not be worried" rather than 'you do not deserve' or are not qualified enough to be worried. Again in Buddhist lore the word *arhat* bears an entirely different meaning when it was applied to a true seeker of the ultimate truth or *nirvāṇa.* One-sided rather than a holistic explanation of the word meaning would not suffice to understand the actualities of things and events. It could thus be well construed that Manu never meant to impose 'slavery' on woman as argued by modern feminist theorists and disparagers of ancient Indian culture. Manu proscribed inordinate freedom to woman lest it should hamper them. By doing that he was drawing a *saumitrirékha* (circular line Lakshmana drew around Sita in *Ramayana* so that nothing and none could cross the circle and do any harm to her) or the line of protection. Unlimited freedom, Manu feared, might do away with chastity which determined the serenity of womanhood and he wanted to see this sublime aspect of womanhood preserved as the bedrock of culture, a belief common throughout India across time and place. It is interesting to notice the concern of Arjuna who told to Sri Krishna while at Kurukshetra that if woman would become corrupt the longstanding traditions would be destroyed.[68] Thus Manu always wanted to preserve woman and womanhood as the foundations of culture rather than a mere object of sensual pleasure. To this law giver of ancient India womanhood betokened a higher ideal not to be approached in a dilettantish manner. She was the divinity incarnate, the manifestation of culture or the highest principle and was to be treated like that. Hence his firm conviction that

> *yatra nāryāstu pūjyanté ramanté tatra dévataḥ*
> *ytratāstu na pūjyanté sarvastatrāphalaha kriya*

śōchanti jāmayō yatra vinaśyatyāśu tatkulam
na śōchanti tu yatraitā vardḥanté taddḥi sarvadā.[69]
Where women are honoured, there the gods are pleased; but where they are not honoured there all works turn fruitless.
Where the female relations live in grief, the family soon wholly perishes; but that family where they are happy ever prospers.[70]

Womanhood was thus something to be much valued according to Indian tradition. There might of course be instances of women having been ill-treated or harassed. But they were not commonplace and also not in line with the social ideals. The laws never gave their imprimatur to such things. Generally speaking, woman enjoyed a respectable social status in ancient India which continued down the centuries.

References

1. *Brahadaranyaka Upanishad*, IV. 4. 18.
2. *Manu Smruti*, IX. 18.
3. *Ramayana*, Ayodhya kanda. XVI.
4. *Ibid*, Ayodhya kanda, XXI.
5. *Atharva Véda.* 19, 71.
6. *Mahabhashya.* IV,1,14; 3,155.
7. Anjali Chatterji, 'Social Status of Women in Dharmasastras', in Chandrakala Padia (Ed), *The women in Dharmasastras*, New Delhi, 2009, P-149.
8. *Bruhadaranyaka Upanishad*, III. 6,8.
9. *Ibid*, III. 6, 1.
10. *Ramayana.* II. 118. 34.
11. *Ibid*, II. 118. 35-36.
12. *Vasishta Dharma Sutra*, XVII, 70.
13. *Rk. Véda.* X, 85.
14. *Manusmruti* IX- 89.
15. A. S. Altekar, *The Position of Women in Hindu Civilization*, p. 65.
16. Anjali Chatterji, *Op. Cit*, P-169).
17. *Manu*, III. 21.
18. *Ibid*, III. 24.
19. *Ibid*, III. 27.
20. Grorge Buhler, *Laws of Manu*, Delhi, 1988, p. 80.

21. *Manu*, III. 51, 54.
22. *Ibid*, III. 30.
23. *Ibid*, III. 32.
24. *Ibid*, III. 33.
25. *Ibid*, III. 31.
26. *Ibid*, III. 34.
27. *Ibid*, III. 4.
28. *Ibid*, III. 5.
29. *Ibid*, XI. 172, 173.
30. A. S. Altekar, *Op. Cit*, p. 69.
31. *Ibid*, P. 70.
32. *Ibid*, IX. 130.
33. *Ibid*, IX. 131.
34. *Ibid*, IX. 194.
35. *Ibid*, III. 52.
36. Quoted in A. S. Altekar, *Op. Cit*, p. 144.
37. *Manu*. IX. 59; G. Buhler, *Laws of Manu*, p. 337.
38. *Baudhayana Dharma sutra*, II, 1, 20.
39. *Narada*. XII, 80-88.
40. *Manu*, IX. 60.
41. *Ibid*, IX. 66.
42. A. S. Altekar, *Op. Cit*, p. 150.
43. *Atharva Veda*, XIV. 1, 43.
44. *Manu*, V. 153.
45. *Ibid*, V. 154.
46. *Ibid*, V. 155.
47. *Ibid*, V. 156.
48. *Ibid*, V. 157.
49. Swami Vivekananda, *Op. Cit*, Vol. IV, p. 82.
50. K. M. Kapadia, *Marriage and Family in India*, Bombay, 1966, p. 55.
51. *Mahabharata*, I. 374, 73.
52. V. S. Srinivasa Sasri, *Lectures on the Ramayana*, Madras, 1986, p. 366.
53. C. Rajagopalachari, *Ramayana*, Mumbai, 2006, p. 96.
54. Swami Vivekananda, Op. Cit. Vol. IV, p. 89.
55. *Ramayana*. III. 9. 24.
56. *Manu*, IX, 28.
57. George Buhler, *Op. Cit*, P. 332.
58. *Manu*, III. 60.

59. *Ibid,* V. 150.
60. *Ibid,* V. 158.
61. *Ibid,* II, 145.
62. Ananda K Coomaraswamy, *Op. Cit,* p. 117.
63. *Manu.* IX. 3.
64. G. Buhler, *Op. Cit,* p. 328.
65. *Manu,* V. 148.
66. G. Buhler, *OP. Cit,* p. 195.
67. *Gita.* II. 26, 27.
68. *Ibid,* I. 40, 41, 42.
69. *Manu,* III, 56, 57.
70. G. Buhler, *Op. Cit,* p. 85.

9

Vedic Economy : Was it Pastoral

Some modern historians are tended to describe Vedic economy as merely pastoral. Their thesis is supported by some references here and there to some terms associated with kine. These are *paśu*, *gau*, *gōmat*, *gāvisti*, *gavyat*, *gavyu*, *gōpa*, *gōpati*, *gōjāta*, *duhitur*, etc. According to R S Sarma these terms indicate the existence of an economy with cattle wealth as its mainstay. "As opposed to wild animals (*mruga*), they domesticated *paśu*, mainly cattle which were evidently valued for non-vegetarian food and diary products, although the term also indicated horses and some times even human beings," he says.[1] But the word *paśu,* taken in the Vedic sense, was applied to all creatures and beasts, or animal world as a whole. Vedas define the word *paśu* as onc tied with *paśa* or rope or the one tied to worldly pursuit. Sarma is right when he is of the opinion that the word *paśu* included human beings, too. So it can be inferred that the word *paśu* does not exclusively mean cow though this also could be included among the many meanings of the word. Sarma's argument that cows were valued for non-vegetarian food during Vedic times is also untenable because of the absence of any evidence to buttress it up. In Vedas beef eating is seldom heard.

In Vedas we come across reference to *saptagāva* or the seven cows, which are associated with *surya* or sun. In some contexts Sun is pictured as associated with the seven horses. The Sun, the Dawn, the *gāva* (cow) and the *aswat* (horse) are mentioned together in many places in the Vedas. It would indeed be foolish to believe that Sun had domesticated cows or horses. Then what does this mean. According to some commentators of Vedas both on historical and spiritual lines, the seven cows or the seven horses referred to in *Ṛk Véda* are symbolic of the rays or seven colours in the light. R N Dandekar observes that the number 'seven' has got a significant meaning in Vedic context. *Agni*, which expresses itself in *sūryarūpa* in the atmospheric plain, is described in Vedas as of *saptamānava* (seven people), *saptaraśmi* (seven rays), etc. *Saptagāva* or the seven cows associated with Sun must be nothing other than the seven rays symbolically represented through the givers of white coloured milk. White or the word *sweta* is often used in Vedas to denote light, bliss or enlightenment of mind and soul. Sun is *padmaprabōdha* or one who makes the lotus of mind bloom or who imparts *bōdha* or enlightenment. Sun is the giver of enlightenment, and the cows associated with him are rays of light. They are the 'shining herds,' enlightening dark corners of mind. The image of cow is constantly associated in Vedas with Dawn and Sun. Vedas refer to the legend of the recovery of the lost cows by Indra and Brahaspati with the aid of divine haunt *Sarama* and Rishi Angirasa. Here the Vala, the enemy conceals the cows and withholds light. But Indra restores this light to the sacrificer. The cows concealed by Vala and restored by Indra thus represent the spiritual light concealed by the force of darkness which Indra, the lord of the world of light or the shining ones restores to the seekers (*dēva, div, divākara, deo, dyuthi*, etc., are rooted in the common meaning, the 'light'). And we have still more conclusive verse where it is said: "Thy cows (rays) remove the darkness and extent the light" (*sam té gāvas tama āvartyanti jyotir yçchanti*).[2] By restoring the 'shining herds' Indra helps the sacrificer enjoy the immortality and bliss of the *sōma* (*sāuma* or the bliss derivative of the union of *prakruti* and *purusha*). The cows referred to in Vedas are not quadrupeds of the ordinary sense.[3] And the *gāvisti* of the kind fought between Indra and Vala is no ordinary fight for the so-called cattle wealth. Therefore it is quiet clear that the meaning of cows as well as *gāvisti* referred to in Vedas are far away from what RS Sarma would have us believe. Through dilettantish approach one would only miss the meaning of *gāva* and *gāvisti* of Vedas.

But it should not be understood that there was no pastoral economy. Economy referred to in Vedic literature was to a good extent pastoral just as it was agro-based as well as commercial. Indeed agriculture and cattle rearing went hand in hand. It cannot be said that the people who symbolically used the term *gava* did not know about cows. They domesticated kine of various kind and size, and milk and its products constituted the lion share of their food products. The milk (*dugdha*), ghee (*ghrutha*), etc., were in common use. *Gavya* or products of cow were the staple food items. We come to hear of the bread and cake items including *apupa*, probably made of milk-corn mix. Cattle rearing developed into a profession, with the result that long pastures and the related professional groups emerged. The literature is replete with references to cattle rearing. Both in Mahabharata and Bhagavata Purana the *vraja*, *gōkula* and *gōpāla* are alluded to. The community of cowherds was a reputed social formation of ancient India, which engaged in active profession associated with rearing of kine. Bhagavata Purana waxes eloquent over this professional class. It alludes to the sound of milking, and churning of curd by *gōpis* as heard by Akrura on his way to Gokula to invite Krishna to Kamsa's Mathura. It speaks about the houses of *gōpis*, abounding in milk and its products which the mischievous Krishna in his childhood days is said to have stolen and eaten. References abound to cows of Krishna, identified as blacky, spotty, splashy, brownie, and the story of his rearing them around the Govardhana is well known. There were of course battles for cows (*gāvisti*), too, as referred to in the story of the fight between king Virata and Kurus. The story has it that king Virata, peeved at the audacious stealing of the cows by the Kurus, wanted to avenge the adversaries, and that the soldiers were led by Uttara who was charioted by Arjuna disguised as Brihannala. All these refer to the importance of cattle wealth as the main stay of Vedic economy. Cow and milk were units betokening wealth and prosperity. For instance, the literature calls the daughter *duhita* or the one who milks away the prosperity of the house when she leaves for her husband's after marriage.

Besides, cattle were used as beasts of burden. Tied to the vehicles, they were used to pull both goods as well as passengers. Bullock carts carrying people and goods are alluded to in the literature. The story of Bhima going to finish the demon Baka with a cartful of food drawn by bullocks is really interesting. So many are the references of this type, and we may well conclude that cattle wealth augmented transporting, too, of the time. Bullocks were again set at work in rice paddies and cornfields. As agricultural profession was conducted on a large scale, help of the cattle was much availed to prepare fields for cultivation. Ploughs and ploughshares were widely used, most of them drawn by oxen. References abound to ploughs drawn by more than two bullocks. Literature makes mention of *urvara* and *kshétra* with *sita* or the one got ready with the help of *sīra* or plough for sowing seeds. For food as well as food producing work cattle was of much utility. Cow was the symbol of prosperity as it was the unit of wealth and it may not be astonishing that people prayed for getting many more cattle or struggled to retrieve the lost ones. Cow was to Vedic people precious and sacred. It is in this context that Manu's admonition not to offend cow (*na himsyāth brāhmaṇāngāśchá*)[4] or his classification of the slaying of cow (*gōvadḥa*) among unpardonable offences[5] comes to have relevance.

References

1. R.S. Sarma, *Material Culture and Social Formations in Ancient India*, Delhi, 200, p. 24.
2. *Ṛk Véda*, VII. 79. 2.
3. Sri Aurobindo, *The Secret of the Veda*, Pondicherry, 1987, pp. 119-121.
4. *Manu.* IV. 162.
5. *Ibid*, XI. 59, 60.

10

Materialism

The lofty metaphysical thoughts apart, the Vedic age produced a smattering of reckless and imbalanced materialistic ideas, too, which concerned only with the world as one sees it. The followers of these ideas gave credence only to the visible world or appearance (*pratyaksha*) and would not accept perceptions (*anumāna*). Everything is as it is and the nature of the world with its inherent qualities is predetermined or in-built and not imposed on it by any external or invisible agency, they believed. A type of natural determinism thus evolved. *Swabhāvavāda* as it is generally called in Indian philosophy rejected the idea that nature reveals a divine power that works behind it or any transcendental being that controls or conceals in it. It did not accept the principle of transmigration of soul though it admitted a self lasting till death. This idea is discussed in *Katha Upanishad* wherein out of its general context it skirts the question whether the soul survives the body. One *Mahabharata* section states, "Death is the end of beings just as ocean is of the rivers" (*bhūtānām nidhanam nishṭhā srōtasāmiva sāgaraḥ*). The doctrine thus refutes the existence of any transcendental entity and rejects the idea of a permanent soul and the law of *karma*. Regarding the ultimate source of the material universe there is no means of deciding whether it was conceived as one or many. While in one context the animal organism is traced to five elements, in another context *swabhāvavāda* is associated with the ultimacy of the elements. This 'mundane metaphysics' thus explains the original significance of the system that evolved later into *Lokayata Vada*, which is restricted to the experienced world as referred to in later literature.[1] Of the noted materialistic views of ancient India *Chārvāka darśana* looms important.[2] What signifies the term *Chārvāka* is controversial. While one version has it that *Chārvāka* was the name of the disciple to whom the exponent of this school first communicated his doctrines, the other one goes to explain the sweet-tongued (*chāru-vāka*) and superficial attractiveness of its tenets. Whatever teaching this school disseminated appeared sweet and easy for ordinary people to follow. Hence the word *Chārvāka* that derived from *chāru- vākya* or beautiful and sweet saying that could be followed without equanimity of thought and action required for a moral life. That its philosophy is concerned only with conveniences and comforts of life, a kind of high living and no thinking, an animal-like spendthrift life couched in reckless and audacious luxury appears to be more plausible explanation behind the origin of the name of this school. "As indicated by the other name, *Lōkāyata darśana* sometimes given to it, there seems to have merged in it the *swabhāva* doctrine, which also had only an empirical basis."[3] It is also believed that this ideology is related to Brahaspati who was the *Guru* or spiritual teacher of *Dévas* or the celestial ones. According to the lore king Somadeva kidnapped the wife of Brahaspati. Annoyed at this, Brahaspati had defeated the king with the help of *Asuras* or demons and finally became the enemy of divine qualities. The demonic tastes finally made him an enjoyer of sensual pleasures. The teachings of *Chārvāka* are not available in their original, but from references given in other source especially by opponents of the school who take them up for criticism. *Sarva Darśana Samgraha* contains a chapter, which briefly describes *Chārvāka* philosophy, but adds nothing to what is already given in other sources. References abound to those who gave utmost importance to material pleasures like Virochana who zeroed in on the need of a happy and prosperous mundane life and Jabali who counseled Sri Rama to leave the miseries of forest life and return to Ayodhya to enjoy the royal pleasures. Mahabharata also refers to a conversation between a Charvaka scholar and Yudhishthira while the latter was returning victorious from the battle of Kurukshetra.

Charvakas believed only in the present and refuted the possibility of a past or future life and rejected the theory of transmigration of soul through concatenation of death and birth. They exhorted to live in pleasure without wasting time to perceptively prod into the nonexistent invisible. So long as man lives he is to enjoy it to the brim. Basing on the *swabhāvavāda darśana*, as mentioned earlier, they believed that the world has neither a creator, nor there an effort, rhythm and continuity behind process of creation. They would not deliberate with meaningless queries like why the fire has burn, water its coolness, sugarcane its sweetness, or rose flower its beauty. They would not mind answer that the dance is inherent with the peacock or music is one with the cuckoo. They would not acquiesce in with the metaphysical conclusion that qualities are expressions of the ultimate beauty or divinity latent in all beings. They would of course believe in the four constituents of creation, earth, water, fire and air, but would not accept the existence of ether or *akasa* because it is invisible. What is visible alone is real and the concepts like the netherworld and rebirth are myths, they would argue.

Having no respect to the Vedic concepts like knowledge, rebirth and ultimate deliverance, Charvakas disparaged the Vedas in the most humiliating tongue. They condemned Vedic scholars as:

trayō védasya kartārō
bhanḍa dḥūrta niśāchara
jjurpharirturpharītyādi
panḍitānām vacham smrutam.

"Authors of the three Vedas are jesters, spendthrifts and goblins. They use high sounding nefarious words like *turphari* and *jurphari.*

agnihōtram trayōvéda
tridanḍam bhasmaguntanam
buddhi paurushahīnānām
jīvika dhātrunirmitaḥ.

"The *agnihotra yaga*, the three Vedas, asceticism and smearing ash on the body are means of livelihood of those devoid of manliness and intellect."

They always employed a type of twisted logic, which for the time being may appear genuine to the hearers and established their views however untenable they were. Some of them are as follows. The *Charvakas* used to question the time old belief that animal sacrificed at rituals would directly reach heaven with the counter question that if the killed one on such an auspicious occasion would reach heaven why that the *Yajamana* or performer of sacrifice would not use the same method to send his father to heaven.

paśuśchénnihata swargam
jyōtishṭōma gamishyati
swapitā yajamānéna
tatra kasmānna himsyaté.

They condemned the tradition of *sraddha* or annual rituals performed to propitiate the souls of the departed. Because this would be as foolish as cooking and symbolically serving food to those on journey who left home without taking food at the time of departure, the Charvakas would joke. They refuted the idea of rebirth and the belief that soul of the dead rests in heaven and ask, why these souls do not come down to earth to help the relatives from misery.

yadi gachhét param lōkam
déhadésha vinirgata
kasmāt bhūyō nachāyāti
bandhusnéhasamākula.

"Giving away of gifts would not please and satisfy those in heaven like the food cooked and served below doesn't do away the hunger of those in upstairs, they argued."

na swargō nāpavargō vā
naivātmā paralaukika
naiva varṇāsramādīnām
kriyāścha phaladāyikā.

"There is neither *swarga* or heaven nor *mōksha,* or eternal deliverance, and no soul that resides in transcendental world. The *varṇa* and *āsrama* systems that are considered as of high spiritual value are indeed useless."

Hence their exhortations to enjoy life without the waste intellectual exercise on what are mere imaginary. This is how *Sarva Darśana Samgraha* concludes the *Chārvaka* views on the pleasures of life:

yāvajjīvét sukham jīvét
rinam krutvā ghrutam pibét
bhasmībhūtasya déhasya
punarāgamanam kuta.

"Live happily so long as one lives. Borrow to dine with ghee. After death the body would be burnt to ashes. None would come back for recovering the debt."

Charvakas' fascination for sensual pleasures is further revealed from their addiction to drinks, which they deemed as the best means to be free of pain and sorrow. The *Sarva Darsana Samgraha* thus gives their opinion about using intoxicating drinks:

pītvā pītvā punapītvā
yāvat patati bhūtalé
punaruddhāya punapītvā
punarjanmana vidyaté.

"Drink and drink as much as possible and drink again till one falls flat on the ground. Take drinks soon after one regains consciousness and thus attain deliverance."

The *Chārvākas* thus do not accept any type of ethical bond. They would satisfy the needs through any means irrespective of whether it is fair or foul.

References

1. M. Hiriyanna, *Outlines of Indian Philosophy*, Delhi, 1932, pp. 104-105.
2. Usually the word *Darsana* has a spiritual connotation in Indian tradition. The word meaning of *Darsana* itself is 'auspicious vision' or vision of a higher reality, or the ultimate truth or God. Naturally *shaddarśanas* or the six systems of Indian philosophy became *darśanas* since they were spiritual subjects. But the word *darśana* had never been used to denote a non-auspicious subject, leave alone one which argued against the existence of God and pooh-poohed noble values. However as time passed the later generations without much care or any significance to the rules of tradition turned lax in usages and called the idea of Charvaka a *darśana.*
3. M. Hiriyanna, *op. cit*, p. 187.

PART - II

SARASWATI-SINDHU CIVILIZATION

11

Saraswati : the Lost River

An Indus Valley site

Right from early times India has been the cradle of cultural florescence. Her north-western parts gave birth to one of the ancient civilizations. Differently called as Harappan Culture or Sindhu Valley Civilization, this early civilization of India has been of much historical interest to archaeologists, geologists and even space researchers. However, as

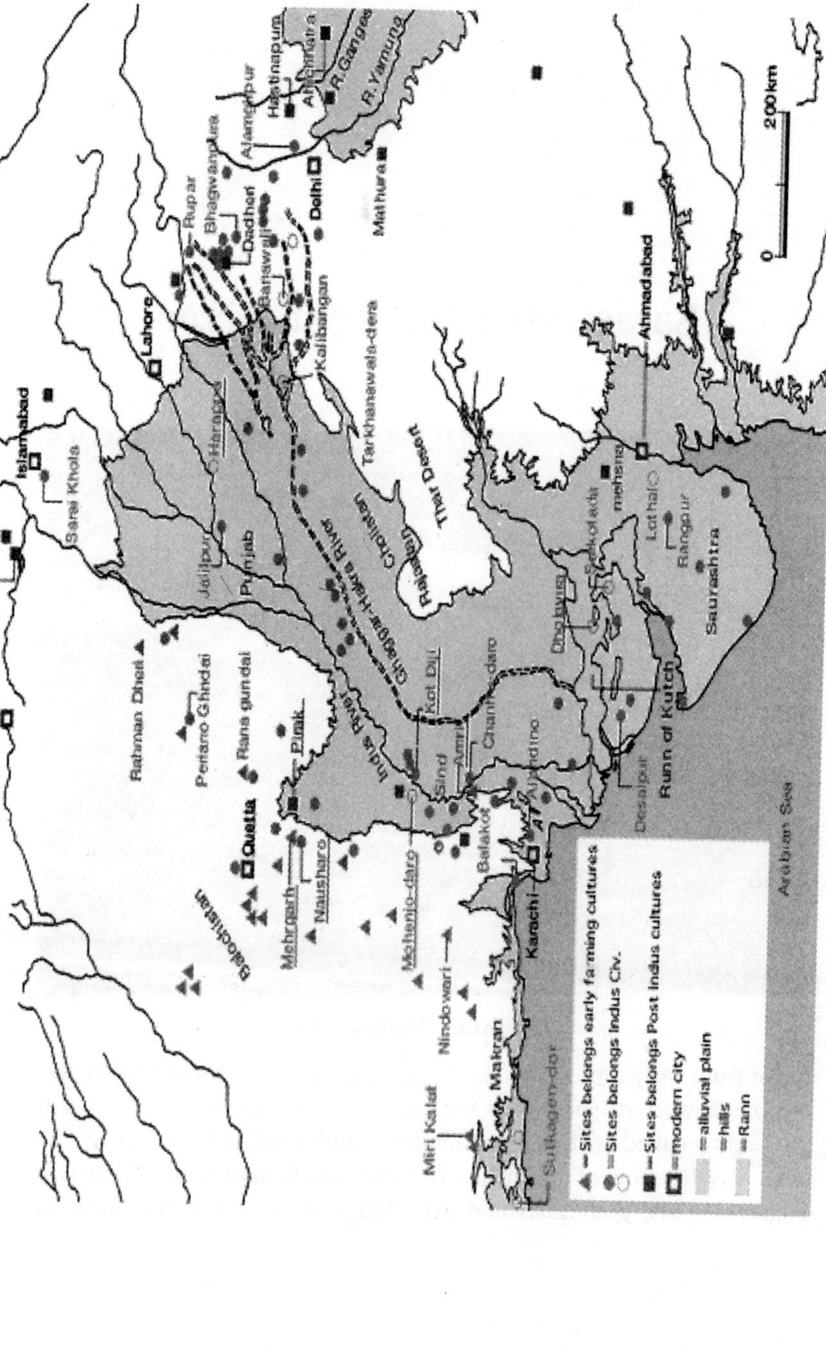

Map of Saraswati-Sindhu civilization

archaeological research progressed, the very name Indus Civilization proved to be a misnomer since the remains of this civilization unearthed from various parts of India reveal that it was not confined exclusively to Indus Valley. Its cultural dissemination took place in an area of about 2.5 million sq. km. of India. The northern most of Indus sites is Manda located on river Beas near Jammu. The southern most is Bhagatrav on river Tapti in Maharashtra. The eastern most sites are Alamgirpur on river Hindon near Delhi and Mandoli near Nandanagari in North Delhi. In the west it extended to Sutkagendor on the ancient shore of Arabian Sea near the eastern border of Iran. The main sites include Harappa, Mohenjodaro, Chanhudaro, Lothal, Ropar, Kalibangan, Banavali, Kunal, Kotdiji, Dholavira, Surkothada, Mehrgarh, Rahmandheri, Ranagundai, Amri, Kil Gul Mohamad and a host of other major and minor ones. However, what is most astonishing is the concentration of these sites in the vast tract lying between Indus on the west and Ganges on the east, where the archaeologists and geologists alike have discovered the paleo-channels of a lost river with more than twenty two km. breadth at some places. This according to D.N. Wadia is the "old bed of Saraswati ... at a time when it and the Sutlej flowed independently of the Indus to the sea, i.e., the Rann of Kutch"[1]. By 1886, itself R. D. Oldham, the then Deputy Superintendent of the Geological Survey of India had pointed to the existence of this river. He observed the paleo-channels of a river that flowed in between Yamuna and Sutlej and that this river had two channels one of which passed through Haryana (Khaggar-Saraswati channel). He also observed some shifts in the channels of this river, which according to geological findings had changed its course many times. Analyzing the fossils unearthed from the beds of these lost rivers, he concluded that these were of the creatures, which floated in the same river.[2] C. F. Oldham also took notice of the paleo-channels of this river. He traced an old river bed, the Hakra or Sotra (Ghaggar) or Wahind, more than thousand km. in length, the channel of a lost river, traceable from Ambala near the foot of the Hymalayas through Bhatinda, Bikaner and Bahawalpur to Sind and thence onwards to the Rann of Kutch. Quoting from the *Ṛk Vëda*, *Mahabharata* and *Manusmruti*, he concluded that this was the channel of the ancient river Saraswati which nourished a great civilization. Beside the river, all along its course he came across remains of highly civilized centers. He wrote:

> The existence of this river at no very remote period and the truth of the legend which assert the ancient fertility of the lands through which it flowed, are attested by the ruins which everywhere overspread what is now an arid sandy waste.
>
> Throughout this tract are scattered mounts, marking the sites of cities and towns. And there are strongholds still remaining, in a very decayed state, which were places of importance...
>
> Amongst these ruins are found, not only the huge bricks used by the Hindus of the remote past, but others of much later make, too.

Taking the once urban nature of these areas and the unerring geological findings about the long and wide river bed of this lost river, he concluded that this was nothing other than the Vedic Saraswati referred

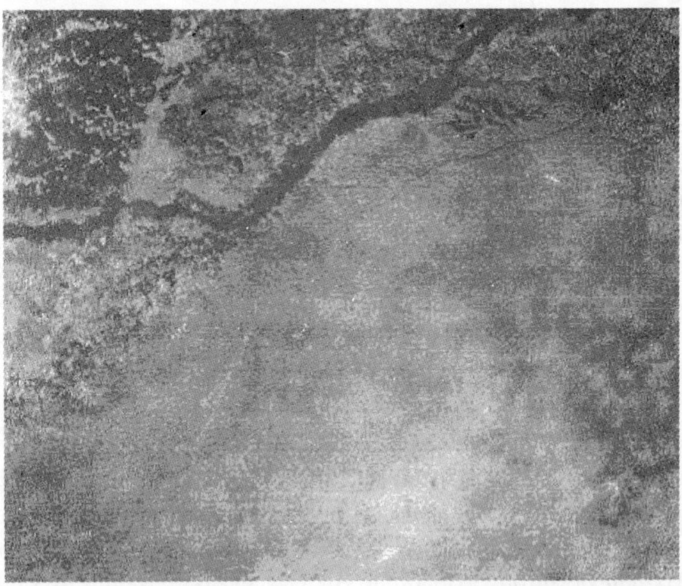

South-westerly swing of Saraswati at Anupgarh; LANDSAT image (1982) from University of California, San Diego, obtained by Dr.S. Kalyanaraman; the black spots are near Suratgarh, north-east of Anupgarh, representing the formation of hard pans (gypsum and lime deposition) due to water-logging.

Near Jaisalmer (see the image in the middle of the left margin)

to in ancient Indian literature.[3] Later the geologists engaged in geomorphologic survey on the eve of launching the Fakra-Nangal project also came across the old bed of a long river, which flowed in the south

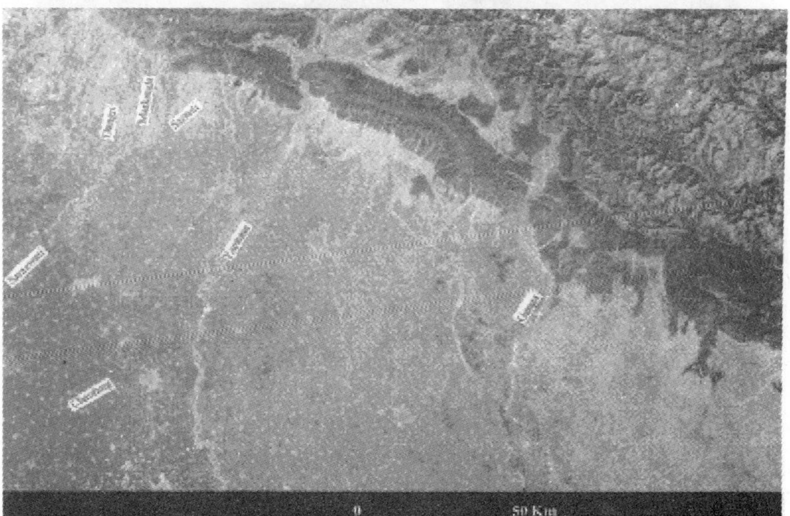

An IRS-ID satellite image of Paonta Sahab Dun in the Sivalik domain and the foothill showing the Sarsuti and its tributaries springing from the Sivalik hills. (Picture of National Remote Sensing Agency, Hyderabad)

west direction and ended up in the desert.[4] The evidence from the *Manusmruti* about the existence of the rivers Saraswati and Drishadwati, which flanked the area it calls Brahmavarta is further attested by the most modern geological findings and also imageries sent by the earth sensing satellites of both NASA and ISRO. They give information about the ancient geological structure of north-west India based on the pictures of the paleo-channels of the rivers that flowed and ended up in Thar Desert.[5] According to Geological and hydrological findings, this area, though now appears arid, was in ancient times watered by a group of mighty

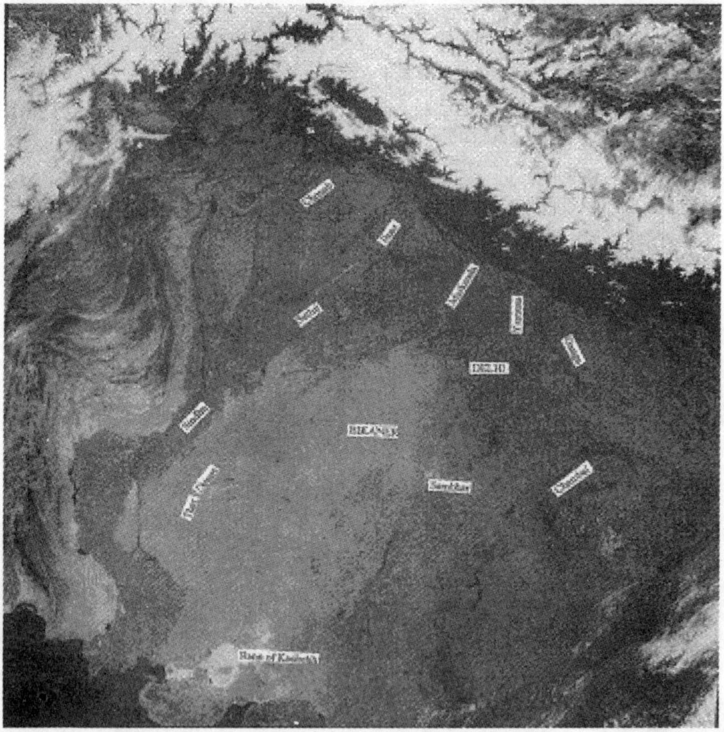

Satellite image of north-western India, showing the land of Sindhu and Saraswati rivers. The sweeping arm of the arcuate Himalaya and the straight stretch of the Aravali enclose it. Saraswati is shown by the two dimly visible channels that fade out into the desert sand of Marwar at the centre of the picture. (Picture of National Remote Sensing Agency, Hyderabad)

rivers that flowed in between the Sindhu in the west and Ganga on the east. The long channel of the river sourcing off the foot of Sivalik ranges and coursing south-west was junctioned with many streams having considerable volume of water. The main Khaggar-Saraswati channel was enriched from the west by Sutlej while from the east rivers like Drishadwati (the present Chautang), Yamuna and Markanda combined flowed into the Saraswati-Khaggar channel which took its mighty south-western course till it emptied itself into sea at Rann of Kutch.[6] Consequently the areas between Saraswati and Drishadwati became resourceful to support the all-round prosperity of the people there. According to Manu this place, being the most auspicious, was suitable for all kinds of spiritual activities and he calls it *Brahmavarta*, the divine land:

saraswatidrushadvatyōr dévanadyōr yadanantaram
tam dévanirmitamdéśam brahmāvartam prachakshaté[7].

This opinion of Geology has not changed till date and it continued only to be buttressed up by similar findings of archaeology and space research later. Interestingly, most of the sites of what was so far called Indus Valley Civilization have been excavated from the areas this lost river with its many feeder sources had flowed and changed its course many times. Indeed most of the archaeological finds regarding what we call Harappan civilization have been unearthed from the Cholistan desert area where a Pakistani team of archaeologists headed by M.Rafique Mughal concentrated its surveys along 300 miles of the dry bed of Hakra river.

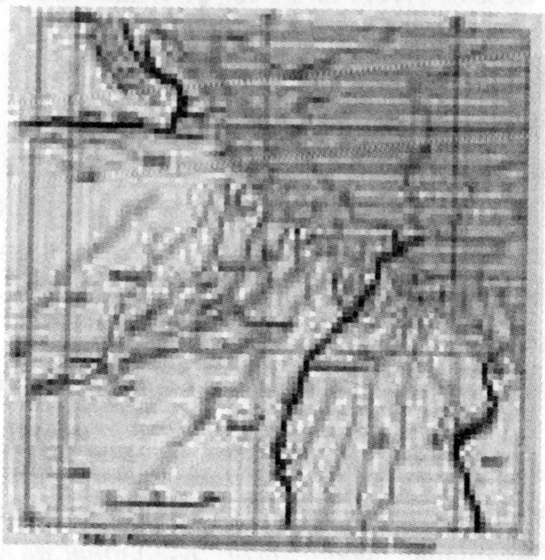

Watershed between Sutlej and Jamuna

The Cholistan discoveries, Mughal says, have given a "new perspective and orientation for planning future research on Indus Valley Civilization," because "sites of various periods, and their concentration or distribution, provides a reliable basis for reconstructing various changes in the course of the Hakra river, often identified with the Saraswati of the Vedic period"[8]. Further excavations in Cholistan and other sites which dot all across the regions where this lost river had flowed have brought to light that what has been thus far described as Indus Valley Civilization had only a few sites on the Indus. Most sites of this civilization including the maritime and other navigational centers were concentrated on the strands of the once mighty river Saraswati or were connected to it.

One may wonder as to whether this lost river was so big that its sand beds and valleys helped flower so great a civilization and fostered it for a long time till it ceased to have its mighty flow and ended up in the desert. According to geologists the two thousand year period, between 6000 B.C and 4000 B.C., witnessed the full splendour of Saraswati when as a great river it watered the plains of Punjab, Rajasthan, Gujarat and Haryana. Definitely this mighty river became an object of much praise and veneration and was deified and eulogized by the seers who authored the Vedic hymns. The river is described in the *Ṛk Vēda* as:

ekācetat saraswatī nadiinam śuchiryati giribhya ā samudrāt[9].

"She is flowing from the mountains to the ocean".

So great was she to the Vedic people that they praised her as the best of mothers, best of rivers and best of Goddesses and invoked her blessings:

ambītamé nadītamé dévītamé saraswati
apraśasta iva smasi praśastim amba naskridhi[10]

"Best of mothers, best of rivers, best of Goddesses, Saraswati, we are ignorant and untrained, give us wisdom and knowledge.

She is described as the river whose unlimited and uninterrupted flow with its swift movement and speedy rush gushes forth with tempestuous roar:

yasya ananto ahnuta stvesha ścharisṇurarṇava amaścharati rorūvat[11].

Her mighty current is described to have broken the boulders on either side easily like breaking the lotus stems.[12] Similarly *Yajur Vēda*, *Atharva Vēda*, *Brahmanas*, *Manusmruti*, *Mahabharata* and *Puranas* wax eloquent in praise of the river Saraswati, which was the lifeline of the versatile progress of ancient north-west India. But all the available sources say that this river gradually dried up and lost its course in later time and the civilization that flowered on its banks turned lackluster with its industrious population migrating to elsewhere. Plate tectonics, according to geology, had done away with the existing earth structure resulting in the hydro changes of the area leading to aridity. A comparative study of the paleo-channels of Sutlej and Yamuna as found in the imageries sent by the satellites and the geological graphs with their present courses would reveal that some catastrophes like an earthquake resultant of plate-tectonics caused Sutlej to take a westerly course to join the Sindhu, and Yamuna an easterly one to flow into the Ganga. Consequently the main channels with no feeder streams, dried up in the desert sands. What remained were only the Ghaggar, Chautang and some insignificant channels, which could not help Saraswati and Drishadwati flow with as much waters as in the time fed by Sutlej and Yamuna. Literary sources like *Panchavimsá Brahmana, Latyayana Srauta Sutra, Baudhayana Dharmasutra, etc.,* state that Saraswati in later times had only a little water. According to *Mahabharata* Saraswati dried up with its fishes dieing and the occupants of its valley migrating to other places in search of safe settlements.[13] *Manusmruti* says that Saraswati lost its flow and went underground at the place called Vinasana (*vinasýati antardadhāti saraswati atréti vinaśanam*)[14] which the scholars identify as somewhere at Kalibangan, one of the major sites of Saraswati-Sindhu civilization. The oral tradition that Saraswati is *vilupta* or completely hidden at Prayag is thus testified right by archaeological, geological, literary and other sources. According to S. P. Gupta:

> "It may also be noted that from Adi Badri in the Sivaliks supposed to be the source of Saraswati, to the site of Bahar, running past Kapalmochana, Bhagawanpura, Thanesar-Kurukshetra and Pehoa, the river is still seasonably alive. At Bahar it meets the river Ghaggar. Its old course, which is now seen running parallel to that of the Ghaggar, is still visible on the ground in the form of a long and wide depression, some four to five km. At the widest, called Sottar Valley. This old channel runs through the districts of Jind, Hissar, and Sirsa in Haryana until it meets the modern Ghaggar near the Rajasthan border. The old channel of Saraswati is popularly known as Rangoi, Nai, Nadi, Hakra, Ban, Sarsuti, etc"[15].

Thus on the basis of all these findings what may be assumed is that the earliest cradle of civilization of north-west India was Saraswati Valley which accommodated almost all sites of what historians have been calling Indus Valley Civilization. Indus, as famous as Saraswati in the time when Vedas were composed, compiled and classified, was no less than any other river in caressing the cultural growth of ancient India. Nonetheless it was Saraswati that top-ranked. It was the Vedic civilization that flourished on her valley, and it is from Saraswati valley region that archaeologists unearthed the relics of the civilization whose chronology goes back, in some cases, to periods prior to 10.000 B.C. Indeed it is in the light of these findings and developments that many historians and archaeologists like B.B. Lal have concluded that it was the people of Indus-Saraswati Valley who authored the Vedas. And this is again supported by many facts and also similarities between what have been so far written off as entirely different civilizations in race, nature, religion and many other ways of life - Indus and Vedic cultures.

The new discoveries have brought to light more data regarding this civilization that challenged many early views and beliefs. First, they have undone many false notions about the differences between Indus culture and Vedic culture, which have thus far been a stereotyped discussion in ancient Indian history. Second, these findings help us recast the chronology of ancient Indian history. Third, the readings in Indus script, the findings of archaeology, both land and marine and reliance on astronomical data and modern space research combined with a bit mathematics help us look at the history of ancient India from a new angle.

Reference

1. D.N. Wadia, *Geology of India*, Delhi, 1984, p. 368 (First published in 1919).
2. R.D. Oldham, 'On Probable Changes in the Geography of the Punjab and its Rivers an Historico-Geographical Study', *Journal of Asiatic Society of Bengal*, 1886, Vol.55, pp.322-343.
3. C.F. Oldahm, 'The Saraswati and the Lost River of the Indian Desert', *Journal of the Royal Asiatic Society*, 1893, Vol.34, pp.49-76.
4. B C Roy, 'Geological Map of Rajasthan', *Geological Survey of India*, Vol. 86; 'Lost Course of Saraswati River in the Indian Desert', *Geographical Journal*, Vol-145 (3), 1979.

5. Yas Pal, 'Remote Sensing of the Saraswati River', *Frontiers of Harappan Civilization*, (Ed. B.B. Lal and S.P. Gupta), New Delhi, 1984, pp. 491-498.
6. K.S. Valdia, *Saraswati : The River that Disappeared*, Orient Longman, Hyderabad, 2002, pp. 23-36.
7. *Manu.* 2. 17.
8. M Rafique Mughal, 'Recent Archaeological Research in the Cholistan Desert', *Harappan Civilization*, (Ed. Gregory L. Possehl) New Delhi, Oxford & IBH, 1993, pp. 85-94.
9. *Ṛk Véda*, 7:95:2.
10. *Ibid*, 2:41:16.
11. *Ibid*, 6:61:8.
12. *Ibid*, 6: 61:2.
13. *Mahabharata*, Vanaparvan, LXXXII, CXXX, etc.
14. *Manusmruti*, II, 21.
15. S.P. Gupta, *The Indus-Saraswati Civilization*, pp. 13-14.

12

Indus Town-Planning

Indus culture had an antiquity with many millennia of human endeavour behind it. Chronology of this civilization is now broadly bracketed between 4000 BC and 1400 BC. This culture which had its genesis during 4000-3500 BC, had its formative period during 3500-3000 BC. Having seen the full bloom during 2600-1900 BC, this civilization saw its evening during 1700-1400 BC. There were also the pre-ceramic Neolithic cultures that existed in Mehrgarh and Kile Gul Mohamad areas with their nuclear agricultural villages. Archaeological discoveries from Fatehbad district in Haryana gave valuable information about pre-Harappan civilization. The artifacts unearthed from Kunal on the Saraswati bed are inordinately antique. These discoveries "have striking similarities with the finds excavated so far in Pakistan and dated to the pre-Harappan period," claimed the team of archaeologists including Dasarath Sing Malik, former Deputy Director of Haryana State Archaeology Department. Carbon dating exercise carried out by the University of Pennsylvania dates some of these artifacts to 3100 BC or before. Some of them belonged to the period prior to 3500 BC.[1] Ceramic Neolithic cultures flourished in these areas during 6000-5000 BC. There were the Nagwad and Lotheswar cultures, which may be dated back to 5000 BC or much earlier. It is thus archaeologically proved that a very large area of north India comprising 2.5 million sq. km. had more than 7000 years of cultural heritage. Again it

Harappan sites

is to be noted that even after the period usually assigned to Sindhu-Saraswati civilization of north-west India continued to be the center of cultural and commercial activities, proving that the civilization that flourished here continued and lasted for generations, though it could not maintain the vigour it had in its heydays. What can be definitely stated is that the cultural foundations ancient India laid on the valleys of her sacred rivers, Sindhu and Saraswati, continued to be the bedrocks of her life system down the millennia. As Romila Thapar very rightly puts it, there "is little doubt now that certain facets of Indus Valley Civilization survived into the second and first millennium cultures, in spite of the decline of the cities"[2]. In fact these "certain facets" continued to influence the Indian culture in the millennia to come. And if the present culture of India is analyzed to the core one could see the systems and practices India developed on the Saraswati-Sindhu valleys still in force.

The most outstanding feature of their civilization was the skilled town planning, which had a perfect blueprint. Most of the Indus cities are built on the same basic principles though in details each one is found widely different from the other. Mohenjodaro is typical of the Indus cities. The basic plan includes two major sections of the city. The smaller section is generally located on a high ground, which is often called 'citadel'. The second, the larger section, located on the lower ground, is called 'township'. Or they are respectively called 'upper town' and 'lower town' for convenience. 'Upper town' or the 'citadel' part of the city contains large buildings of public utility like the 'granary', 'pillared hall' and the 'great bath'. The 'lower town' contains large and small houses of common men, both rich and poor. These are 'two-unit' sites. The cities of Harappa and Kalibenga had two or more distinct units, each one very often surrounded by separate fortification walls. Surkotada, Lothal and Dholavira are single unit sites because the so-called 'citadel' and 'lower town' are not separated with large gap as at Harappa.[3]

The most noted features of these cities are the structures of public utility like the 'great bath', 'granary,' and the 'pillared hall'. Situated in a courtyard within the citadel of Mohenjodaro, the public bath is an important attraction of the civilization. Measuring 11.89 m (north-south) and 7.01 m (east-west) with a depth of 2.44 m, it is surrounded by *verandas* at the back of which are arranged rooms on three sides.[4] The flights of steps made of bricks on both the northern and southern sides lead to the bottom of the bath. There is a double-ringed well in one of the rooms,

Remains of the Great Bath, Mohenjodaro

which supplied water. An outlet near one of the corners led to a large drain, which had flown out the polluted water. It is to be noticed that all houses in the city had their own private baths and that the public bath was constructed in addition to this is a matter of special interest to historians as well as sociologists. It may be presumed that the public bath was used for public functions or any such purpose. Or otherwise what was the necessity of constructing such a great bath in spite of the numerous house-baths. Some writers in their unbound enthusiasm to denigrate the culture of ancient India, overlooking all the canons of reason, have slap dashed to the reckless conclusion that the place was used for amorous activities. Interestingly D.D. Kosambi has gone up to the audacious extent of opining that the rooms around the bath were used for the sexual cohabitation between the nymphs and the priests of Indus Valley, a conclusion that is not supported by any literary or archaeological evidence.[5] He did not even think about how livings beings as priests could keep physical relationship with supernatural beings as nymphs whom no materialistic interpretation including that of Karl Marx can accept as historical realities. Certainly his assertion regarding this, as if he was an eyewitness cannot be taken in face value since it lacks historical evidence. Imagination cannot be the basis of historical writing. It might be noticed that Indus people led a life of entertainment bristling with festive gatherings and celebrations. They might have used the Great Bath as a venue for such occasions including religious ablutions, which were usually performed in ancient India in connection with spiritual ceremonies.

Mehrgarh - Store rooms of a granary 5000-4000 BC Period. (Pre-Indus-Saraswati)

From Harappa have been unearthed the remains of rows of dwellings and granaries standing on a riveted platform. These rows of dwellings, each of them consisting of two rooms and a courtyard with partially brick-paved floors, might have accommodated the labourers of the granary. Probably these rows of dwellings which excavators call "Coolie lines" are indicative of some kind of government planning. Several dehusking platforms, which situated north of this "Coolie lines," give the remains of "concentric rings of bricks laid on edge around a central hole, which originally contained a wooden mortar." Bits of straw, husked and charred wheat and husked barley found from this platform show that it was used for pounding grains. Granaries that situated near the river bed measure 15.25 x 6.10 m and are arranged symmetrically into two rows of six each on the sides of a central passage 7.01 m wide. The approach to the granaries extending from river side, points to the use of boats transporting grain. This has semblance in planning and construction with the warehouse of Lothal. At Lothal the citadel had a 'warehouse' comparable to Harappa's 'granary' in basic structure. Yet another structure that arrests attention at Mohenjodaro is the large hall which archaeologists opine was an assembly hall. 27.44 m square, it was divided into five aisles by four rows of bricks. The granary, the Great Bath, the Assembly Hall, the Palace building and other structures including temples make it clear that these Indus cities

Dholavira : East gate way structures and polished pillar with mushroom shaped top of mature Indus-Saraswati

A fortified settlement

A Dholavira settlement

A Dholavira site

were the seats of power which must have monitored a highly developed urban life. At Dholavira, Surkotada and Kalibāngan houses had large rooms and the roads were broader than those at Kalibāngan. Dholavira, which started undergoing excavation from 1990 onwards, was one of the major centers of Harappan civilization. The most noted feature of all these Harappan sites was the commonly seen fortifications around the cities, which protected them from recurring floods as well as tidal attacks of which the evidences are found at many places. With archaeology and geology having made unprecedented advance, the old and imaginative argument of European scholars like Mortimer Wheeler that these fortifications were for defending the Indus cities from Aryan invasion has proved completely untenable. It may be noticed that even Wheeler could not overlook the massive anti-flood measures Harappans undertook though he through out his life continued to be the camp leader of Aryan invasion theorists and propagandists.

One may wonder at the town planning in the city of Dholavira. This great city that situated in Kutch, though now rocky and bare, accommodated a highly industrious, agricultural and pastoral people between 2500 BC and 1900 BC, opine the archaeologists who speak about the unique features of the relics found there, the red pottery with black designs, seals with Harappan writings, stone blades and beads of various kinds.[6] Skirted on both sides by the streams, Mansar and Manhar, and surrounded by massive fortification walls, it was carefully designed. Though usually described as single-unite city, Dholavira had three parts the Acropolis, Middle Town and Lower Town. The Acropolis was built on a raised platform. Remains of structures made of well-cut stone blocks, a carefully planned system of drains and a large well were found here. Archaeologists conclude that this might have been an administrative building occupied by the rulers, and they call it 'Castle'. Surrounded by a massive wall, the Acropolis had gates on at least three sides. To the north of Acropolis was the Middle Town crowded with neatly arranged streets and buildings within the surrounding wall. Well-to-do group must have peopled this place. The third part of the city, the Lower Town, was left open to ordinary dwellers including artisans engaged in pottery and bead work, farmers and other manual labourers. Those who designed this city were careful to leave wide and open spaces between different sections of the city. The vast expanse between Acropolis and middle town resembles a huge open-air stadium where important activities or

Conception of ancient Harappa's Mound E Gateway

ceremonies attended by people must have been held. One important feature of the city that differentiates it from other Harappan cities is the large-scale use of stones for building houses, drains and water reservoirs. Broken parts of pillars and their bases, their surfaces smooth and polished, which have been found near gateways of Acropolis, recall the Harappans' skill to make grand and impressive stone structures. Even in that remote age of Saraswati-Sindhu Civilization Indians knew the art of cutting and polishing stones for building imposing architectural wonders. It seems that people of Dholavira decked their gateways with name boards. They had set pieces of gypsum to form ten large letters on a big wooden board.

A Computer-generated reconstruction has brought a small area of Mohenjodaro back to life. (*Lost Civilizations* by Austen Atkinson, pp. 179-188)

Though the wooden board had fallen flat and decayed, the arrangement of letters survived. Archaeologists presume this as a board which bore the name of the place, or a signboard providing some sort of information to the people approaching the city.[7] This huge city on the island of the Rann of Kutch according to archaeologists was an important center on the route between cities of the Indus Valley and those of Gujarat. It was the hub of trade that connected several Harappan cities along the coast of Kutch and the trade between Persian Gulf and Indus Valley.

The Indus cities, as noticed earlier, had an excellent fortification system. The massive walls, normally situated on riverbanks, might have been erected to save the townships from the entry of unauthorized persons as well as floods as surmised by S R Rao in the case of Lothal. They might have also protected the city dwellers from wild animals.[8]

References

1. Mukesh Bharadwaj, 'A New Page From History', *The Indian Express*, Thiruvanantapuram, 3 March, 2002.
2. Romila Thapar, *Interpreting Early India*, New Delhi, 1992, p11.
3. S.P. Gupta, *The Indus-Saraswati Civilization*, Delhi, 1996, p. 103.
4. S. R. Rao, *Dawn and Devolution of the Indus Civilization*, p. 49.
5. D. D. Kosambi, *The Culture and Civilization of India in Historical Outline*, New Delhi, 1977, p. 68.
6. Upinder Singh, *Mysteries of the Past Archaeological Sites in India*, New Delhi 2002, p. 22.
7. *Ibid*, p. 24.
8. S. P. Gupta, *Op. Cit*, p. 108.

13

Water Management

There was an excellent water management system. The Indus, and to some extent the Saraswati, had unpredictable courses. Saraswati is said to have changed it course many times as confirmed by literary, archaeological and geological evidences. Indus is well known for having shifted its course continuously before a barrage was built near Sukkhar during the British times. Most of the Punjab rivers have frequently shifted their channels. It is interesting to note that in the time of Akbar Chenab and Jhelum joined the Indus at Uch, instead of Mithankot, almost 100 km. downstream, as at present.[1] It was clear therefore that the cities could not always depend upon the river water to meet their every day demands.

A Mohenjodaro well

Hence a careful arrangement for water supply in the city that became a striking feature. It seemed that people and administration built wells with double rings of wedge-shaped bricks at public places, near crossroads. Individuals dug wells in their own houses. A number of such wells have been found at Mohenjodaro, Kalibengan, Banawali, Harappa and other places both within and outside the houses. Indus cities abounded in the construction of very huge water saving devises. There were two very large water reservoirs made of carefully and evenly-cut stone pieces. Cisterns and wells to store and use the precious rainwater and groundwater could be seen everywhere in the cities. At sites like Dholavira in Kutch large open spaces or rectangular tanks with stone bunds were created to store rainwater for prolonged use. People also built a large stone dam across the Mansar stream, probably to store water or to divert it to a reservoir.[2]

There were a number of anti-flood devices. There were mud brick walls at Lothal, Banawali, Kalibengan and other Indus cities to protect them from recurring floods likely to happen owing to the unpredictable course of Indus and Saraswati. These walls were sometimes 14 m thick. At Lothal the Lower Town also had mud brick walls. The tidal locking system of the dock at this place adds to our knowledge about the anti-flood means of Indus people.[3] According to Prof G.F. Dales "the inhabitants had to constantly raise the occupation level as defense against floods." Wheeler himself wrote, "... it is increasingly clear that massive flood defenses were undertaken".[4] Mackay also points to the thick flood debris capping the ruined buildings. In almost all the cities, towns and villages

A Lothal drainage system

in the flood plains of Indus, Ravi and Saraswati (Ghaggar-Hakra) solid platforms of mud brick and mud, one to two m high, served as high plinths for a group of houses and for the granary and warehouse. All blocks of the citadel and 'Lower-City' or the 'Lower-Town' were served with a network of underground and surface drains to flush out waste matter. The drains from the individual houses emptied into the covered common drain. "The fact that even smaller towns and villages had impressive drainage systems indicates that removing polluted water and sewage was an important part of the daily concerns of Indus people," says Kenoyer.[5] The cities had thus all the amenities a civilized life called for.

References

1. D.N. Wadia, *Geology of India*, New Delhi, 1984, p. 368.
2. Upinder Singh, *Mysteries of the Past Archaeological Sites in India*, New Delhi, 2002, p. 23.
3. S.R. Rao, *New Frontiers of Archaeology*, Bombay, 1994, pp. 4-5.
4. Mortimer Wheeler, *The Indus Civilization*, Cambridge, 1968, p. 47.
5. Kenoyer, Jonathan Mark, *Ancient Cities of the Indus Valley Civilization*, Karachi and Islamabad 1998, p. 61.

14

Religion

The people of Saraswati-Sindhu culture have unmistakably possessed a highly developed and systematic religion with very strong and sublime philosophical foundations. It may be noted that many of the archaeological remains unearthed point to the existence of Vedic religion in Indus Valley. B.B. Lal opines that the southern rhomb of the citadel at Kalibengan served ritualistic purposes. In one of the platforms archaeologists have come across a row of seven oblong fire altars with

A Kalibengan fire altar

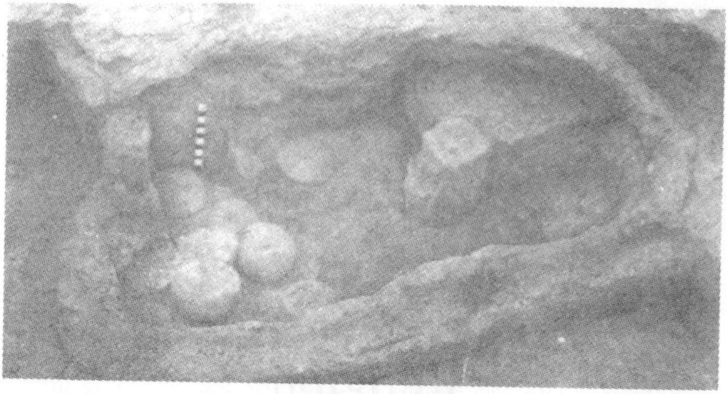

- Kalibengan : A typical fire altar with brick on-edge in the center and terracotta cakes. (Mature Indus-Saraswati)

stele in the centre. According to S. R. Rao, the lower part of a jar containing ash and charcoal placed near the altars was associated with fire worship.[1] B. B. Lal says that the northern rhomb of the citadel was the residential area of priests and that the paved path through a gateway leading to the lower town was the ceremonial pathway. Some of the private houses too had sacrificial altars, which were rectangular in plan, consisting stele of cylindrical blocks. At Banawali an apsidal brick temple has an altar in front.[2] The remains of Kalibengan : Bricklined pit with skeletons of a sacrificed bovine animal. (Mature Indus-Saraswati)

Kalibengan : Bricklined pit with skeletons of a sacrificed bovine animal. (Mature Indus-Saraswati)

Kalibengan point to the existence of animal sacrifice also. A rectangular pit made of kiln burnt bricks containing bovine bones and antlers has been unearthed. This according to S. R. Rao represents nothing other than animal sacrifice. He cites the instance of a terracotta triangular cake from Kalibengan. Partly damaged, it is engraved with the picture of a horned deity with a twig tucked in the headgear. Its reverse contains the motif of a man leading an animal. Similar terracotta cakes have been found from the fire altars of Lothal too, suggesting that animals were led to sacrificial altars to please gods. According to Rao, "the twig tucked in the headgear of the God indicates that he is the Vedic Fire God" or *Agni* who is described as *dārutishṭha*, supporting the plants (*ōshadḥi*) as related in *Satapatha Brahmana*.[3] Kalibengan gives the remains of seven fire altars which many scholars relate to seven types of *Soma* sacrifices (*sōmayāgas*) like *Agnisthoma*, *Atyagnisthoma*, *Uktya*, *Shodasi*, *Aptoryama*, *Vajapeya* and *Atiratra*, as referred to in Vedic literature. From the lower town of Lothal as many as six fire altars have been found. The presence of potsherds in some of the Lothal altars is significant. They might have been used to prepare sacrificial cakes (*Purōḍāśa*). People of Lothal also performed a sacrifice similar to *gavamayana*, which in the time of *Aitareya Brahmana* was performed symbolically.

The seals discovered from Mohenjodaro sites also point to the existence of Vedic tradition and religion. One seal depicts seven chieftains standing below a deity who stands between the two branches of a pipal tree. Archaeologists opine that this god is none other than *Agni* who in the *Ṛk Véda* bears the epithet *Saptamānusha* with the meaning that he belongs to seven people.[4] The famous *Paśupati* seal contains the picture of a tricephalic deity, wearing a horned headgear. Seated cross-legged (*padmāsana*), he wears bangles and wristlets, and is surrounded by a

The 'seven sage' seal

host of animals. Seven lines in the form of 'V' are drawn on his chest and seven more in the central part of his headgear. The seal bears an inscription, which reads (from left to right) *rama-trida-ōsha* or 'pleased and shining (or burning) in three ways'.[5] This three-headed deity shining in three ways, Dr Rao says, is none other than Agni, conceived in three forms. The seven lines shown on his chest are symbolic of the seven rays, *Saptatantu* or *Saptaraśmi* referred to in *Ṛk Véda*. The pictures of beasts that surround the deity give the meaning that Agni is also lord of the beasts or *Pasupati* as described in *Satapatha Brahmana*'.[6] R.N. Dandekar's observations regarding Agni in three forms is relevant: "One of the commonest features of Agni mythology is the emphasis placed in the *Ṛk Véda* on the triple character of Agni." It is indeed asserted that no cosmological fact is more frequently alluded to than this three-fold division of fire.

An Indus Valley seal with the seated figure termed *pasupati*

There are many contexts in the Vedic literature where 'Agni' is referred to with some forms of numerical 'three'. Agni has three faces according to *Ṛk Véda*. He is fire on earth, lightening in *vāyumanḍala* and is *sūryamanḍala* in *antarīksha* or atmosphere. These three forms symbolized by three faces of the God on the seal describe him as burning in three ways.[7] *Ṛk Véda* identifies Agni's three bodies (*tisra*) as *pārthiva, vaidyuta* and *sūryarūpa.*[8] Agni was thus the central figure of Indus religion in which fire worship and performance of sacrifices were common.

Another important aspect of Indus religion was its deep spiritual basis involving meditation and attainment of ultimate salvation. Indus thinkers gave much importance to ideas of enlightenment and salvation with the result that philosophy of Yoga became familiar to the Indus people. Many Indus seals are found bearing pictures of deities seated or standing in yogic pose. The image of the three-faced deity seated in yogic pose or *padmāsana* is worth mentioning. Several Indus sites brought out terracotta human figurines depicting *yōgasana.* "The stone statue of a priest more likely a 'yogi' shows him in deep concentration, his half closed eyes fixed on the tip of his nose"[9]. The discovery of seals depicting yogic aspect is of much significance since it refutes for good the early arguments that Indus culture was pre-Vedic or pre-Aryan and that the cultures as found in the Vedas and brought out by the Saraswati-Sindhu archaeology are entirely different. In fact the presence of Yoga in both the cultures does help confirm that Indus culture was not pre-Aryan and that both were coevals or one and the same. If Vedas and allied literatures give literary and philosophical explanation to the philosophy of Yoga, one could only say that the seals and clay tablets found from Saraswati-Sindhu Valley containing Yoga postures are archaeological evidences to that, Yoga was the dominant spiritual practice of Saraswati-Sindhu Valley which cradled the Vedic culture. Indeed this and many other similarities do confirm that what prevailed in Indus Valley was none other than Vedic culture.

Saraswati-Sindhu religion was a multifaceted one, encompassing within it many popular traditions and cultural streams. Archaeologists have come across innumerable seals like the one with *paśupati* representation, seals depicting yogic posture and figures with headgear decorated with bullhorns. Kunal, Burzahom and Padri have given Terracotta images of bull and bullheads painted on pottery. Dales had located a 'Proto-Siva' image among the paintings on pottery. Already Sir John Marshall, and V. S. Agarwal and others later, pointed out that these figures represent the 'Proto-Siva' imagery, which could be unmistakably identified with the Vedic Rudra or Siva of the later Hindu tradition. Indeed the idea of an all renouncing God, ash-smeared, always seated in Yoga, at times performing the great mission of annihilation through his cosmic dance to which he calls all the seasons and beings of the universe, awe-inspiring but with *abhaya-mudra* or the symbol of reassurance, has been at the core of Indian thought throughout the formative periods of religion and philosophy in the sub-continent. India's memory and her tradition, both written and oral, were vibrant with the idea of Siva's cosmic dance, the harmonizing link between destruction and creation.

Siva is inseparable from *Sakti* or female energy or Goddess. Naturally from Saraswati sites have been discovered images of 'mother goddess' also. It is to be noticed that the cult of worshipping female deity occupied prominent position in the chalcolithic cultures of Baluchistan from about 5000 BC and also in the beliefs of the Bronze Age cities of Saraswati-Sindhu Valleys from 3500 BC.[10] Many figurines depicting female fertility which indicate worship of a Mother goddess (like *Śakti* and *Kāḷī*) have been unearthed. Indus seals depict animals, perhaps as the object of veneration, comparable to the zoomorphic aspects of some Hindu gods. Definitely these images must have been the iconic representations of the female power referred to in Vedas and other allied literature as 'Aditi', 'Ma devata', 'Ambika' of the Buddhist and Jain traditions and 'Mai', 'Mata', 'Devi' and 'Durga' of the innumerable other traditions of the land. People worshipped different objects of nature including various natural phenomena. As in all the Indian traditions, especially the Vedic, the religion of Saraswati-Sindhu people gave importance to the worship of water. Water worship in ancient India was invariably associated with the worship of Siva or Rudra, as found in the *Rudrādhyāya* of *Yajur Véda.*[11] Trees were personified and worshipped. The *nāga* (snake) worship, which even today forms an important part of all Hindu traditions, including Buddhist faith, was popular in Indus Valley. Thus analyzing to the core of Indus religion one may be inferred that it was not different from the main religious system that existed in India from time immemorial.

References

1. S. R. Rao, 'The Aryans in the Indus Civilization', *The Aryan Problem* (Ed. S. B. Deo and Suryanath Kamath), Pune, 1993, P. 174.
2. S. R. Rao, *New Frontiers of Archaeology*, Bombay, 1994, p. 51.
3. S. R. Rao, 'The Aryans in Indus Civilization', *Op. Cit*, p. 175.
4. *Ibid*, p. 177.
5. S.R. Rao, *Dawn and Devolution of the Indus Civilization*, New Delhi, 1991, p. 288.

6. *Satapatha Brahmana*, VI 1, 3, 8 to 18.
7. Rao, *Dawn and Devolution of the Indus Civilization*, p. 289.
8. *Ṛk Véda* III. 1, 2.
9. Michel Danino, *The Invasion that Never Was*, Mysore, 1996, pp. 66-67.
10. S. P. Gupta, *Indus-Saraswati Civilization*, p. 149.
11. Appendix II.

15

Harappan Trade and Commerce

The Saraswati-Sindhu people practised different occupations, trades, arts and crafts. The food economy they developed, advanced style of life they pursued, ornaments they wore, and the implements and utensils they used in their daily life, all recall the high degree of perfection they maintained in different activities.

It should be born in mind that the urban life is always supported by a very rich rural economy. Indeed a civilization can progress only if the industrial urban life goes in perfect harmony with its agro-based rural economy. Because it is always the rural economy blessed with its crops potential that sustains India's urban life. India's rural economy performed its historic mission of supporting urban life down the millennia. Indeed from the very Saraswati-Sindhu days India lived in her villages.

The urban centers like Mohenjodaro, Harappa, Kalibenga and Lothal were supported by the surplus of agricultural produce from the market towns like Surkotada, Kot-diji, Rangpur, Banavali, Rehman Dheri, Manda etc., which were surrounded by agro-rich areas. The granaries of Mohenjodaro and Harappa clearly indicate the level the food economy of Indus people rose to. Archaeologists have come across traces of irrigation canals in Saraswati valley and evidences of plough fields have been found at Kalibenga.[1] Their food crops included wheat, jujube, and barley. "The oldest excavated site, Mehrgarh, at the foot of the Bolan pass in Baluchistan, which extents over an area of more than 200 hectares, goes back to 7000 BC and shows a veritable agricultural economy solidly established as early as 6000 BC"[2]. During Indus days this place produced wild barley with its different variety and wild species of cereals. While Harappans cultivated wheat, barley, peas and sesame, the fields of Mohenjodaro and Chanhudaro gave wheat-mixed barley and other items like *Brassica juncea.* Harappan sites of Sind and Punjab, and Rangpur and Lothal are reported to have given evidence regarding the production of rice and bajra. Waterlogged condition that existed in many places like Bhal in Gujarat was very much conducive to rice cultivation. By the late Harappan period food system progressed much. Savalda became the center of Jowar and Lentil cultivation. Chalcolithic levels of Prakash yielded barley and horsegrain. The latter formed an important produce in many parts of India. Lentil, mung or urd and Indian jujube were other food items. Harappans' was a balanced vegetarian diet; "carbohydrate derived from cereals like wheat, barley and millets, proteins from peas, chickpea and horsegram, and fats from seeds of sesame and mustard." In addition to these they consumed rice and jujube, meat and fish. From all Harappan and late Harappan sites bones of sheep, pig, cattle, and of birds like fowl have been discovered.[3] Commercial crops, too, were cultivated on a large scale. Mehrgarh was the center of cotton and barley production during the 5th millennium BC. Charred seeds of cotton in huge quantity belonging to pre-Harappan and Neolithic-Chalcolithic periods have been found from this place. Saurashtra was another center of cotton cultivation.[4] "The impressions of textile items and twisted strings on sealings and the presence of terracotta whorls, bobbins, spools etc., used in spinning and weaving at Lothal suggest that cotton was grown and made into cloth," opines S.R. Rao. From Mohenjodaro pieces of cotton cloth with its fiber produced from *Gossypium arboreum* were excavated.

Saraswati-Sindhu people were familiar with agricultural implements like ploughs and seed-drill. B. B. Lal observes that farmers of Kalibenga were perhaps the early people used to prepare the field through furrowing. Alluvium resulting from annual inundation added to the natural fertility of Sindhu Valley. Indus farmers seem to have cultivated wheat and maize without tilling the land. Tilling was required only to control the weed. They applied bio-fertilizers to soil which was helped by their animal domestication. Use of chemical fertilizers has also been traced. Kalibenga gave potsherd with gypsum crystals, which might have been stored to reclaim saline lands and render them productive. "Gypsum occurs profusely in Rajasthan desert. There are also a large number of deposits in Bikaner. Ground gypsum is used in agriculture as a surface plaster for covering moisture in the soil and for aiding nitrogen absorption from manures. It is also used to reduce the salinity and alkalinity of the soils where the sodium iron is replaced by a calcium iron, since gypsum is calcium sulphate (Ca $SO_4 2H_2O$). The soils of Rajasthan desert are usually saline, with sodium forming 90 percent of the total cations"[5]. In view of this the scholars conclude that the Harappans have possibly used gypsum as a fertilizer.

Indus-Saraswati people, it appears, were familiar with rotation of crops and mixed cropping of wheat and barley so that if wheat fails the hardier crop, barley would yield. Steven Weber identified a plant based subsistence system at Rojdi, which was a food producing settlement through out the year. Rojdi was the hub of cultivation, animal domestication, pastoral activities, plant gathering and hunting.[6] Excavators also point to the collection of many types of seeds of grasses, sedges, *Polygnum* and other weeds at Surkotada, which might have been used to prepare gruel or medicine or to feed cage birds. If to believe Gordon Childe fish regularly imported from the Arabian Sea coast augmented the food supplies of Mohenjodaro.

Along with farming Saraswati-Sindhu people domesticated various animals, which helped them in many of their activities including agriculture and transportation. Archaeological remains tell a great deal about the animal wealth, which the north-west India had from so antique a period as 14000 years ago. They domesticated bull, cow, goat, sheep, buffalo, elephant, cat and dog. The bull images seen on many seals point to the special significance the people had given to that animal. But this does not mean that cow was least cared. Significance to bull can't be construed, as evidence to the general belief the historians have so far been on with that cow was a neglected animal in Indus civilization. In fact according the Vedic literature, which eulogizes the greatness of river Saraswati and the culture that blossomed on its banks cow was venerable which should not be killed (*akhnya*). That cow (*gov*) is *akhnya* is the opinion of no less a Vedic thinker than Manu who speaks of Saraswati-Drishadwati doab or *Brahmāvarta* as the holy venue for all spiritual activities. It should be noticed that the very same *Manusmruti*, which deals at length with river Saraswati, its spiritual significance and its disappearance at Vinasana, that speaks about the religious importance of cows. She was the venerable

'Cow-Mother' or *Gomata* to the Saraswati-Sindhu people. It would also be idiotic to believe that the people who worshipped bull neglected cow, which is the very regeneration link of the species itself.

Horse in Harappa: The fauna was so wide-ranging that it included a variety of wild animals, too, which Indus people seem to have tamed and domesticated. Archaeological discoveries now run in contrast to the early conclusion of historians that horse was absent in Sindhu valley. On the contrary they prove that the place-name Sindhu or *Saindhava* (the word

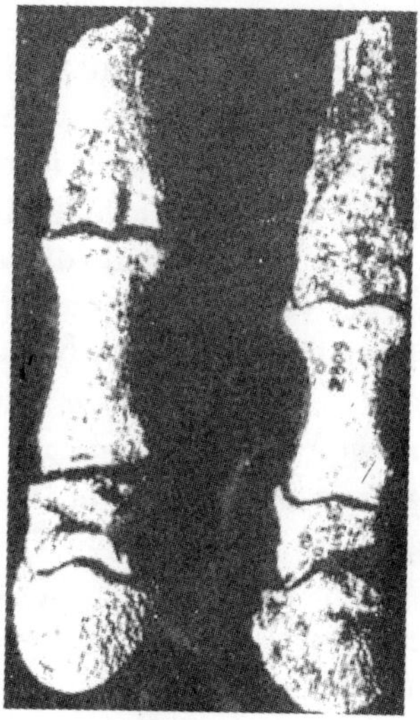

Surkotada : Leg bones of 'domesticated' horse, *Equus Cabalus* Linn. (Mature Indus-Saraswati)

saindhava in Sanskrit means 'of horse') was meaningful by all means. It may be noticed that many of the early historians based their arguments on the absence of horse to prove that Indus culture was pre-Vedic. Indeed this negative evidence proved the basis for at least three generations of historians including the present one, of R. S. Sarma and Romila Thapar to build up their hypothesis that this culture was non-Aryan because Vedic people were familiar with horse right from the beginning of what they call the 'Vedic Period'. That the Vedic civilization's familiarity with horse is no proof to conclude that horse was absent in Sindhu valley proved something unintelligible to these scholars. Again, absence of evidence is no evidence of absence. Even these hairsplitting arguments prove irrelevant to the study of Indus Valley horse. In fact evidences abound to prove that Indus people knew about horse. Already in 1946 Col Ross had identified the bones of horse at Rana Gundai. That Mackay (1943) had found a terracotta figurine of a domesticated horse from the upper levels of Mohenjodaro is also well known.[7] According to John Marshall "... the Mohenjodaro horse and, and the example of *Equus Caballus* of the Zoological Survey of India, are all of the type of the "Indian country bred..."[8] Archaeological discoveries of S. R. Rao, too, had brought out remains of horses from various sites.[9] Bhola Nath, a leading archaeo-zoologist of India identified in 1968 some of the bones from Lothal as of domesticated horse - *Equus Cabalus Linn.* He examined a lot of animal bones from Harappa among which he found the bones of true domesticated horse.[10] Bhola Nath also identified horse bones from Ropar, excavated by Y. D. Sarma. Similarly V. V. Rao had reported the discovery of bones of true horse from Kalibenga excavated by B. B. Lal and B. K. Thapar.[11] J. P. Joshi and Madhu Bala had referred to the discovery of the remains of *Equus Cabalus Linn.*[12] In 1972 A. K. Sarma had identified bones of true horse from the site of Malvan in Gujarat excavated by J. P. Joshi and F. R. Alchin. The veracity of this identification was confirmed in 1991 by Prof. Sandor Bokonyi, an acknowledged authority on horse in the world of archaeology, in a report he gave to M. C. Joshi, the then Director General of the Archaeological Survey of India.[13] Discovery regarding domestication of horse in Sindhu Valley proved a big breakthrough. It for good set aside arguments regarding one of the differences between Indus civilization and Vedic culture.

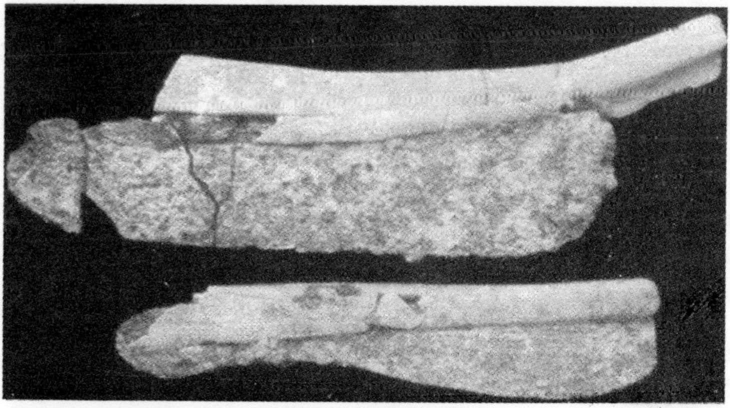

Copper blade with bone handles or protection sheath, unique of its kind

Side by side with developing an agro-based economy Indus-Saraswati Valley bristled with a variety of industrial activities. Indus tools and ornaments made of copper and bronze recall a high degree of excellence in mining and metallurgy. All the Indus sites of Punjab, Sind, Jammu and Gujarat used copper and bronze tools and ornaments.

Harappa, Mohenjodaro, Lothal and Rehman Dheri were great industrial cities, which produced agricultural implements and craftsmen's tools made of copper and copper alloy. Khetri mines of Rajasthan seems to have met the requirements and it is interesting to note that R. C. Agarwal has discovered from around Khetri simple tools and weapons including flat celts and arrowheads. S. R. Rao points to the probability of copper having been brought from Agnigundala in Kurnool of Andhra and Chitradurga of Karnataka. "The occurrence of steatite beads and chert blades at Maski in Raichur," he says, "may suggest Harappan contact." Afghanistan as well as Oman with their hundreds of copper smelting sites also gave Harappans essential raw material. "Owing to the scarcity of tin, bronze objects were limited in numbers." More than 70 per cent were unalloyed copper articles. However, the Indus technicians were familiar with alloying to harden copper and its hardness was further increased using cold hammering technique. From Rangpur have been discovered tin-alloyed and nickel-alloyed objects. Tin was imported from Khorosan. At Lothal archaeologists have discovered a copper jar, which was processed through these techniques including *sinking* and *raising* to pressure the metal disk into pot form. There were open stone moulds to cast flat axes, pins, needles, and chisels, and closed moulds to make fish hooks and mid-ribbed swords.[14] The most sophisticated casting technique of *cire perdue* as revealed from the dancing girl of Mohenjodaro, the chariot of Diamabad, and the dog and bird of Lothal apart, the Harappan smiths knew the techniques such as lapping for joining two parts of tubular handles, pouring molten bronze and riveting for joining parts of vessels. We have also got a number of Harappan copper daggers, 3 to 10 cm long, some of them having folded socket and others with perforated tang as seen on one from Surkotada.

In bead making the Harappans met the demand of domestic and international markets. Harappan beads have captured the markets of Bahrain, Failaka and Mesopotamian cities. The Ur clay tablets refer to the Dilmun boats carrying beads of gemstones. Lothal and Chanhu-daro were the noted centers of bead making. Indus craftsmen were well versed

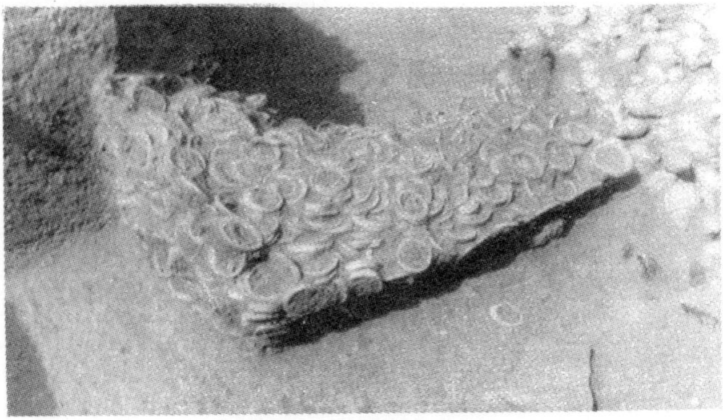

Details of pile of unfinished shell bangles perhaps kept in a leather or cloth sack

in cooking the pebble and grinding and polishing them. Indus bead makers used rough stones to grind beads and polished them in leather drums containing sand. The beads of Lothal were far famed for their perfection and superb finish and the bead factory there excelled all others. The Lothal bead factory consisted of a working platform in an open courtyard

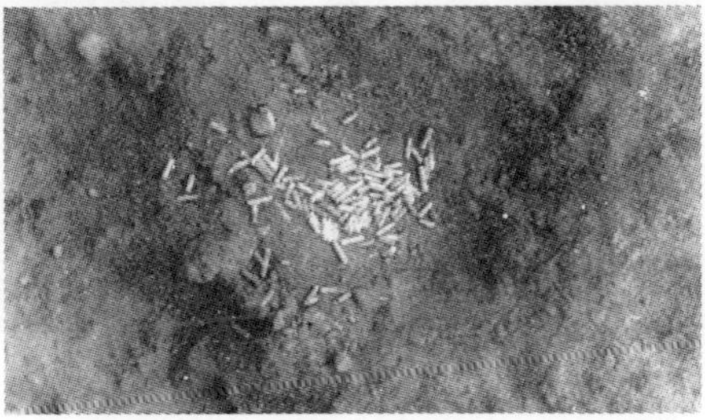

Faience beads from a faience kiln area

from where archaeologist have discovered jars of beads, and remains of kiln, used probably for heating raw materials and finished beads.[15] Goldsmiths of Lothal produced necklaces of micro gold beads which are of rare quality. Lothal bead makers made boot-shaped, plano-convex beads, double-eyed beads of agate, gold-caped beads of jasper and etched beads of carnelian. Thousands of micro-beads, three hundred of them weighing just one gram, have been discovered from Harappan sites like Rangpur, Lothal, Mohenjodaro, Rojdi, and Zekhada.

Handicraft reached its excellence. Along with bead making and bronze casting Indus-Saraswati people carved ivory, worked shells, baked

Stockpiling area of variegated jasper in clay bins

pottery and engraved their seals with remarkable artistic perfection. They used standardized bricks and tools and evolved a perfect system of units for lengths and weight, and in fact were familiar with the decimal system of measurement that helped them in town planning. Compasses made of conch shell, which might have helped them measure angles between stars for navigation, have been discovered.

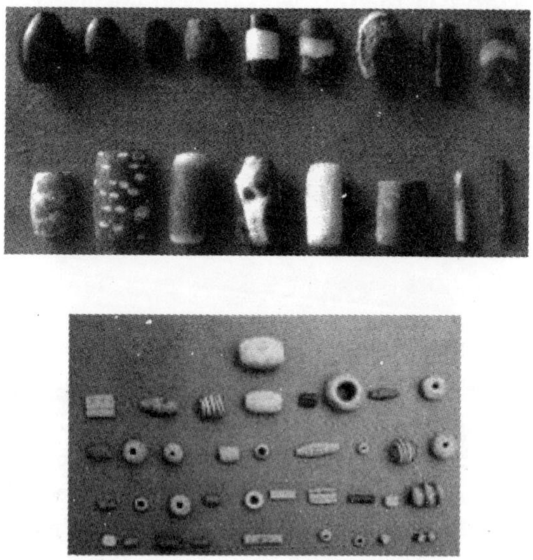

Beads in various stages of production

Bead chains

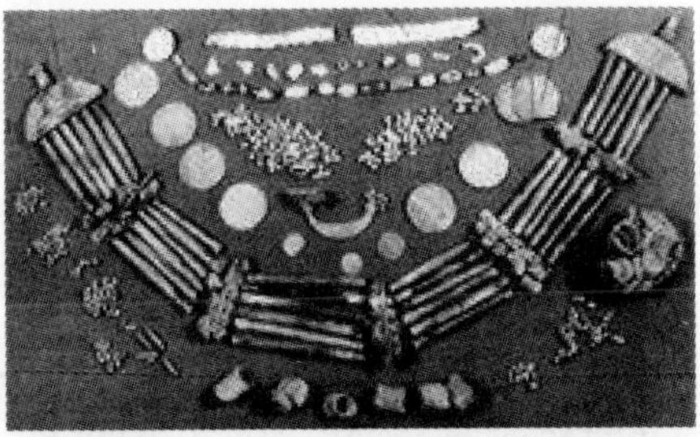

Bead necklaces and ornaments

The Harappans appear to have been well dressed as they were well ornamented. Fragments of cloths from Mohenjodaro and impressions of loosely woven cloths on Lothal sealings indicate that cloths made of cotton, wool and perhaps also flax were used. The seven figures found on a Mohenjodaro seal give some idea of their dress. They wear long tunics and headgears flowing behind their back. Men and women of nobility might have worn costly garments of various shades and hues often noted for their perfection and grace. Stitching and embroidery works were common. Women were fully clad with both upper and lower garments made of cotton, silk and wool. Men had worn a pair of dress consisting both upper and lower garments. But we have also evidences of male figurines wearing only lower garment and a shawl covering the chest. Priests have worn along with the lower garment an upper garment that corresponded to the *uttarīya* referred to in the Vedic texts. The toilet set of middle class family included ivory kohl rod and combs, copper mirror and shell containers for unguents. We have evidence of red pigment on the tip of an ivory rod from Lothal, which suggests that women painted

Mohenjodaro binary weights

their lips. Traces of black eye paint or *kājal* have been found in a vessel. Women applied, as they do in modern India, face paints, turmeric, costly oils and many such cosmetic items to beautify the face. Applying vermilion at the hair-parting (*sīmantarékha*) as an auspicious mark of married women was common. They were fond of jewellery and their ornaments reveal a high degree of aesthetic excellence. The figure of the dancing girl from Mohenjodaro is depicted as wearing several bangles and bracelets. Jewellers of Mohenjodaro were well versed in producing ornaments of gold, precious stones and beads. The people wore gold and silver ornaments along with those made of copper and bronze of a wide variety. Necklaces of micro-beads, chains, bangles, earrings made of shell, bracelets, armlets, anklets, girdles, waistbands etc., were commonly worn. Men, too, wore ornaments. All these were studded with precious beads, especially the black glass beads, which the women who follow *Sanātana Dharma* have been using as a symbol of *Sausti.* "Abundance of beads at nearly all Harappan sites makes one wonder if the tradition of wearing beads as a symbol of *Sausti* originated in the Harappan Civilization"[16]. Evidences of painted pottery, stringed instruments and the images of dancers infer that painting, dancing, music and sculpture were well within their aesthetic life. Recreations included a number of games like playing at balls, wrestling, swimming, and a spate of festive gatherings that added spontaneity and vitality to Indus life. They had a number of indoor games, too, like chess, dice and puppetry. A probable ancestor of the game of chess had been discovered. Remains of innumerable toys infer that children were not a neglected lot. The exquisite care of toy making brings out that children were cared and loved so much so that they never felt any juvenile delinquency.

Highly maritime, the Indus-Saraswati people were experts in the art of building ships and docks. It is to be noticed that India has an excellent tradition of navigation as referred to both by archaeological finds as well as literature. The *Rajavalliya* and *Yuktikalpataru* elaborate on various types of boats. However, we don't have any remains of Indus Valley boats except some terracotta models found from Lothal where archaeologists have discovered the remains of a large dock. These terracotta models depict three types of boats. One is flat-based like the river rafts while two others were with high keels, all fitted with high pointed stem and stern that monitored the turning and direction of vessels by steering oars. The ships, broad and strong, were safe on the high seas even without outriggers. "The prow was often decorated with fanciful animal figures" as in the case of boats pictured at Ajanta and Sanchi.[17]

The people's knowledge of shipping, ship building and seafaring activities are further attested by the remains of the huge docks they constructed. Archaeologists have discovered a massive, dredged canal and docking facility at the coastal city of Lothal. Indeed the dock at Lothal forms one of the valuable assets Harappans have bequeathed to posterity. This trapezoidal brickwall structure measuring an average 219 metres north-south and 38 metres east-west was built of kiln-burnt precious bricks which could not be spared for building even the houses of wealthy merchants. The dock was protected from the attack of sea water by the surrounding brick wall with its original height measuring probably 4. 15 metres, and was provided with offsets at necessary intervals to resist the overturning movement due to the water thrust as seen on the outerface of the western wall. Definitely Harappans were the early people to make full use of the tide in the construction and operation of a dock which was instrumental in coastal and overseas trade. Ships coming to the Gulf of Cambay must have been moored along the river quay on the western side of the town and "sluiced into the basin at high tide through the first inlet (12 m wide) provided in the northern arm." There was a spillway with 1. 5 m thick brick walls built at right angle to the southern arm for the excess water at high tide to flow out. The water-locking device arranged to the spillway ensured the minimum draught of water for the ships to enter the dock. Also it could see the basin effectively desilted by the inflow of tide which would sweep out all the dirt through the spillway.

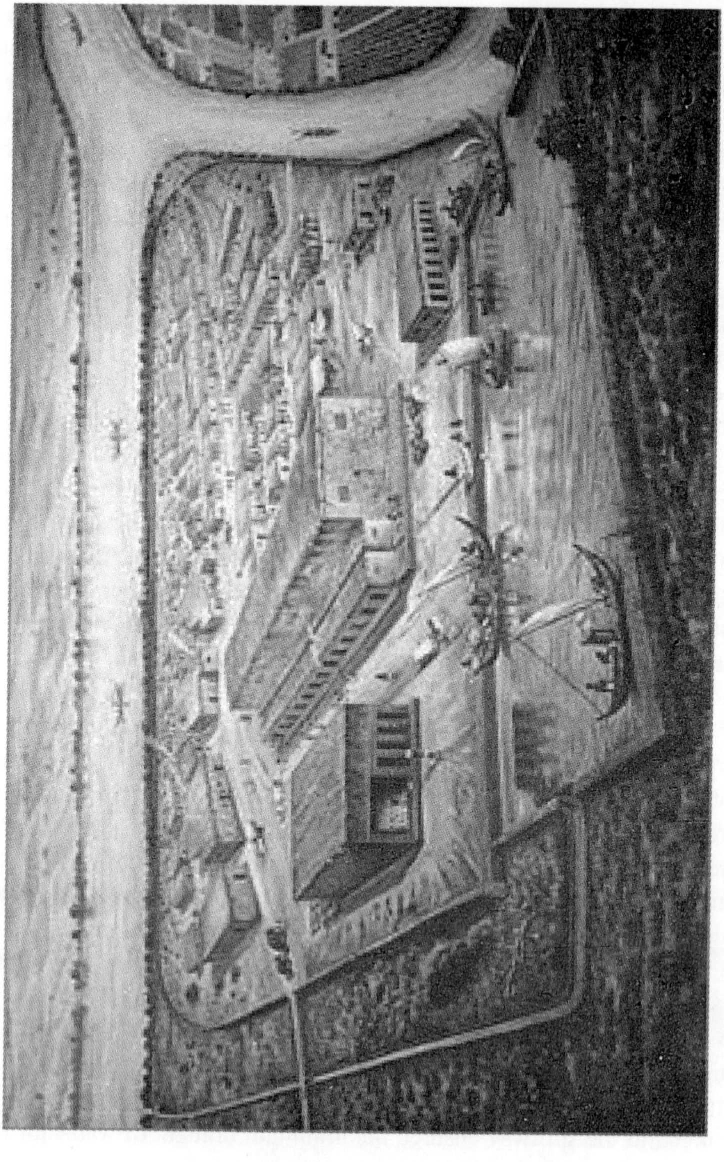

Ancient Dockyard at Lothal as envisaged by the Archaeological Survey of India.

Approximately 60 to 75 tones capacity ships measuring 18 to 20 m long could easily enter the basin from the shorter side and move along the longer side and anchor at the wharf where they could load and offload the cargo. From the dock were found stone anchors to which the ships could be tied and allowed to berth. Five perforated stone anchors weighing 100 to 150 kg, three on the floor of the dock and two outside, found at the dock had shallow grooves to tie the rope and lower them. The warehouse was built quiet near to the basin so that the cargo unloaded at the wharf could conveniently be taken to it and stored. According to Dr S. R. Rao, it was a great maritime and cultural complex with a great tradition on the Arabian Sea. He testifies to its long drawn tradition by pointing out to people's continued worship of the sea goddess called Vanuvatimata until the Archaeological Survey started excavations there in 1955. Definitely this was a huge complex graced with the invisible presence of their sea mother goddess; it was the main center of overseas activities of Saraswati-Sindhu people.

An outstanding feature of Indus civilization was the trade and cultural contacts with other coeval cultures. Indus-made objects and seals, discovered from many archaeological sites, substantiate this. A number of Indus seals have been found in Mesopotamian towns like Umma, Lagash, Ur, etc. and Oman, Bahrain and Failaka islands in Persian Gulf. According to Tosi this trade contact existed during pre-Hammurabi period. The Akkadian terracotta tablet inscription referring to the port 'Meluha', found in Mesopotamia throws light on the Indian trade with Persian Gulf and Mediterranean regions. According to this inscription Persians and Sumerians obtained from India ivory objects, stone and shell inlay work, gold ornaments, ornaments of carnelian and other semiprecious stones, hard woods, rare animals, hunting dogs, birds and slaves. A commemorative inscription of Sargon of Akkad (2334 BC - 2279 BC) boasts of the ship from 'Meluha' (identified as Indus Valley) together with "those of other two countries along the shores of Arabia, Dilmun and Magan, moored at the wharfs of his new capital, Agade"[18]. Another cylindrical seal with Cuneiform script and Acadian-Sumerian language belonging to the same period is of much significance. It bears the inscription *su-i-li-sụeme-bal me-luh-ha* meaning "Su-ilisu, Meluha interpreter" and the representation of an audience with a kinglike person who listens to a short statured person with hand posture indicating or interpreting the conversation of the man who sits opposite to the king with a goat in his lap. Lamberg-Karlovsky identifies this as the pictorial representation of an Acadian ruler being presented with a goat brought by a Meluhan whose conversations were translated or interpreted by the short statured man found on the seal who is identified as an 'interpreter from Meluha'[19]. The painted pottery belonging to Indus Valley having striking similarity with those unearthed from Iran and Mesopotamia throws further light on the subject. Reserved Slip Ware of the Sargonid period has been found from some of the Indus sites like Mohenjodaro, Harappa, Surkotada, Lothal and Kalibenga[20]. An Indus seal with the carving of a bull and manger was found from Kish. Long biconical red carnelian beads of Indus-Saraswati origin have been discovered from the royal graves of Ur. Macky points out the striking similarity between the feeding cups (with spouts projecting onwards from the base) found from Harappa and Ur. There are again similarities between the handless dishes commonly found in Sumer and those discovered from Mohenjodaro and Harappa. Gordon Childe opines that some of the pieces of vases found at Al'Ubaid were made of Indian soapstone.[21] The discoveries from Susa have given representations of horned bull, which resemble a number of such figurines made of clay, faience, bone and copper discovered from Harappan sites. Many steatite seals were discovered from Persian Gulf sites like Failaka and Bahrain. Belonging to 3rd millennium BC, they depict the picture of horned bulls in front of the manger while another piece of sculpture probably belonging to the period of the ruler called Gudea (BC 2400) represents a humped bull of the type usually found at Mohenjodaro, Harappa, Kalibenga, Lothal and other related sites. John Marshall opines that the humped bulls were of Indian origin and introduced later to Elam, Egypt, Anatolia and Syria. Tosi has it that Indus trade network included as its centers the West Asian cities like Tello and Susa and many other spots of Asia Minor and Central Asia. He states further that Indus merchants or Meluhans had settled in Sumer by the end of the third millennium BC and got assimilated with the native culture there so much so that they supplied 'wood and other raw materials' they brought from their distant lands for the construction of a temple at Lagash by Gudea. Irrespective of whether Tosi's argument about the Meluhans having been assimilated to Sumerian culture could be taken in face value or not, one may appreciate the civilian sense, humanitarian attitude and the secular character of these ancient mariners.[22] Economic texts of Ur III Dynasty bristle with references to a Meluha village (*e-duru me-luh-ha*) and Meluhan sons (*duma meluha*) and lists of persons, their debts and dealing with rations and deliveries of cereals etc. Interestingly from some Omani sites along the coast as well as in the interior oases were discovered many Harappan artifacts, especially Harappan ceramics. According to Tosi, "Harappan ceramics are found in affluent oases settlements like Hili and in tiny seasonal camp sites like Ghannada, on the western coastland between Dubai and Abu Dhabi"[23]. The discovery of various types of beads and jewelry from many sites also go to establish the existence of trade links connecting India, Mesopotamia and Egypt. Indus relics, among others, bristle with carnelian beads, which had been made at Lothal where a bead factory specialized in producing beads of various types of stones, including onyx. According to Wooly, similar types of beads were recovered from the grave at Ur. A bead from Shah Tepe in Iran was found ornate with typical Indus design. Basing on these discoveries Childe concluded that Indus region was the center of beads manufacturing and that the Indus craftsmen had run a beads factory at Ur also.[24] Indus made carnelian beads differing in shapes and designs made their way to Kish, Tel Asmar and other regions, too. There was thus a commercial network around the Persian Gulf region involving Lothal in Gujarat, Rasal-Juniz in Oman, Ur in Mesopotamia and half a dozen minor commercial entrepots where mercantile communities might have had their temporary settlements and lived in line with the laws of the respective regions. Interestingly a Sargonid text relates the story of a Meluhan called Lu-Sunzida who had to remit to Urur, son of Amar-Luku 10 shekels of silver to compensate for a broken tooth.

The most interesting aspect related to Indus-Saraswati commerce was the importance of seals and 'agent system' as pointed out by Sasi

A unique inscribed steatite seal with a socket perhaps with a lid

Asthana. Persian Gulf cylindrical seals with Indus motifs and inscriptions, and a number of Indus seals, too, have been discovered from West Asian sites, and we could definitely conceive some authorized agents of the Indian merchants who carried the seals to these trade centers to stamp the goods which they sent to the Indian ports. It may also be construed that they were licensed agents authorized to use these seals by well-knit and well orchestrated guilds or trade departments at home that must have been part of a well established administrative setup which was characteristic of Indus polity if some such ever existed. From the Persian Gulf made cylindrical seals with Indus motifs and signs it also appears that the Indus merchants have engaged the service of Gulf merchants,

These fragments of early Indus writing are about 5,500 years old

Indus Seals

too, a practice which could still be seen in international trade transactions. The cargo thus stamped by both Gulf agents and Indian merchants could easily be identified when they reached the Indus ports of Dholavira, Lothal and the like and kept in warehouses.

Indus Valley Seals. The first one shows a Swastika, a prominent symbol in Hinduism

Lothal : A Persian Gulf steatite seal showing Animal motif (Mature Indus-Saraswati level)

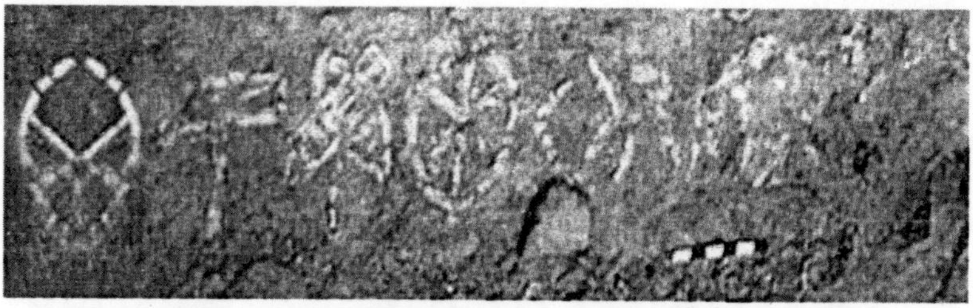

An inscription of ten characters found in the north gate chamber (Dholavira) with letters measuring 33x27 approximate (mature Indus-Saraswati)

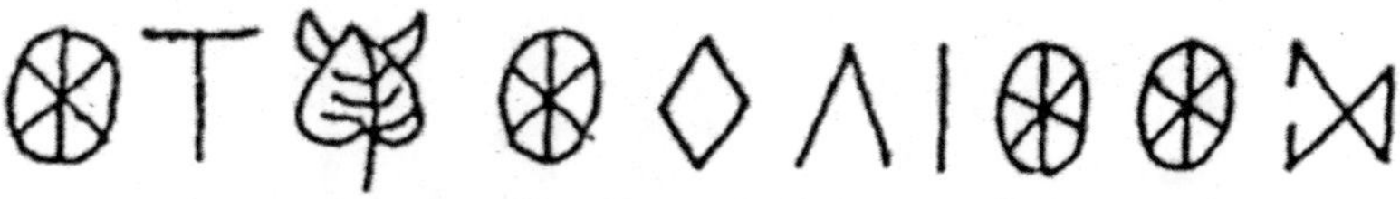

Reading from left to right

ma-dha-dha-ra-ga-va-dha-śvai-sahasra-dha

mad-dvaidhaḥ-rāga-vedhāśvaiḥ-sahasra-dhā

So much was the continuity of cultural and trade connections that even after the heyday of Indus-Saraswati civilization Indian traders visited far-off regions, and their early contact with Western world is further attested by literary evidences. Some Indian scholars categorically stated that Indians traded with Babylonian and African regions. During the peak times of the Babylonian civilization Indian mercantile community frequented the royal court of Babylonia. The Old Testament's story of the 'Writing on the Wall' of King Belshaser is of much interest. The writing *mene mene tekel upersin*, as explained by Daniel which meant, "God has counted and balanced you, but still found wanting" appears to have unambiguous resemblance with Sanskrit usage. *Mana* in Sanskrit means scaling and *Tugalai*, weighing. Even after being scaled and weighed the King was found wanting, and he is found *uparsin* (*apaharshiṅi*) without happiness (or *harsha*). The script of the writing found on the wall was nothing other than that of an Indian who spoke a language, which resembled Sanskrit though not as refined and perfect as the latter. They also traded with African coasts and seem to have established their commercial colonies there. According to Ayaswami Kalyanaraman, the *Panis* referred to in *Ṛk Véda* in their risky seafaring activities established the Phoenician Civilization, which was purely a commercial one. The commercial nature of Phoenicians and the verbal similarity between 'Pani' and 'phoeni' by all means can buttress up this argument.

References

1. S. R. Rao, *Dawn and Devolution of the Indus Civilization*, p. 168.
2. Michel Danino, *The Invasion that never Was*, p. 59.
3. S. R. Rao, *Dawn and Devolution of the Indus Civilization*, p. 169.
4. B. B. Lal, 'Report on the Chemical Analysis and Examination of the metallic and other objects from Lothal', in S. R. Rao, *Lothal: A Harappan Port Town II*, Memoir of the Archaeological Survey of India, No. 78, New Delhi, 1985, pp. 651-666.
5. Vishnu-Mittre and R. Savitri, 'Food Economy of the Harappans', *Harappan-Civilization*, Ed. G. L. Possehl, pp. 206-221.
6. Steven A. Weber, 'Changes in Plant Use at Rojdi: Implications for Early South Asian-Subsistence Systems', *Harappan Civilization*, Ed. G. Possehl, pp. 287-293.
7. S. P. Gupta, *Indus-Saraswati Civilization*, p. 159.
8. John Marshall, *Mohenjodaro and the Indus Civilization*, Vol. 2, p. 654.
9. S. R. Rao, *Dawn and Devolution of the Indus Civilization*, pp. 255-269.
10. S. P. Gupta, *Indus-Saraswati Civilization*, p. 160.
11. S. P. Gupta, *Op. Cit*, p. 160.
12. J. P. Joshi and Madhu Bala, 'Manda: A Harappan Site in Jammu and Kashmir,' *Harappan Civilization*, Ed G. L. Possehl, p. 129.
13. S. P. Gupta, *Op. cit*, p. 161.
14. S. R. Rao, *Dawn and Devolution of the Indus Civilization*, pp. 172-173.
15. *Ibid*, p. 182-183.
16. K. T. M. Hegde, R. V. Karanth and S. P. Sychanthavong, 'On the Composition and Technology of Harappan Microbeads', Possehl, *Harappan Civilization*, P. 239.
17. S. R. Rao, 'Shipping in Ancient India', *India's Contribution to World Thought and-Culture*, Vivekananda Kendra, Chennai, 2003, p. 99.
18. Maurizio Tosi, The Harappan Civilization beyond the Indian Subcontinent" *Harappan Civilization*, Possehl Ed., pp. 365-377; also see Oppenheim, A. L. "Seafaring merchants of Ur," *Journal of the American Oriental Society*, Vol. 74, pp. 6-17.
19. S. P. Gupta, *The Indus-Saraswati Civilization, Op. cit*, p. 116.

20. Sashi Asthana, *History and Archaeology of India's Contact with other Countries*, Delhi, 1976, p.42.
21. *Ibid*, p.45.
22. For the refutation of Tosi's assimilation theory see S. P. Gupta, *Indus-Saraswati Civilization*, p. 120.
23. Maurizio Tosi, 'The Harappan Civilization beyond the Indian Subcontinent' *Harappan Civilization*, Possehl Ed., pp. 365-377.
24. Gordon Childe, "India and the West before Darius," *Antiquity*, Vol.XVIII, 1939, p. 12.

16

The End

What might possibly have led to the decline of the material prosperity and urban gaiety of Saraswati-Sindhu civilization. The submerging of river Saraswati and its end owing to the changes in the courses of its big feeder channels have already been mentioned. Geology speaks about the plate tectonics that happened in north-west India and adjoining sub-Himalayan regions. It is noticed that Saraswati changed its course many times and the remaining channels were lost in the Rajasthan desert. The Khaggar-Hakra river system is considered to be a part of the ancient river Saraswati. With large volumes of water, it was, as already mentioned, located with the Sutlej to its west and Yamuna to its east. It may again be noticed that though the earlier hymns of *Ṛk Véda* praise Saraswati, the later hymns mention the river to be meandering and sluggish, and praise river Sindhu instead. It is not unlikely that the center of civillzation moved from the bed of drying Saraswati to Sindhu valley. It is natural that the one time industrious group who peopled the valley of Saraswati quit this place and migrated to Sindhu valley when they saw Saraswati drying up. The theory is supported by the Mahabharata, which mentions that river Saraswati ends in a desert (the present Rajasthan area). Around 1900 BC there were signs of gradual decline. People started to leave the cities. Those who remained were poorly nourished. Even fishes died out in Saraswati. The crucial factor may have been the disappearance of substantial portions of the Ghaggar-Hakra river system. Geology has it that a tectonic event had diverted the system's sources toward the Ganges plane, though there is a little uncertainty about the date of this event. Such a statement may seem dubious if one does not realize that the transition between the Indus and Gangetic plains amounts to a matter of inches. The region in which the river's waters formerly arose is known to be geologically active, and there is evidence of major tectonic events at the time the Indus civilization collapsed. After all, the geostructural changes that led to the disappearance of Saraswati was only a part of the major tectonic change that took place on India's north-western cost. This, as already noted, is referred to in Mahabharata and the literary evidence is amply shored up by geology of the area. According to Mahabharata thirty six years after the Kuru-Pandava war the people of Indraprastha-Hasthinapur region saw the great river running in opposite direction and the birds overhead wheeling in circles. Similarly, they saw anomalous animal behaviour along the cost during the same time. The Musala Parva thus says: "streets swarmed with rats, and mice which came out of their holes looked dazed, earthen pots showed cracks and were broken from no apparent cause, birds chirped ceaselessly, cattle and goats cried themselves hoarse, and horses bolted away from their carriages." The city of Dwaraka was shortly engulfed by marshes due to ground subsidence. Foreseeing the possibility of a natural calamity Sri krishna sent all his people to safer places including Prabhas. Soon after the departure of the people, Mahabharata says, "the sea, the abode of the monsters, engulfed the gem-filled Dwaraka." The city thus sank into the sea "presumably due to a tectonic movement accompanied by an earthquake"[1]. Thus in the light of literary, archaeological and geological evidences it could be construed that by around 1800 BC, most of the cities were abandoned, allowing the regional cultures showing the influence of Indus civilization to emerge like the 'Cemetery H culture' of Harappa and the 'Ochre Coloured Pottery culture'.

A possible natural reason of this civilization's decline is connected with the climate change, too. In 2600 BC, the Indus Valley was verdant, forested, and teeming with wildlife. It was wetter, too; floods were a problem and appear, on more than one occasion, to have overwhelmed certain settlements. As a result, Indus people supplemented their diet with hunting. By 1800 BC, the climate is known to have changed. It became significantly cooler and drier. Besides, there was the problem of the recurring floods, and as evident from archaeological remains it compelled the inhabitants to erect mud walls and fortifications around their cities which some western historians in their early stages of research have taken for the walls of defence against the invading Aryans. In fact the recurring floods that submerged the layers of construction forced the people to build new cities over the ruins of the old which required the felling of trees in abundance both for wood to construct buildings as well as firewood for baking bricks. This certainly must have resulted in the deforestation of the area, turning it arid and dry. Naturally, the place slowly turned sparse in vegetation and human habitation, and the Saraswati civilization began to find new pastures on the bed of river Indus to continue as a living civilization in times to come.

Aryan invasion - A myth : It is in this context of the aftermath of a civilization's collapse that the Indo-Aryan migration hypothesis into northern India may be discussed. In the early twentieth century, this migration was forwarded in the guise of an "Aryan invasion," and when the Indus civilization was discovered in the 1920s, its collapse at precisely the time of the conjectured invasion was seen as an independent confirmation. In the words of archaeologist Mortimer Wheeler, the Indo-Aryan war god Indra "stands accused" of the destruction. Indra, otherwise called Purandara or the shaker of the forts, is accused by the Wheeler-type historians of having destroyed the forts of the *Dasyus* or *Dasas* who were supposedly dark-skinned. But this is only a derivative of the misreading of *Ṛk Véda* as pointed out by many Vedic scholars. *Purandara* of the *Ṛk Véda* or the 'shaker of the forts' as translated by the English scholars is referred to in the Veda as the one who appears in the form of sun god and shatters the *śāradīyapura* or the snow-fort (It is interesting to notice *Ṛk Véda* identifying one deity with the other since the Vedic seers took all gods as the manifestations of the one supreme spirit, the Brahman. Therefore Indra is identified with Pushan or the Sun or Varuna or the rain god). Certainly this is nothing other than the poetic description of sun melting the mountain snow in the Himalayas which the European scholars in their ignorance and unbound enthusiasm to project India as a conglomeration of races and its history a story of racial fight, took as an evidence for Arya-Dravida fight.

Besides, evidences from the Saraswati-Sindhu sites make it clear that the cultural elements associated with the people whom European indologists used to call Aryan were well inlaid in the flowerbed of Indus culture. Right from its beginning Saraswati-Sindhu culture had in it all the elements of what is called Aryan civilization : the fire worship, the Yogasana, the Swastika, the cult of Mother Goddess, the Phallic worship, worship of cow and all the healthy precedents the Hindu civilization now observes. One may again take for instance the Harappan geometry which set the patterns of town planning and design of sacrificial altars. Advocates of Aryan invasion theory would make one believe that Indians borrowed geometry and astronomy from the Greeks following Alexander's invasion of India. But it is to be noticed that from time immemorial town planning with carefully laid out cities arranged with drainage system had been the hallmark of Indian cities as revealed from Mohenjodaro and Harappa or the cities like Ayodhya whose graphic description is given in the Ramayana. Even the building style of the *chaitya* halls which could later be seen in the Buddhist structures with sanctum at the centre of the one end and long aisle in the midst, a style which the Europeans later inducted into their Church structures, is referred to in Ramayana. It is evident that people of Indus Valley were well at home with methods of geometry which helped them design *yajñaśāla* or sacrificial altar. In fact the remains of Vedic sacrificial altars discovered from Indus sites prove the existence of Vedic religion there. Indians had also been in possession of the theoretical knowledge of geometry as revealed from the mathematical text, *Sulbasutra* which must have existed long before the 2nd millennium BC which is considered to be the time of the Vedas. Interestingly the argument that the construction of the Vedic altars was done by the so called Dravidians of the Harappan civilization whereas the literature which contains the instructions for building them was the creation of the invading Aryans appears paradoxical. The only tenable argument is that Indus Valley architects and the *yajñaśāla* designers followed this ancient treatise of geometry in the north-western part of the subcontinent which, as could be believed from the chronology of both Harappan structures and Vedic literature, formed the part of the Vedic India. All these evidences go to convince researchers that the cultural elements found in Indus Valley were already prevalent in India, and as John Marshall observes there was millennia of cultural endeavour before they evolved into the state they were found in at Indus sites.

After all, the difference between South and North India said to be based on the Arya-Dravida difference is a myth rather than a historical reality just like the myth it is based on. The South and North had never been at poles apart in cultural life. Both had common gods, common traditions and a common cultural background. One may take for instance the tradition of Siva worship which is referred to in history textbooks as the religion of South India, again said to be the Dravidian stronghold. But this argument proves only a travesty of facts. Siva worship, just like the worship of other Gods of the Hindu Trinity, had been a part of Indian religion irrespective of North-South difference. From Mount Kailash or the temple of Pasupatinath at Katmandu in the North to Rameswaram in the South Saivism was a potent force that strengthened the spiritual unity. Looked further, it could again be seen that North India gave more importance to Siva worship than the South did as could be seen in the Himalayan regions like Nepal, Kashmir and the northern parts of the Uttar Pradesh and Himalchal Pradesh. The story of the 'Dravidian God' Siva destroying the forts of Tripuras is only the fabrication born of European Indologists' dilettantish approach which falls wide off any accurate historical knowledge. Even geographical distance or political difference never hindered the progress of India's cultural nationalism. North had warmly welcomed and accepted many gems of Hindu thought that sprang from the South. Chanakya, the leading exponent of early Hindu polity hailed from South just as Agastya who took the sacred lore to the South came from north. Sankara, Madhvacharya and Ramanuja were southerners, wholeheartedly accepted in North India. Temples in North accepted priests from Kerala while the Kashmiris recruited priests from Karnataka. South, described as the Dravidian stronghold was the citadel of Vedic learning with its far famed centers like Kanchi, Rameswaram, Sringeri and Kalady. Even in times the Indian kings stood at dagger heads the current of cultural unity flowed silent and strong. What else could be understood from the enthusiasm with which the ancient metros of India like Nalanda, Vatapi and Kanchi turned up to celebrate the visit of Huien Tzang, the Chinese sage who came to learn Buddhist teachings at the very time their political heads were fighting each other. The cultural current that encircled India in its mighty and soothing embrace was thus invincible and irresistible.

After all, the term Arya as found in Indian lore of any period doesn't connote anything racial. One may take for instance the definition Amarakosa, the authoritative Sanskrit lexicon gives to the term Arya. According to it an Arya is one who hails from a noble family, of gentle behaviour and demeanour, good natured and of righteous conduct (*mahākula-kulīnārya-sabhya-sajjana-sādhavah*). Even Manu draws the difference between an Arya and Non-Arya when he speaks of the spiritual plummeting of people. Thus he observes:

> ...in consequence of the omission of sacred rites, and of their not heeding the sages, the following people of the noble class [Arya Kshatriyas] have gradually sunk to the state of servants : the Paundrakas, Chodas, Dravidas [Dravidas, according to the lore were people of the country called Dramida or Dramila whose last king Satyavrata was rescued by the fish incarnation of Vishnu during the deluge], Kambojas, Yavanas, Sakas, Paradas, Pahlavas, Chinas, Kiratas and Daradas.

It is thus clear that Aryans were not a race but people noted for their universally respected qualities. Even Dravidas themselves were, if to take Manu's view, Aryans who for their having failed to observe the spiritual rites fell from the heights they occupied. Aryas were indeed highly spiritual and cultured people guided by the supreme light. Children of Arya seek and are led by *jyōti* or light, says *Ṛk Véda* (*...prajā ārya jyōtiragraḥ*).[2] Again it should be understood that the word Arya was honorific to address people. *Arya* and *Aryé* were thus commonly used to address man and woman with respect. Arya-Dravida difference and enmity was only the product of imagination and ignorance rather than of any meticulous research. The late George F. Dales thus refutes the Aryan invasion theory:

> Nine years of extensive excavations at Mohenjo-Daro ... have yielded a total of some 37 skeletons which can be attributed to the Indus period. None of these skeletons were found in the area of the fortified citadel, where reasonably the last defense of this city would have taken place [If such an alleged foreign invasion by the Aryans ever occurred] ... Despite extensive excavations at the largest Harappan sites, there is not a single bit of evidence that can be brought forth as unconditional proof of an armed conquest and destruction on the scale of the supposed Aryan invasion.[3]

The skeletal remains found at Harappan sites that date from 4,000 years ago, show the same basic racial types as are found today in Gujarat and Punjab. This is interesting, because if a foreign light-skinned people entered and took over, it would seem likely that there would be genetic

Sample of skeletal remains from Harappa

evidence for this. The long continuity of ethnic groups in this region would indicate that the people living there had not seen an influx of a different ethnic group that would have mixed with their own.[4]

It is thus certain that the collapse of Indus Valley Civilization was not the result of an Indo-Aryan migration about which there is no evidence. On the contrary it seems rather likely that the hypothized Indo-Aryan migration was the product of an imaginary collapse, comparable with the decline of Roman Empire and the incursions of relatively primitive peoples during the Migration period. This fallacious argument is just the result of applying European paradigm in Indian history. True in case of the fall of Roman empire, Toynbee's idea regarding the external and internal proletariats is resultant of an exhaustive and meticulous research. But generalizing Toynbee's theory in all cases of historical developments is idiotic. After all so long as the Indian culture maintains its continuity and contemporanity it can't be plainly stated that the Indus Valley Civilization had completely kissed the dust. Besides, the exponent of the theory of the external proletariat, Toynbee himself agrees that Indian culture is a living one and not dead like that of Greece or Rome. If to quote a modern writer :

> Both the Swastika and Shiv Lingum have been symbols closely related to the Hindu religion (even to the present day), indicating continuity of the Saraswati civilization rather than a complete collapse or destruction… Swastika, a symbol associated with the Indo-Aryans by early historians, has been found in large numbers over several Indus sites. Similarly, several Shiv Lingum type structures have been found at several Saraswati-Sindhu sites... The discovery of

> Swastikas has put to question the theory of an Aryan invasion of Indian subcontinent... there was no Indo-Aryan invasion...

Or we may ask, were there Aryans and their systems in the Saraswati-Sindhu valley prior to the Aryan invasion Intelligence alone would answer. After all, the Aryan theory itself was the product of European imperialistic design. Germany which was an emerging power during the first and second World Wars was in search of an identity and a theoretical background to support and justify its dominance urge. It was this dominance urge which Max Muller supported through his Aryan theory that was much used by Nazi Germany which claimed to be the land of the Arya, the nobler race born to rule others. This resulted in the Nazi idea of German racial superiority and arrogance which Hitler tom-tomed in his campaign against the other European powers. Suffice it to say, the Aryan theory Max Muller coined had badly mutilated European peace and checkmated the Anglo-French interest for a good number of years. But the very same Max Muller, the self-styled Sanskrit scholar who once vehemently argued that Aryan is a race made a summersault. Gobbling down the 'racial nature' of the term Aryan he later said, "Aryan is a language." This was to appease Great Britain whose newly constituted Boden Chair of Sanskrit at Landon lured the wily Max Muller. This he thought was the only way to please the English and occupy this world's most prestigious professorial chair of Sanskrit. Besides, he was the Christian missionary number one who continued to vilify the British government's slow process of Christian proselytizing in India. Hinduism in India is in doom, he once said and "if Christianity is not stepping into its shoes whose fault it is," he blamingly asked the British Government. Aryan invasion theory was thus an expression of European imperialism sworn to divide India politically, racially and psychically. It is a travesty of historical truth, a vicious idea that emanated from an evil mind.

References

1. K. S. Valdiya, *Saraswati : The River that Disappeared, Op. cit*, p. 80.
2. *Ṛk Véda*, VII. 33.7.
3. Dales, George F. *The Mythical Massacre at Mohenjodaro.*
4. Stephen Knapp, *Proof of Vedic Culture's Global Existence*, Michigan, 2000, p. 43.

Conclusion

Indian culture was always characterized with its amalgamating, all embracing and acommodative nature. Many foreigners were amazed at this unifying nature that threaded together as if in a single garland all the diversities which made India an epitome of the world. Down the lanes of its history it fostered a life system rich in its long tradition of give and take, inform and get informed and accept and be accepted. Not only indigenous but foreign cultures, too, found acceptance and assylum in India and its culture. India's is the civilization which whole heartedly welcomed and gave assylum to the civilization of the Isralites the very time, if to quote Swami Vivekananda's address at the Parliament of Religions, their temple was shattered to pieces by Roman tyranny. Even in recent times India witnessed mass exodus of foreigners into her territory whom she had accommodated. So much was India's all embracing nature that by imbibing the universal ideas and accommodating the foreign elements she could forge a unity out of diversities. But what was the secret behind this rare and unexampled all encompassing broadness is something the student of Indian history and culture is to learn. This idea of unity was inherent in Indian thought right from the time of the Vedas which could be deemed the first spring of human thought and culture. She, as found in her Vedas, realised the oneness of everything. The philosophy of monism or advaita as well as the idea regarding the universal or undifferentiated consciousness as the indwelling spirit of everything worldly was well within her vision. India realized this truth and her philosophers and seers loudly proclaimed it and carried it down the generations reminding them that it is the national mission to see the idea of oneness propagated and realized. Unity rather than disunity is the desirable law of human progress. Coherence rather than decoherence is the ideal law of existence. Coherence at mental, social, national and international level can help humanity realize itself as one undivided family. Making world one family - *vasudhaiva kudumbakam* is the the law or *dharma* for which India has been striving in her right earnest from the dawn of her history. If men are the reflections of the very same divine, they are a fraternity bound together in enlightenment. Long before the modern sciences began speculating and theorizing on the one indwelling energy, India's Upanishads sang and sublimated the human soul, enlightened it with the ambrosia of the devine oneness. Consequently, notwithstanding all the external differences the idea of unity worked underground weaving everything into one single whole, irrespective of all the diversities among religions, political ideologies and social differences. As already described, there was nothing to be identified as difference between the Saraswati civilization and the culture that sprang up from the Vedas. Indeed that they were one and the same is well attested by all the available literary and archaeological data. The very same civilizational aspects continued down the millennia with the result that whatever religion that sparng up from India found itself in harmony with the entireity of Indian socio-religious fabric. Buddha for instance was a product of the Indian spiritual tradition and whatever he taught did not ran in contrast to the existing religious ethos. And whatever ideas about such difference are only the exaggerations predicated on meaningless premises. The same was the case of Varddhamana Mahavira who just like any other teacher of ancient India showed his followers the path towards Kaivalya or the ultimate enlightenment, where there is no differences, where every individual soul finds itself identified with the entireity. All of them thus taught the philosophy of *advaita* or the oneness of all. If everything is emenation of the samc ultimate thare cannot be any difference, all Indian teachings believed alike. One may take for instance the teachings of Jesus Christ himself who studied philosophy of monism or adavita from the Buddhist monastries of north-west India. Teachings of Jesus Christ come in perfect harmony with the precepts of all Indian systems, especially his philosophy of unattachment, renunciation and monism. That the West has henously hijacked him and misused his name for colonising the New World is of course another thing. But the philosophy of Christ still remain perfectly Indian and finds itsef in perfect agreement with Indian monism. So long as the idea that "I and my Father are one" continues to be the cardinal philosophy of Christ it would remain in harmony with the spirit of India. The opinion of Swami Vivekananda that he belongs to "the religion of which Christianity is an offshoot and Buddhism its rebel child" is worth mentioning. India at all times taught the philosophy of oneness and it is this oneness among humanity that any one studying the history of India learns.

Appendix - I

Sheet Anchor of Indian Chronology : A Critique

Western scholars like William Jones, Pargiter, James Princep, George Turnour, etc., have commendably contributed to Oriental studies. Sir William Jones, a judicial officer of East India Company was the founder and President of the Royal Asiatic Society established in Bengal in 1784. Widely traveled in North India, Kashmir and Western Asia, he studied the history of these areas. He collected from Kashmir a text of the history of Bactria called Dabistan Document and concluded that kings of Indian origin ruled Bactria many years before Alexander's invasion of India. In 1793 he declared that he had solved the riddle of ancient Indian chronology, stating that Sandrokottas referred to in the accounts of Megasthanese (Greek writer of the 4th century BC) was Chandragupta Maurya of the Indian Puranas and other literatures like Mahavamsa. According to Greek accounts Alexander's invasion of India lasted from 327 BC to 323 BC. As per Greek accounts an Indian king named Sandrokottas who defeated Alexander's successor Selukos took over as king of Palibothra during 320 BC. Basing on these Greek accounts William Jones concluded that Sandrokottas and Palibothra of Greek accounts were Chandragupta Maurya and Pataliputra respectively. Jones took 320 BC as the year of Chandragupta Maurya's coronation. Jones thus laid the sheet anchor of ancient Indian chronology. Thus having bridged the chronologies of

India and Europe, European Indologists prepared the chronology of ancient India on the basis of this sheet anchor.

First of all it may be noticed that primary sources are of cardinal importance in historical research. Secondary sources regarding a *datum* could of course be relied upon but only if the primary source is available. But in the case of Megasthanese' *Indica* nobody ever had seen or read it in original. Suffice it to say, there is no such a work as *Indica.* In fact our knowledge about the said *Indica* is based just on hearsay. We come to hear of the *Indica* just from the information provided by the later Classical scholars like Arrien, Strabo, Plutarch, Curtius etc. And whatever smattering we have about *Indica* is from the few quotations later classical writers gave in their writings. *Indica* as we get it at present is thus only a collection of the copious extracts which these classical writers say they quoted from Megasthanese.

Authenticity itself of the *Indica* could thus be questioned on the basis of its own absence, leave alone any statement or finding based on it. *Indica* is just a myth and any writing based on this myth could be none other than fiction. Myth would not make history. This is the opinion of the methodology of history.

Even if just hearsay about the Indica shall be used to write the history of ancient India overlooking the inevitability of the primary source, still Jones' Sheet Anchor of Indian Chronology remains a Grope in the dark. It is the conclusion of a reckless slap dash rather than meticulous research. Mere verbal semblances between 'Palibothra' and Pataliputra, and 'Sandrokottas' and Chandragupta (Maurya) made Jones conclude that 'Palibothra' was nothing other than Pataliputra and 'Sandrokottas', Chandragupta Maurya. But had Jones been a bit keener in his observations and reasonable in his research he would not have concluded so. It was indeed an inattentive conclusion, a lax finding. To prove this argument right we may take some of the following and relevant portions from Classical accounts.

1. *Prassi surpasses in power ... their capital being Palibothra, a very large and wealthy city, after which some call the people itself Palibothri ... nay even the whole tract along the Ganges.*[1]

Arrein, depending on Megasthenese' and other Greek writers' accounts writes, "Megasthanese stayed in the court of Sandrokottas. He also stayed in the court of Porus. Porus was a mightier king than Sandrokottas." This means that Sandrokottas was only an insignificant king before Porus who was the ruler of a territory comprising only two districts. Thus the Sandrokottas referred to in Classical accounts was only a dwarf compared to the Emperor Chandragupta Maurya of Puranic and Buddhist accounts. Sandrokottas of Classical accounts was not Chandragupta Maurya. According to this statement Palibothra's location was (while traveling from the North-West) before the Ganges-Yamuna confluence. But Pataliputra or modern Patna lies south-east of the confluence.

2. *The situation of Palibothra is given as 425 miles from the confluence of Ganges and Jomanese and 738 miles from the mouth of Ganges where it meets the sea.*[2]

This argument is again buttressed up by Arrein's account that "Thence to the confluence the Jomanese and Ganges 625 miles and to the town of Palibothra 425 miles." This means that the confluence was 200 miles ahead of Palibothra. But Pataliputra was ahead of the confluence and not 200 miles before it. Thus taking the geographical location of Palibothra as given in Classical accounts it may be concluded that Palibothra of Megasthanese and Arrein was not Pataliputra.

3. *The people in whose country this city - Palibotra is situated, is the most distinguished in all India and is called Prassi. The king in addition to his family name must adopt the surname Palibothras, as Sandrokottas for instance did, to whom Megasthanese was sent as an embassy.*[3]

But nowhere in Indian literature or any other source material related to the Maurya dynasty it is mentioned that the Maurya kings assumed any dynastic title. Here also it is fallacious to assume that Sandrokottas was Chandragupta Maurya.

4. *About Sandrokottas, it is said that he was the greatest among the Indian kings and he was the king of Prassi whose capital was Palibothra.*[4]
5. *Sandrokottas killed the previous king and became king himself*[5].

It is true that Chandragupta Maurya had defeated the early Magadhan king Dhana Nanda. But he did not kill the latter. The literature on the other hand informs that Chandragupta Maurya had allowed him to quit Magadha taking as much money and material as could be carried in a cart.

6. *Seleukas Nikator had given his daughter in marriage to Sandrokottas.*[6]

But this reference is also not agreeable with the history of Chandragupta Maurya. Contemporary Indian evidences never refer to Chandragupta Maurya as having married a Greek Princess.

7. *Heracles (identified by historians as Surakulesh Vishnu) was the founder ... of no small number of cities, the most renowned and greatest of which was Palibothra.*[7]

Here it is mentioned that Palibothra was founded by Surakulesh Vishnu. It may be noted that Pataliputra on the other hand was founded by Udain. Again it might be noticed that the capital of Magadha up to the time of the Andhras was Girivraja or Rajagriha and not Pataliputra (which, too, however was not Palibothra of Megasthenese).

8. *The river Jomanese flows through the Palibothra into the Ganges between the towns of Methora (Mathura) and Carisobaras (Kalisarovar* according to the British Indologists*).*[8]

But it may be noticed that Yamuna is not flowing through Pataliputra. Yamuna flows into the Ganges even before the Ganges reaches Patna or Pataliputra.

Besides, here it is good to have an understanding of the Greek pronunciation of the Sanskrit name. It is to be noticed that Pataliputra can't be written as Palibothra if to ground our argument regarding this on the Greek word Palibothra itself. The letter 'p' in Patali is written in Greek as English 'p' only. Then why the 'p' in Putra is changed into Greek 'b' is surprising. There is no instance of the Sanskrit 'p' changed into Greek 'b'. It is thus clear that 'putra' is not 'bothra'. Pataliputra is not Palibothra of the Greek accounts.

All these possible and convincing arguments likely to come up against the sheet anchor given by European Indologists notwithstanding, this chronological setting still continues to dominate the study of ancient Indian history. Classical accounts are still relied to study the history of India's past and its chronology even as they often disagree with each other and contain mutually contradictory statements regarding incidents or places and persons. Even the very question regarding the originality of *Indica* as noted earlier combined with the ambiguity of these accounts would suffice to make one doubt the reliability of these accounts. Yet the modern Indologists continue to stereotype William Jones fallacy.

Dr R. C. Majumdar, an authority of Ancient Indian history states that "... a perusal of the different accounts [of the Greek writers] raises grave doubts whether they are all derived from a common reliable source."

He says that though Megasthanes' "Indica, or collection of fragments preserved in later writings, has long enjoyed the reputation of being a rich mine of useful and authentic information about India, ... the question of how far the fragments usually ascribed to him, can really be accepted as such, and may be relied upon as authentic" is something to be addressed with utmost caution.[9]

In fact many authorities including H.C. Raychaudhuri doubted the reliability of the Classical accounts of India though he, too, followed the British Indologists in many of his writings including his masterpiece, *Political History of Ancient India.* The fallacy of Jones' Sheet anchor being thus clearly established in the light of the Classical accounts, it would be interesting to enquire whether there was a place in India that would agree with Palibothra of the Greek accounts.

Jones and his followers took Prassi for *Prachya* which in Sanskrit means the Eastern country. Jones took the statement in the Greek accounts that "Palibothra stood at the junction of Ganges and Erannoboas" and believed that Erannoboas was Hiranyabahu which was also called Sone. River Sone no doubt was also known as Hiranyabahu.[10]

The conclusion of Jones thus appears correct and justifiable but for another statement of Megasthenese wherein he describes Erannoboas and Sone as different rivers. Megasthenese has stated, "Nineteen rivers are said to flow into it (Ganges), of which ... the Condochates, Erannoboas, Coseagus and Sonus are navigable."[11]

Thus with Megasthenese himself having described Erannoboas and Sone as different rivers Jones' attempt at identifying Erannoboas with river Sone to locate Palibothra near the latter in Eastern India proves untenable. Megasthenese Palibothra was not in Eastern India. His identification of the city of Palibothra, the country of Prassi and the river Erannoboas thus proves the best examples of the hasty conclusions he jumped to without checks and counterchecks of data.

Jones calls Megasthenese ignorant and inattentive. But it could hardly be believed that Megasthenese, a person of such a high office i.e., an ambassador was ignorant and inattentive. Megasthenese was well familiar with the places he visited in India. According to him, "Indus skirts the frontiers of Prassi"[12].

It may be noticed that Mahabharata refers to the country of Sindhu Pulindakas along with Chedi, Vatsa, Karusha and Bhoja (*chedivatsa kārushaśchabhōja sindhupulindaka*) which situated in Madhyadesa.

Megasthenese might have meant this Sindhu-Pulinda of Madhyadesa which in later times was called Kali Sindh. It is interesting to note that Mac Crindle's English translation of Schwanbeck's *Indica* shows one Sindhu river to the south of Parnasha and Chambal which join Yamuna. The Prassi of Megasthenese must have situated near the Sindhu Pulindaka country and around this Sindhu river. It may again be noticed that there was no river called Sindhu near Patna or Pataliputra. Sindhu and its tributaries flow or end up in the North-western India itself. Besides, archaeology has it that many rivers of North-western India changed their course, and some of them even submerged or dried up.

Archaeological finds excavated by the Indian and Pakistani archaeologists and geologists prove that river Yamuna and some of the present tributaries of the river Indus flowed into river Saraswati of which some remaining channels are still called Saraswati, Sarsuti etc. Taking these archaeological, geological and other findings which have come up so far we may believe that there might have been a certain minor river which the people of Kali-Sindh called Sindhu. Though unknown to other parts of India and insignificant before the then mighty Sindhu or Indus river, Megasthenese who stayed in Palibothra for a good number of days must have noticed this minor river that skirted the frontiers of Prassi.

According to Classical accounts river Jomanese flows through Palibothra into the Ganges between the towns of Methora (Mathura) and Carisobaras (not Kalisarovar as taken by European Indologists but Karushasarovara).[13] Thus as previously said Karusha was also located in Madhyadesa, quiet near to Sindhu Pulinda, i.e., between Sindhu Pulinda and Prayaga. Taking Classical accounts in corroboration with the study of the geography of Madhyadesa it could be concluded that Palibothra, the Prassi capital was near Mathura, Karushasarovara and Sindhu Pulinda or Kali Sindh. Palibothra was not Pataliputra as William Jones mistook.

Then, was there an ancient kingdom in the Madhyadesa that agrees with the Megasthenese description of Palibothra. The question brings us to the country of Prabhadraka, Prabhadra or Paribhadra which reigned in Madhyadesa from the very Mahabharata times. Certainly it must be the Palibothra of Megasthenese where he is said to have stayed as an ambassador. The *Mahabharata*, Parasara's *Jyotisha-Samhita*, Varahamihira's *Brihatsamhita* and *Puranas* refer to the kingdom of *Prabhadrakas*. As the post-Mahabharata literary works make mention of the Paribhadrakas it could well be assumed that they continued to rule and were known to the writers of the Gupta period. They also allude to the king called Chandraketu as the head of the Prabhadraka Kshatriyas. But it is yet to be ascertained whether he was the Sandrokottas of the Greek accounts. The Bhadraka kingdom or Paribhadra and its people, the Paribhadrakas or Palibhadrakas might be the Palibothra and, the Palibothris of Megasthenese accounts.

Thus while studying the Megasthenese accounts one comes up with the following conclusions. Yamuna was flowing through Prabhadra or Palibhadra, the capital of the Prassi kingdom which was 200 miles from Prayaga on the way to Mathura. Paribhadra or Palibhadra was near Sindhu-Pulinda or Kali Sindh. The Karushasarovara was between Sindhu-Pulinda and Prayaga. Palibothra might thus be Paribhadra rather than Pataliputra.

Hence the need to neglect a non-existing datum like Indica and restructure the chronology of ancient India depending on original and authentic sources.

References

1. Pliny, II, 22; Pandit Bhagavadatta, *Bharatavarsha ka brihat itihas*, quoted by Shriram Sathe, *Dates of the Buddha*, Hyderabad, 1987, p. 16.
2. R. C. Majumdar, *Classical Accounts*, Calcutta, 1960, p. 130.
3. *Ibid.*
4. *Ibid.* pp. 4, 12.
5. V. A. Smith, *Early History of India*, Oxford, 1924, p. 124.
6. Mac Crindle, *Ancient India as described by Megasthanese and Arrian*, Calcutta, 1926.
7. Diodorus Selucos, *General Description of India*, Book II, 39. Also see Pandit Bhagavadatta, *Bharatavarsha ka brihat itihas*, quoted by Shriram Sathe, *Dates of the Buddha*, Hyderabad, 1987, p. 16.
8. Shriram Sathe, *Op cit*, p. 16.
9. R. C. Majumdar, *Op cit*, pp. XX-XXVI; also see its appendix - I, p. 461.
10. *śōṇō hiraṇyabāhū syāt*, *Amarakosa*. 1-10-33.
11. Pliny, VI. 22, John Bostock and T. R. Riley (trans.), *The Natural History of Pliny*, London, 1890; R. C. Majumdar, op. cit, p. 341.
12. Frag. LVI, Pliny, 22, Quoted in Shriram Sathe, *op. cit.* p. 104.
13. Shriram Sathe, *Op cit*, p. 16.

Appendix - II

Ogastantra or the Indian art of living in tune with nature

It is appropriate to begin quoting an excerpt from the Red Indians' Chief Seattle's 1885 speech to a White Governor who had come to occupy the Red Indians' land:

"What is it that the White Man wants to buy, my people will ask. It is difficult for us to understand.

"How can one buy or sell the air, the warmth of the land. That is difficult for us to imagine. If we don't own the sweet air and the bubbling water, how can you buy it from us. Each pine tree shining in the sun, each sandy beach, the mist hanging in the dark woods, every space, each humming bee is holy in the thoughts and memory of our people... Every part of this soil is sacred in the estimation of my people...

"We are part of the earth, and the earth is part of us. The fragrant flowers are our sisters, the reindeer, the horse, the great eagle our brothers...

"We know that the White Man does not understand our way of life. To him, one piece of land is like the other. He is a stranger coming in the night taking from the land what he needs. The earth is not his brother but his enemy, and when he has conquered it, he moves on... He treats his mother the Earth and his brother the sky like merchandise. His hunger will eat the earth bare and leave only a desert...

"Your God is not our God!... Our people are ebbing away like a rapidly receding tide that will never return. The White Man's God cannot love our people, or he would protect them...

"But why should I mourn at the untimely fate of my people Tribe follows tribe, and nation follows nation, like the waves of the sea. It is the order of nature, and regret is useless. Your time of decay may be distant, but it will certainly come, for even the White Man... cannot be exempt from the common destiny. We may be brothers after all. We will see[1].

"This Western trend to exploit nature was resultant of the fatal divorce brought about by the new religion of the West between God on the one side and his creation, nature, on the other. Many Western thinkers including Voltaire, Jefferson and Thomas Paine have recognized this. In fact in pre-Christian or 'Pagan' religions (as modern Europeans call them) no such divorce existed. It would not be off the mark to quote Pierre Thuillier, the French historian of science who writes:

"Christian theology defined a conception of nature perfectly adapted to technicist ambitions. As a matter of fact, in Paganism, natural realities were perceived to be living inhabited by "soul".... A spring (or a tree) was not reduced to a physical reality, a material reality. It was something more, an entity with a life of its own. It was therefore perfectly natural for a spring to be respected and even revered. It was seen as a marvelous manifestation of Nature, herself regarded as living. The earth, let us recall, was perceived as one great organism; the Greeks called her as "Mother Earth." Even minerals appeared endowed with certain life, and all individual existences mysteriously associated with one another amidst the whole, of which humanity itself was but one fragment.

With Christianity, a supposedly "superior" religion that attitude towards nature was totally disqualified. Henceforth, it was forbidden to revere springs as if they had a dignity of their own. People's whole adoration had to be turned to the Christian God and to him alone... It is true that nature, created by God, retained a certain spiritual value. But a radical transformation had taken place: earth, air, water and fire, now theologically striped of all "soul," were no more than objects which *Homo technicus* was free to manipulate as he wished... Through its doctrine, the Judeo-Christian tradition somehow legitimized officially the most daring technical enterprises.[2]

The whole pre-Christian world seems to have worshipped earth as the sacred abode of the Divine that manifested in every object. It is also to be noticed what prevailed on the global face prior to the origin of the modern Western and Middle Eastern religions, was a universal religion with its characteristics more or less similar irrespective of regional and continental variations. Recent archaeological findings from Honduras, Mexico etc. established the similarities of the ancient American cultures, Mayas, Incas or Aztecs with those of the ancient culture that flowered on Saraswati-Sindhu Valleys. Both, like the people referred to in *Rk. Veda* and *Zend-Avesta*, were the worshippers of nature, especially of fire. Of all these cultures India offered a highly admirable world view that zeros in on the importance of nature. But all these cultures were swept away by the steamroller of the Judeo-Christian advance, as also of Islam, and with the passage of time they became aborted civilizations. *Siva Purana* says, the Kali Yuga or the age of *kali* would witness many signs of growing chaos among which the noted would be the merchant class' abandonment of the "holy rites such as digging wells and tanks, and planting trees and parks."[3]

It is the European trend that sprang up with the Renaissance, which prompted man to have a microscopic approach to each and every problem of life. With industrial development making nature the target of exploitation, a particular ideology, too, was evolved as a moral support to this exploitation. It was all in with the Semitic belief to have a systematic approach for the brutal enjoyment of nature. According to Francis Bacon, "The secrets of nature reveal themselves under the vexation of art [i.e., artisantry, technology] than when they go their own way." The Baconian method thus suggests haunting the nature, enslaving her, and pressurizing her like an inert plastic material into a mechanical mould or any form and to torture her to reveal all her secrets. Such a process of perception calls for a change of mentality, a change from its natural state to a mechanical one. This superiority of man over nature, a reflection of the Old Testament belief that nature with all its living beings is for the enjoyment of man, is the cardinal aspect of the Baconian spirit and all the later mechanical approaches to nature. The next development in this approach appeared in the 'Discourse on Method' of Rene Descartes, who advocates a mechanical way of thought in experimenting with the nature, which according to him has a mathematical structure or pattern.

Mind is a machine, man is different from the entirety, and knowledge results from the association of fragments of ideas. Everything according to this view is an isolated entity which conflicts with the other, and produces a mind-matter duality. This schizoid duality, which can't accept the idea of unity and harmony in universe and the resultant 'Beauty' thereof, is the basis of this world view. He elaborates this further in his *Principles of Philosophy* and looks to the world as a machine of matter and movement. In his thought even non-material aspects have only material basis, and natural and artificial things cease to have difference. "I do not recognize any difference between machines made by craftsman and the various bodies that nature alone composes," he observes. Animals are machines made of wheels and coils; and human body, too, is a machine. The result is a deductive logic and a mechanical world view. This evolved further into the Galilean idea that nature could be controlled only if it is taken as dead and useless. To understand this mechanical nature, a mechanical mind which can vivisect nature into separate units is called for. To know is to control; truth is only that which is useful, and this new method of perception expelled from within its range elements of values and experience. Newtonian concept of 'Dead matter' also added to this mechanical world view. Thus with the Cartesian paradigm seeing nature as an object of exploitation, technological and economic systems ruthlessly torturing and looting the nature began to gain ground.[4] Irrespective of any difference in economic ideologies, the thought that nature is an aimless and lifeless object that awaits exploitation by man has become one of the cornerstones of both capitalist and socialist thoughts.

The approach and attitude to nature depends on the mindset of a people with the result that it could be looked either as a dry machine or a vibrant life system. It is here that Indian outlook to nature differs. Indian tradition had developed an integral and holistic approach to the entire faculty of knowledge of which ecology constituted an important part. According to ancient literature, India developed a desirable and admirable type of corporate existence, a state of nature working on the principles of morality or *Dharma.* It led man and his thoughts from de-coherence to coherence.

The state of nature is not a fiction but a historical reality. Rousseau and Montesquieu have theorized about that archaic state of nature with no ruler, nor the ruled. In it man found himself in perfect harmony with nature, an opinion, which is again shored up by the like oriental theories, too. *Mahabharata* thus says:

na rājyam na rājāsid
nadandyō nachadāndika
dharméṇaiva prajāsarva
rakshanthisma parasparam.

According to this version, in this state where natural laws were in vogue there was neither kingdom nor the king, no body was punished, nor was there wielder of rod. Protecting each other, the people led a life of *Dharma* and lived in harmony with nature.

Indian world view upholds a holistic approach to man and nature, which are inseparable parts of the totality. To ancient Indians, nature and its other living systems were venerable objects. Nothing was considered as dead matter. Indian thought upholds nature as the manifestation of the *Brahman* or the divine spirit. Naturally nature became a revered object. Nature or *Prakruti* is the universal appearance (*viswarūpa*) of the *Brahman* which encompasses in its *viratpurusha* (all-encompassing) aspect all the worldly beings - trees, beasts, birds and the like which are deemed its organs. *Purushasukta* describes the *Brahman* or the *Purusha* as with many heads, thousand eyes and thousand feet.

sahasrasīrsha purusha
sahasrākshā sahasrapād.[5]

Whatever was found in nature or cosmic body was taken as the manifestation of the divine with the result that each and every phenomenon in nature became as venerable as the *Brahman* itself. It was not out of fear, as is falsely believed, but out of love and affection to an object, which the culture of the land held dear and near to it that such an approach to nature was developed. It could see a divine manifestation in everything and worshiped it.

If nature and ecosystem were the expressions of the divine, it was the earth, which sustained them. The mother of all the flora and fauna, she was the most sacred, and was worshipped as the consort of God *Vishnu.* The seers imagined of her as ocean-clad and decked with beautiful mountains, and to trample upon her with feet was sinful to be apologized.

samudravasané dévī
parvatastana mandité
vishnupriyé namōstubhyam
pādaspsarśam kshamasvamé.

"Forgive me for my touching you with my feet. I salute thee oh goddess! Thou who art ocean-clad and with mountains as thy breasts and thou who art the beloved of Vishnu, the supreme God.

Charms were often composed to invoke the blessings of mother earth and special rites were performed at the time of any new initiative:

yatté bhūmé vikhnāmi
kshipram tadapi rōhutu
māté marma vimrugiri
māté hridayamarpipam.[6]

"Let whatever I dig up from the earth grow in size. Let not my spade oh! Mother earth, wound thy heart or such important parts.

The lore looks to trees as the flying curls of the God or Hari:

namasté vrukshébhya harikéśébhya.[7]
nama saspinjarāya tvishémité.[8]

According to the *Rudradhyaya* of *Yajur Veda* tree is God itself. It abounds in hymns to praise and worship the trees and all sources of water as incarnations of Lord Rudra:

nama kāṭyaya nīchyāyacha.[9]
"I salute the waters of small brook (*kāṭya*) and cascade (*nīchya*)
nama sudyāyacha sarasyāyacha.[10]
"Salutations oh! the waters of muddy place (*sudya*) and lake (*saras*).
namō nadyāyacha vaiśantāyacha.[11]
"Waters of river (*nadi*) and small lake (*vaisanta*), I salute.
nama kūpyāyachāvaṭyāyacha.[12]
"I salute the waters of well (*kūpa*) and ditches (*avaṭya*).

There was prayer for the peace and tranquility of the atmosphere, earth, vegetation and forest.

dyō śānti antarīksham śānti apa śānti
oushadhayé śānti vanaspatayé śānti.
sarvam śānti.

"Let tranquility be to the sky, atmosphere, earth, water, and the entire flora and for everything.

Planting trees was considered sacred which would help one attain heaven, since they were reckoned as the divine incarnate or the embodiment of *Veda*. It is interesting to note Jambavanta's briefing to Hanumana on the eve of his trip to fetch *mrutasanjivani* to rejuvenate Rama in the battle field. He described the medicinal plants as the icons of the highest knowledge, *vedasvarupa*.

According to Kamandakiya *Nitisara* :
aśvaddḥmēkam pichumandamēkam
nyāgrōdhamēkam daśatintriṇiścha
kapithhavilvāmalakatrayancha
panchāmranaḷi narakam nayāti.

"One who plants one pipal tree, one neem tree, one banyan tree, ten tamarind trees, three jackfruit trees, and five coconut trees would never go to hell.

The teachings of the Buddha laid great significance on nature and all animals associated with it. In fact it is not wholly a Buddhist ideal, but something the Buddha himself had drawn from traditions. For, the literature of the time including *Arthasastra* of Kautillya refers to the importance of trees and flower gardens as inseparable parts of the cities and towns. Naturally the Buddhist teachings, as reflections of the time, signified the importance of nature, and in course of time there developed stories about the birth (*Jatakas*) of Buddha wherein nature, its beasts and birds found their harmonious commingling. One comes across how the Buddha himself was protected by the *Naga Muchalinda* by spreading its hood over him while lost in a long trance. We see the images of *nagas* and *naginis* in the Buddhist art at Sanchi, Saranath, Barhut or Amaravati where the *stupa* railings bristle with images of serpent Gods and relief motifs of so many other beings of nature like the *Bodhi* tree or even the nature spirits, *Yakshas* who lay hanging on either side of the gate ways on the four sides. These *Yakshas* according the far famed philosopher and art critic, Ananda Kentish Coomaraswamy, are the guardian deities of the four quarters of the universe, symbolizing the theory of balance, rhythm and order (*ṛta*).[13] Nature was according to ancient Indian thought a synthesizer and balancer.

All thesc bring out that India developed the *ōgastantra*, which can be translated into the 'science of adjusting with nature' instead of 'nature management.' Naturally it was impossible for Indian culture to look to nature as a dead matter. Nature was to the Indians a guide disciplining their life that found itself associated with the entirety. It imparted *ṛta* or order to life. Nature was a harmonizing force that made life in ancient India a mutual entertainment leading to the bliss of corporate existence among men as well as between god and man, *yajña* :

sahayajñā prajā srushtvā purōvāchā prajāpati
anēna prasavishyadḥvamēsha vōstvishṭakāmadhuk.[14]

Prajapati, progenitor of all the worlds, creating of yore, beings that co-exist with a sacrifice, said: "By this you multiply, let this yield you covetable objects of desire.

dévān bhāvayatānéna té déva bhāvayantuva
parasparam bhāvayanta śréya paramavāpsyathaḥ.[15]

"By this entertain the gods and let the gods entertain you; entertaining each other you will both attain supreme good.

Nature was a great inspiring force to many human endeavours. Interestingly India's prominent literatures were written in the forest interiors and are set against the backdrop of nature's sylvan surroundings. As already noted Indian tradition looks venerably to earth as a goddess, *Bhūdēvi* and the story of her consort Vishnu incarnating from age to age to relieve her of the burden of *asuric* or demonic forces, an act he does out of his love for the earth, is meaningful in Indian cosmology. Many of the heroes and heroines of Indian tradition are in one way or the other related to the earth. Sita means the daughter of the furrow and she returned to the earth she came from. Siva is bound to the earth through Parvati, daughter of the Himalayas. Earth and heaven are inseparable. *Ṛk Véda* says, "Heaven is my father; my mother is this vast earth, my close kin."[16] Nature is man's defender rather than an adversary to be conquered and despoiled. "Blue water, open space, hills and thick forests constitute a fortress," says Tiru Kural.[17] Rivers from Ganga to Kaveri are goddesses. *Ṛk Véda* looked to the river Saraswati as goddess and mother alike and as the giver of wisdom:

ambītamé nadītamé dévītamé saraswati
apraśastā iva smasi praśastīmamba naskridhi.[18]

"Best of mothers, best of rivers, best of Goddesses, Saraswati we are ignorant and untrained, give us wisdom and knowledge!

Again river valleys were considered auspicious for conducting religious rites. According to Manu the Saraswati-Drishadwati Valley was most auspicious place and hence suitable for all kinds of spiritual activities and he calls it *Brahmavarta*, the divine land:

Saraswatīdrushadvatyōr dévanadyōr yadanantaram
tam dévanirmitamdéśam brahmāvartam prachakshaté.[19]

"Gods created the land between the divine rivers, Saraswati and Drishadwati. It is called *Brahmāvarta.*

The mountains from the Himalayas to the Vindhyas are gods. Trees, as already said, are sacred, so are many plants and flowers, and a number of animals from cow to peacock. And down the millennia nature has been playing a dominant role in shaping India's culture. Its history, literature, culture, religion and all other walks of life were moulded by the influence of nature. Its psyche was cast in the lap of nature, and its religion in the forest retreats, which proved the backdrop for many creative works, literary as well as spiritual. The *Aranyakas* were authored in the forest interiors, and the Vedas were chanted in hermitages, which were the spiritual repositories of India's perennial culture from where sprang the inspiration for the great civilizing efforts. Forests had been the 'place where all creatures find their protection of love' (*śaraṇyam sarva-bhūtānām*) as described in Kalidasa's *Sakuntala* in which we hear the pleading of the forest dwellers with the king to spare the life of a deer, helplessly innocent and beautiful, a pleading that comes from the heart of the whole drama. On many occasions forest was the companion of man, imparting the message of tranquility to his soul. In Ramayana, the poet says, Rama and his companions, in their banishment, faring forest after forest, living in the leaf-thatched huts, and sleeping on bare ground, did not know any rigours of journey, because their hearts felt their kinship with the woodland, hill and stream amidst which they were not in exile. 'When Rama took his abode in the delightful *Chitrakoota*, by the *Malayavati* river, with its easy slopes for landing, he forgot all the pains of leaving his home in the capital at the sight of those woodlands, alive with beasts and birds.' Having enjoyed the beauties of the nature, Rama who was the lover of mountain and forest (*giri-vana-priya*), exuded to Sita an air of exuberance: "When I look upon the beauties of this hill, loss of my kingdom troubles me no longer, nor does the separation from my friends cause me any pang."[20] Thus nature and her surroundings offered solace to many bruised hearts. They were soothing and creatively inspiring.

References

1. Michel Danino, *Indian Mind Now and Then*, Mysore, 2000, pp. 92-94.
2. Pierre Thuillier, *The Great Implosion - Report on the Collapse of the West, 1999-2002*, Paris, 1995.
3. *Siva Purana*, II. 1. 23.
4. Will Durant, *The Story of Philosophy*, New York, 1961, p. 152.
5. *Purusukta*, I.
6. *Atharva Véda*, I. 1, 35.

7. *Yajur Véda*, 2. 2.
8. *Ibid*, 2. 3.
9. *Ibid*, 7. 8.
10. *Ibid*, 7. 9.
11. *Ibid*, 7. 10.
12. *Ibid*, 7. 11.
13. Ananda K. Coomaraswamy, *The Dance of Shiva*, New Delhi, 1982, p. 72.
14. *Gita*, III. 10.
15. *Gita*, III, 11.
16. *Ṛk Véda*, I. 164. 33.
17. *Kural* (translated by C. Rajagopalachari), Bombay, 1981, p. 151.
18. *Ṛk Véda*, 2:41:16.
19. *Manu*, 2. 17.
20. Rabindranath Tagore, *Creative Unity*, New Delhi, 1980, pp. 53-55.

Appendix - III

Buddhism : A Continuation of Vedic Religion

T. S. Kartika
(Associate Professor of Philosophy,
N. S. S. Hindu College, Changanacherry, Kerala)

> The aim of Buddhism was the reform of Vedic religion by standing against ceremonials requiring offerings of animals, against hereditary caste and exclusive priesthood, and against belief against permanent souls. It never attempted to destroy that religion, or overturn the social order. It introduced a vigorous method by organizing a class of sanyasins into a strong monastic brotherhood, and the Brahmavadins into a body of nuns ...[1]

This opinion of Swami Vivekananda may appear queer to an ordinary student of history fed on the conventional approach to the religious history of India set by European Indologists. Looked superficially, Hindu and Buddhist systems as they are differently called, would appear as running in contrast to each other. But a closer look would reveal the untenability of the argument that one is orthodox and the other heterodox. It would be fitting to have a look into the tradition of Gautama the Buddha rather than of Buddhism to have an understanding of how much Siddhartha, the prince of Kapilavastu was influenced and his mental background moulded by the spiritual attitude of the land he was born and brought up in. It is interesting to look into the very name his parents selected for him. Siddhartha, as his name meant, was eligible for all kinds of transcendental powers (*siddḥi*). Born and brought up in the spiritual tradition of India cast in Vedic frame, Siddhartha received the most advanced type of education usually given to the scion of the princely family. Naturally amidst the Vedic rituals and many such ceremonials that might certainly have been the part and parcel of the then religious systems on the one side and the idea regarding the cardinal truth of ultimate deliverance from the meshes of mundane illusions on the other, the young Siddhartha chose the latter rather than the former. His religion therefore was spiritual and not ritualistic. Hence his refutation of the hollow and meaningless sacrifices and Brahmanical practices which were to a good extent decried by the Vedas themselves.

True, ritualism and the resultant priestly supremacy had badly mutilated the Indian society. Those who controlled the rituals controlled the psyches of the superstitious population. Ignorance made a people slaves to the more knowing or seemingly knowing priestly class who resorted to exploitation, a practice totally abominable to Vedic ideals. Naturally a man of *vidya* or real knowledge, if to use the Vedic jargon, would not subscribe himself to the anti-vedic practice of exploiting the lowest and the lost under the pretext of Brahmanism as interpreted by the priestly communities. Hence the search for Truth afresh by the real seekers of the ultimate reality or deliverance. It is interesting to note that Upanishads insist on *vidya* or wisdom or insight into reality, accompanied by control of desire and detachment from earthly ties and interests. "Vidya is not learning, but rapt contemplation; it is a realization of one's unity with the supreme spirit, in the light of which all material attachments and fetters fall away." Buddha definitely subscribed to this view.[2] And it is quite natural that some one in search of this long lost Truth would turn to break the crust of social and cultural customs to look beneath and beyond to know whether there is any glittering ember of Truth underlying the useless cinder mound of rituals and sacrifices. This is what Gautama Buddha did. He was really in search of the *bōdḥa* or enlightenment already envisioned in the Vedas and sought after by many early seers or monks. Definitely Gautama belonged to that unending tradition of the Buddhas or enlightened ones who streamlined and guided India's spiritual tradition down the ages. He was the next one in the long array of great teachers who carried down to posterity the gems of *vidya* and *bōdḥa*, the cardinal aspects of the Vedic tradition. *Vidya* or real knowledge alone would give *bōdha* or enlightenment, Gautama like all the other sages of Indian tradition knew. Hence his refutation of the meaningless ritualism and caste based Brahmanic supremacy that clouded the golden face of Truth with their dark blanket. Naturally he wanted to reform the Vedic religion by rejuvenating its real spirit buried to obscurity by vested interests and greedy trends. Sakyamuni was thus another *muni* (sage) of India's *ārshaparampara* or tradition of *Ṛshis* or seers. That what he taught were heavily drawn from the Vedas is well attested by both his philosophy and practical life.

It has always been the social phenomenon to look down upon any reformer or seeker who stood for cardinal values and attempted to save them from the social decline. Definitely Buddha, too, as alluded to by literary references, must have been vilified for his revolutionary and radical views of the kind once upheld by the Vedas. As one could expect, to a group whose dilettantish approach to things blasphemed the Vedic teachings, teachers like Buddha must have been a thorn in the flesh. In a world where the word *Purōhita* which meant promoter of the likes (*hita*) began to be applied for someone who cared exclusively for his own likes or interests instead of the one who promoted the *hita* or interests of the entire humanity, the latter type would rather be isolated and spurned. Sometimes, as it is known, Gautama Buddha might have been decried by the pristine community who monopolized the Vedas to make them their livelihood; but India's spiritual intelligentsia who once loved the Vedic teachings were now with the Master of Kapilavastu whose teachings were in fact the Vedas retold. The story of an arrogant priest who approached Buddha who was sitting cross legged and enjoying the bliss of salvation after his having emerged from a seven days long meditation, to argue about the nature of a true priest is well known. He asked Buddha: "What are the characteristics of true priests" To this Buddha replied:

> "True priests are those who have abandoned all sins, who are free from arrogance, who are pure and self-controlled, who are wise and learned, who have achieved a high degree of holiness, and his behaviour does no harm to any living beings.[3]"

A true priest according the Vedic interpretation is none other than one who is unassuming, who transcended the sensual and material plain, a sacred one, man of wisdom and knowledge and a lover of the entire universe, a real *Viśwamitra*. Buddha was thus once again redefining the pristine purity of India's priesthood envisioned by its Vedas. The way he followed and prescribed for his disciples to achieve this pristine purity was none other than what had already been well within the Vedic injunctions, meditation which was a part of Yoga. We come to hear of the Buddha sitting in trance under a tree on the bank of river Nerenjana at Uruvela for seven days without interruption, enjoying the bliss of salvation. While staying among the Kurus he addressed his disciples:

> There is only one way to purify yourself, to transcend sorrow and grief, to extinguish suffering and misery, to live serenely, and to realize nirvana: this is through applying the four forms of awareness.
>
> The first is awareness of the body, you may go into the forest, sit at the foot of a tree; or you may go into an empty room. You cross your legs, hold your body erect. You observe yourself while you inhale, and observe yourself as you exhale. Inhaling a long breath, you are aware that a long breath has been inhaled. Exhaling a long breath, you are aware that you are exhaling a long breath. You reflect: "Aware of my whole body, I shall exhale." Then you reflect: "Aware of my whole body, I shall exhale." And then you reflect: "Calming my whole body, I shall exhale." Then you reflect: "Calming my bodily forces, I shall inhale." And then you reflect: "Calming my bodily forces, I shall exhale."
>
> As you become aware of the body in this manner, you understand that body continually comes into being and passes away. This understanding concentrates the mind, and enables the mind to become self-sufficient, not grasping at external objects.[4]

It is again interesting to note Buddha's explanation of the four stages of meditation. He thus elaborated:

> Right concentration consists in entering the first stage of meditation. This requires seclusion, and brings happiness and joy. It involves thought and reflection.
>
> The thought and reflection are set aside, and the second stage of meditation entered. This leads to inner tranquility, in which the mind is fixed on a single point. It, too, brings happiness and joy.

> The happiness and joy are set aside, and the third stage of meditation is entered. This leads to total serenity, and an awareness of complete well-being.
>
> Then all senses of well-being and suffering is set aside, and the forth stage of meditation is entered. This leads to utter purity of awareness.
>
> Those who practise the four stages of meditation for seven years may expect two kinds of fruits. The first is perfect wisdom. The second is no further rebirth. These fruits may come after six years, five years, four, three or two years or even one year. They may come after six months, five months, four, three or two months or even after one month.[5]

Here the enlightened one was explaining to his disciples nothing other than the different steps of controlling body and mind and the yogic practice of getting through different stages of physical, mental and spiritual preparation for attaining the ultimate deliverance, differently called *kaivalya, mukti, nirvāṇa*, etc. Where did he study all these form. Definitely from the tradition and religious systems already in practice in India from time immemorial. Because the system Buddha taught to control body and mind was the same as taught by the philosophy of Yoga. Buddha thus laid emphasis on the middle path or balanced life. According to the Gita "the yogic practices of the person who is balanced in his food habits, in games and in activities, in sleep and in wakefulness become fruitful in taking him beyond sorrow" (*yuktāhāra vihārasya yukta chéshṭasya karmasu yuktāswapnāvabōdhasya yōgō bhavati dukhaḥ*).[6] It was ultimately this middle path that landed him in the realm of enlightenment.[7] Buddha himself hints at this when he refers to his having been familiarized with the preliminary steps in yogic practice like postures, deep breathing, alternate breathing, holding the breath, etc. by Alar Kalam. Having developed high esteem about this Yoga teacher, Buddha keenly followed what the former taught. Thus says Buddha:

> "It is not merely by faith that Alar proclaims his doctrine, that of himself he has comprehended, realized, attained it, and abides in it ...So I approached Alar and said to him, "Friend Kalam, what is the extent of this doctrine which of yourself you have comprehended, realized and attained, and which you proclaim" Thereupon Alar proclaimed the attainment of Nothingness. Then I thought, 'Alar has faith,

but, I, too have. Not only has he energy, I too have energy ... Not only has he wisdom, I, too, have wisdom. What if I strive to realize that doctrine of which Alar proclaims that of himself he has comprehended, realized, attained it and abides in it.' Then in no long time I quickly comprehended, realized, and attained the doctrine, and abode in it.[8]"

It is thus clear that the very background of Buddha's spiritual exercise was truly yogic. In fact it was not a new religion, but "a new revelation which a great teacher was preaching," Says Sardar K. M. Panikker.[9] He further writes:

"The distinction between Hinduism and Buddhism in India was purely sectarian and never more than the difference between Saivism and Vaishnavism. The exclusiveness of religious doctrines is a Semitic conception, which was unknown to India for a long time. The Buddha himself was looked upon in his lifetime and afterwards as a Hindu saint and avatar and his followers were but another sect in the great Aryan tradition.[10]"

One leading step in Buddha's teaching on the different stages of meditation is the control of senses. The Gita has already given the definition regarding a sense-controlled man who like the tortoise has withdrawn his senses from the externalities and concentrates on his own inner self. Such one brings all his senses under control including craze for taste and olfactory sensations. According to Buddha:

... an exemplary monk ... is scrupulous in his conduct and in the food he eats; yet he is aware of the danger which lies in the avoidance of small faults. He abides by the highest principles of good action and speech; he guards the gates of his senses; he is alert and self-aware; and he is content.[11]

And the path, too, was of unattachment i.e. the state between attachment and detachment. Buddha suggested his followers take the middle path or *madhyamikamārga* to attain unattachment and the resultant Nirvana. It is a path between acceptance and negation, love and hate, enjoyment and total renunciation. The Buddha explains the middle path or *madhyamikamārga* thus:

"There are two extremes which should be avoided. First extreme is a life devoted to pleasure; this is degrading and worthless. The second extreme is a life devoted to self-

> mortification.; this is painful and worthless. The middle path between these two extremes, leads to insight, which leads to wisdom, which leads to serenity, which leads to truth, which leads to nirvana.[12]"

This philosophy of *madḥyamikamārga* or the middle path the Buddha preached to his followers had already been taught by the Gita. *Vairāgya* that lies between *kāma* and *krōdha* had already been with the Indian thought. Srikrishna in the *Gita* had dealt with the reactionary chain of *vishayasanga, kāma, krōdḥa, sammōha, smrutivibhramśa* and the ultimate destruction at length. It exhorts the seekers to be endowed with wisdom, get rid of both good and evil (*ubhé sukrutadushkruté*) and lead a perfectly balanced life. Thus one attains the stability of wisdom (*sthitaprajña*). Having control over his senses he withdraws himself from all the externalities like a tortoise who tucks its feet and head inside the shell (See the chapter on *Yoga*). This according to Buddha is the state of *sambōdḥi* or of the highest wisdom. This is also described as the state of *nirvāṇa* or *jīvanmukta,* i.e. freedom from all worldly temptations even while alive. *Nirvāṇa* is thus the state of a living being who having mastered the middle path, practises it.

But what is required to attain the state of *sambōdḥi* is the abandonment of desire, because Buddha said it is *trushṇa* or desire that brings about sorrow. And if the *trushna* is satisfied there also it leads to the just opposite, i.e. pleasure. Pleasure and pain are the two extremes and the both are harmful to the spiritual uplift. Swami Vivekananda thus explains it:

> Liberation means entire freedom - freedom from the bondage of good, as well as from the bondage of evil. A golden chain is as much a chain as an iron one. There is a thorn in my finger, and I use another to take the first one out; and when I have taken it out, I throw both of them aside; I have no necessity for keeping the second thorn, because both are thorns after all. So the bad tendencies are to be counteracted by the good ones, and the bad impressions on the mind should be removed by the fresh wave of good ones, until all that is evil almost disappears, or is subdued and held in control in a corner of the mind; but after that, the good tendencies have also to be conquered. Thus the 'attached' becomes 'unattached'.[13]

Hence Buddha's exhortation to be free of desire because the fulfillment of desire as well as the reverse would bring pleasure and pain respectively, both harmful to the attainment of the ultimate freedom. Buddha went to the extent of exhorting his followers to attain freedom even from the desire to be free of desires because the desire of any kind would bring only sorrow.

To attain this state, along with the *dhyānamārga* or path of meditation Gautama Buddha prescribes the noble eight fold path (*ārya ashṭāngikamārga*). It is interesting to note that *ārya* or what is noble is often described as something a balanced state or *samyak*. The *ashtangas* of the middle paths are *samyak karma* (right action), *samyak vak* (right speech) *samyak samādḥi* (right concentration), *samyak darśana* (right view) etc.[14] The Sanskrit word *samyak* means right, proper, equipoise, equilibrium, balance, etc. Buddha thus envisioned a balanced life or middle path as the means to attain Nirvana. Arya, as the term down the millennia implied, is noble and *aryadharma* which was as old as the Vedic culture, has never been a novel introduction either by Buddha or Sankara later who was dubbed *prachhannabuddha*. *Āryatva* (nobility) and *Veda* (wisdom) were indeed synonymous because only through the former one could attain the latter. And as Buddha himself says the concept of *dharma* is the Aryan path or the eternal *dharma*, a realization he reached through self culture.[15] "Buddha's gospel acquired the name of Aryan eightfold path because Buddha was always particular in emphasizing that it was an Aryan path, a path worthy of Aryans, of the noble people of Bharatavarsha."[16] Buddha thus never deviated from the time tested path India fared down the centuries to reach salvation. What he preached was never a new religion but only another revelation that he got following the path of *dhyāna* or meditation which had already been in vogue in the Vedic tradition.

Such a one who attained nirvana is endowed with extraordinary and immeasurable potential. Thus says the Buddha:

> Through his spiritual disciplines, the monk now possesses great mental powers. He may become many beings; and then he may become one being again. He may become invisible, and then visible again. He may walk through a wall or a mountain. He may penetrate solid ground, as if it were water; and he may walk on water, as if it were solid ground ... Through his spiritual disciplines, the monk's

> hearing now surpasses normal hearing. Not only does he hear earthly sounds; he also hears celestial sounds ... The monk's hearing is so acute that he can hear sound from the farthest end of the universe, as well as the tiniest sound from the smallest atoms of the earth ... understand minds and moods of others ... monk can remember his previous existence ... with clarity and know age of death.[17]

Suffice it to say, the power of monk who attained nirvana is all surpassing. His wisdom which is all comprehending and all piercing has crossed the limitations of time and space. Before him is only the infinite, the illimitable wholeness, a completely coherent entirety. He is in everything and in him is all. He is the all knowing, all surpassing one who is beyond limitations of time and space. This indeed is the state of a yogi who attained *samādhiprajña* or balanced intelligence, whose wisdom has become one with the cosmic wisdom or cosmic consciousness. Everything is thus part of universal consciousness and it is to this consciousness that the microcosmic consciousness is to return. Hence the call of *Gita* to perform all the *karmas* or deeds by seeking refuge in that highest cosmic consciousness (*buddhau śaraṇamanviścha*) or the call of the Buddha to seek refuge in consciousness (*buddham śaraṇam gachhāmi*). Buddha following the teachings of *Gita* exhorts his disciples to be a part of the highest *bodha* or consciousness which is undifferentiated or *akhanda.*

One of the ancient teachers on the idea of dialectics, Buddha believed that change is the basis of existence. Buddha, like the Upanishads, theorized that world which is changing and hence indeterminate is only a fictitious creation of the de-cohered mind. "The mind is unstable and unsteady; it is difficult to guard and control. Those who are wise straighten the mind, as the archer straightens the shaft of his arrow."[18] External world is only a superimposition of the transitory mind which ceases when steadied. According to Upanishads the cause of all existence is *anadi* or without beginning; it does not have beginning or end. Buddha, too, speaks of the one absolute which is without beginning or end, a great zero, *śūnya. śūnya* is described as neither existent, nor non-existent, neither both nor their absence. But it is the source of all existence. "He that is allied to *śūnya* is allied to all that is; he that is removed from *śūnya* is removed from all that is." Buddhist teachings identify *śūnya* with *dharma* also, *dharma* according to the Upanishadic thoughts as well as of Buddha is thus the ultimate reality. *Mimamsa* identifies Dharma as the expression of the Divine or the means to reach it. They are one and the same or inextricably intertwined. Hence the Buddhist prayer, *dharmam śaraṇam gachhāmi* or 'may I take refuge with dharma,' the Ultimate. Indeed Indian philosophy well explains the concept of Zero. *Śūnya* is without beginning or end or *ādyantaśūnya* and is infinite. Whatever was infinite was divine and hence something to be revered. Therefore we find the word *pūjya* or the worshipful in Sanskrit to denote Zero. *Dharma Pūja vidḥāna*, believed to be an eleventh century work, gives the following prayer:

> He that has no beginning nor end, no figure nor form, no birth nor death, who is all pervading and unlimited by purpose, who is stainless and immortal, who is to be realized only through Yoga, may that *śūnyamūrti* be my saviour.

All the Indian lore thus unanimously agrees on the infinite and divine nature of *śūnya. Śūnyadharma* is not negative and non existent or emptiness but positive being which is the primal cause of all existence. It is the primal zero or the zero volume singularity everything proceeds from and recedes to. It is this Zero or the wholeness or entirety Buddha exhorted his disciples to seek refuge in. This is pure *advaita* wherein the seeker and the sought become one.[19]

Buddha like most of the Indian teachers has it that everything is conditional and interrelated. Causes and effects in their unending interrelation determine the texture of existence. Theory of causation plays its dominant role everywhere. Everything is dependent on certain other factors and none is independent of the other. In fact in the ultimate analysis one may end up in the wonderland of confusion to distinguish between cause and effect as they are mutually and inextricably interrelated. Even cause ceases to have a separate entity with the effect because it is for the effect the cause happens. To interpret further, effect is the cause of the cause. Here cause is the effect and vice versa. It is interesting to note the ancient Indian description of God as both cause and effect. All merge together into an infinite whole. Everything has got a dharma of its own to fulfill and it is this dharma that determines its place in the unending chain of causes and effects that determine the texture of the whole. Hence the doctrine of dependent origination, *pratītya samutpāda*, which speaks about a manifest world hooked up in a bootstrap of conditions, a world that ceases with the annihilation of conditions through *samyak jñana* or steadied consciousness or *samādḥi* of the Upanishadic language.

Nature is one continuous vibration, an infinite growth bound by an iron chain of causality. It is a continuous whole, one and indivisible. Anything that happens sends a throb through the whole circle of existence, which is only another name for ceaseless change. In the mechanism of universe there is a procedure guided by eternal cosmic law. It is the human imperfection or ignorance that covers up the reality of oneness and projects as individual persons and separate things. Every thing worldly is subject to dissolution and what dissolves gets transformed into something new. One condition results in a chain of conditions and effects, each effect being the condition of the succeeding effects. Thus for Buddha, Becoming and Being are one and the same.

The world of becoming is the world of *nāma-rūpa* or the world of name and form. According to Buddha's theory of dependent origination consciousness gives rise to *nāma-rūpa*, an idea that agrees with the modern physicist's finding, i.e. the collapse of consciousness. Role of consciousness in forming the world of name and form is thus well explained in the following dialogue between Buddha and Ananda.

> "If consciousness, Ananda, did not enter into the womb, would name and form arise in the womb" "No, Sir" "And if consciousness, Ananda, after it has entered into the womb were again to leave its place, would name and form be born into this life" "No, Sir" "And if consciousnesses, Ananda, were again lost to the boy or to the girl while they were yet small would name and form attain growth, increase and progress" "No, Sir" "If, Ananda, consciousness were not to find name and material form as its resting place, would then birth, old age and death, the origin and development of sorrow, reveal themselves in succession." "No, Sir, they would not."[20]

The role given to consciousness in the formation of the material world is the same as found in Upanishad. In the state of Nirvana the differentiated consciousness merges into the undifferentiated consciousness. It is due to ignorance or *avidya* or the play of maya differentiation or separation of consciousness from the undifferentiated consciousness takes place.

The world thus appears like a bootstrap, one holding the other in a tangled hierarchy. Buddha attributes to *karma* or one's action the role of a catalyst in bringing forth *avidya.* Buddhist doctrine is well defined in the *Nikayas* according to which Buddha had the vision of the whole universe as a system of *karma*, composed of beings noble or mean, happy or unhappy, continually passing away according to their deeds, leaving one form of existence and taking shape in another.[21]

The Buddhist doctrine of karma envisages a world of dynamism and indeterminism, a world of oneness. To attain the eternal bliss one has to eliminate bad *karmas* and be neutral to good *karmas.* One should seek universal liberation rather than individual liberation. One should purify oneself as a means to purify the world. Each and every act of purity one does purifies the entirety and becomes a part of cosmic culture or *samskāra.* This is nothing but Gita's doctrine of *niskāma karma* or selfless work with no desire for the fruit. Instead of mere individual liberation Buddha stands for the *lōkāsamgraha* or the holding together of all. The idea of Bodhisattva or the Buddha reincarnating time and again is interesting. The Bodhisattva is the image of a saint who prays for the opening of the world of salvation for all the creatures of the world before he enters it. Because getting nirvana for oneself and leaving all the fellow beings in the world of misery is not in line with the Buddhist theory of non-ego. Again it is the dynamism of karma that keeps up the world. Death is the state of the body when karmic rotations slow down. Thus physical existence is an illusory impermanence created by the *karma* or force of actions. When the force of karma stops the physical existence ceases altogether. When only the world is completely redeemed of the force of karma the liberation is attained. On the whole Buddha's teachings like those of the Vedas or Upanishads seek the universal unity, a creative unity which is beyond and beneath all the visible and tangible diversity. In all aspects Buddha could well be deemed a luminary in the long array of Vedic teachers.

References

1. Swami Vivekananda, *Complete Works*, Calcutta, 2009, Vol.6, p. 161.
2. P. Nagaraja Rao (Ed.), *Radhakrishnan Reader: An Anthology*, Bombay, 1969, p. 332.
3. *Mahavagga.* 1: 2. 1 : 3: 4. 1: 5.
4. *Ibid.* 1: 24. 5 : 7.
5. *Maha Satipatthana Sutta.* 21: 22.
6. See the pages on Yoga in chapter 7 of this book.
7. R. R. Diwakar, *Bhagawan Buddha*, Bombay, 1980, p. 65.

8. *Ibid*, pp. 55-56.
9. K.M. Panikker, *India Through The Ages*, Delhi, 1985, p.25.
10. K.M. Panikker, *A Survey of Indian History*, 1977, pp. 33-34.
11. *Samana-phala Sutta.* 40 : 42.
12. *Mahavagga.* 1: 6. 17 : 18.
13. Swami Vivekananda, *Op. Cit*, Vol. I, pp. 55-56.
14. *Mahavagga.* 1: 6. 17 : 18.
15. S. Radhakrishnan, *Indian Philosophy*, New Delhi, 1989, volume-1, p. 303.
16. R. R. Diwakar, *Op cit*, p. 88.
17. *Samana-phala Sutta.* 83-84, 87-88, 89-92, 93-96.
18. *Dhammapada.* 33-39.
19. P. Nagaraja Rao, *Op cit*, pp. 454, 455.
20. *Mahanidana Sutta, Mahapadana Sutta* and *Samyutta Nikaya* Quoted in S. Radhakrishnan, *Indian Philosophy*, Vol. I. p. 349.
21. S.R. Goyal, *A Religious History of Ancient India*, Meerut, 1984, Volume. I, p. 246.

Bibliography

Aitareya Upanishad
Amarakosa
Apastambha
Atharva Veda
Baudhayana Dharma sutra
Bhagavad Gita
Bruhadaranyaka Upanishad
Chhandogya Upanishad
Darsanamala of Sree Narayana Guru
Isavasyopanishad
Jaimini
Katha Upanishad
Kautallya Arthasastra
Kena Upanishad
Maitri Upanishad
Mahabharata
Mahabhashya
Mahavagga
Maha Satipatthana Sutta
Mahapadana Sutta
Mahanidana Sutta
Mandukyakarika
Mandukya Upanishad
Manu Smruti
Mundaka Upanishad

Narada
Nirukta
Panchavimsa Brahmana
Prasana Upanishad
Ṛk Véda
Samana-phala Sutta
Samyutta Nikaya
Satapatha Brahmana
Siva Purana
Swetasvatara Upanishad
Taittiriya Upanishad
Vasishta Dharma Sutra
Viduraniti
Yajur Véda

Ajithkumar, M. P. 'Indian Background of Nietzschean Thought,' *Quarterly Journal of the Mythic Society*, Bangalore, July-Sptember, 2007. 'Philosopher King', *Quarterly Journal of the Mythic Society*, Bangalore, January-March, 1998. 'Some Thoughts on Sindhu - Saraswathi Civilisation', *Quarterly Journal of the Mythic Society*, Bangalore, Bangalore, December 2002. Saraswati: The Lost River, *Journal of Indian History*, Tiruvanantapuram, August- December, 2007.

Albert Einstein, 'Science, Philosophy and Religion', A Symposium, published by the *Conference of Science, Philosophy and Religion in their relation to the Democratic ways of Life*, Inc., New York, 1941.

Altekar. A. S., *State and Government in Ancient India*, New Delhi, 1984. *The Position of Women in Hindu Civilization*, New Delhi, 1987.

Ananda K. Coomaraswamy, Christian *and Oriental Philosophy Of Art*, Delhi, 1982. *The Dance of Shiva*, New Delhi, 1982. *History of Indian and Indonesian Art*, New York, 1965. *What is Civilization*, Delhi, 1989.

Ananda K. Coomaraswamy and Horner. I. B., *The Great Thoughts of Gotama The Buddha*, New Delhi, 2000.

Anwar Shaik, *The Vedic Civilization*, Cardiff, UK, 2003.

Aswaghosha, *Awakening of Faith* (Trans. D T Suzuki), Chicago, 1900.

Aswini Kumar Lal, 'Big-Bang: A Critical Review', *Journal of Cosmology*, 2010, Vol. 6, 1533-1547, January 30, 2010.

Bipin Chandra Pal, *The Soul of India*, New Delhi, 2010.

Bhandarkar, R. G. *Early History of the Dekkan*, New Delhi, 1983.

Bohm, D. & Hiley, B. "On the Intuitive Understanding of Non-locality as Implied by Quantum Theory," *Foundations of Physics*, Vol. 5, New York, 1975.

Bose, A. C. *Call of the Vedas*, Bombay, 1988.

Chandrakala Padia (Ed.), *Feminism, Tradition and Modernity*, Shimla, 2002. (Ed.), *The women in Dharmasastras*, New Delhi, 2009.

Chatterji. S. K. (Ed.), *Cultural Heritage of India*, Vol. I, Calcutta, 2001.

Dharma, P. C. *The Ramayana Polity*, Bombay, 1989.

Diwakar, R. R. *Bhagawan Buddha*, Bombay, 1980.

Diodorus Selucos, *General Description of India*, Book II.

Fritjof Capra, *The Tao of Physics*, Colorado, 1984.

George Buhler, *Laws of Manu*, Delhi, 1988.

George F. Dales, *The Mythical Massacre at Mohenjo-Daro.*

Ghosh, A. (Published), *Archaeological Remains, Monuments and Museums*, (ASI), Parts I&II, New Delhi, 1996.

Gordon Childe, "India and the West before Darius," *Antiquity*, Vol. XVIII, 1939.

Goyal, S.R., *A Religious History of Ancient India*, Meerut, 1984.

Gregory, L. Possehl (Ed.), *Harappan Civilization*, New Delhi, 1993.

Ghosal, U. N. *Studies in Indian History and Culture*, New Delhi, 1965.

Gupta. S. P. and Lal. B. B. (Ed.), *Frontiers of Harappan Civilization*, New Delhi, 1984.

Heisenberg, W. *Physics and Philosophy*, New York, 1958.

Hemachandra Raychaudhuri, *Political History of Ancient India*, New Delhi, 1999.

Herman Oldenberg, *Buddha*, Delhi, 2003.

Hiriyanna, M. *Outlines of Indian Philosophy*, Delhi, 1932.

Jayswal, K. P, *Hindu Polity*, Bangalore, 1924.

John Bostock and T. R. Riley (trans.), *The Natural History of Pliny*, London, 1890.

John Marshall, *Mohenjodaro and the Indus Civilization*, Vol. 2.

Kapadia, K. M. *Marriage and Family in India*, Bombay, 1966

Kenoyer, Jonathan Mark, *Ancient Cities of the Indus Valley Civilization*, Karachi and Islamabad, 1998.

Kosambi, D. D. *The Culture and Civilization of India in Historical Outline*, New Delhi, 1977.

Lal, B. B. 'Report on the Chemical Analysis and Examination of the metallic and other objects from Lothal', in S R Rao, *Lothal: A Harappan*

Port Town II, Memoir of the Archaeological Survey of India, No. 78, New Delhi, 1985.

Mac Crindle, *Ancient India as described by Megasthanese and Arrian*, Calcutta, 1926.

Majumdar, R. C. *Classical Accounts*, Calcutta, 1960.

Michel Danino, *Indian Culture and India's Future*, New Delhi, 2011. *Indian Mind Now and Then*, Mysore, 2000. *The Invasion that Never Was*, Mysore, 1996. *The Lost River - On the Trail of the SARASWATI*, New Delhi, 2010.

Mortimer Wheeler, *The Indus Civilization*, Cambridge, 1968.

Mukesh Bharadwaj, 'A New Page From History', *The Indian Express*, Thiruvanantapuram, 3 March, 2002.

Nagaraja Rao, P. (Ed), *Radhakrishnan Reader: An Anthology*, Bombay, 1969.

Nand Kishore Acharya, *The Polity in Sukranitisara*, Bikaner, 1992.

Narendra Nath Law, *Aspects of Ancient Indian Polity*, Calcutta, 1960.

Niels Bohr, *Atomic Physics and Description of Nature*, Cambridge, 1934.

Nilakanta Sastri and others (Ed.), *India's Contribution to World Thought and Culture* Chennai, 2003.

Oldahm, C. F. 'The Saraswati and the Lost River of the Indian Desert,' *Journal of the Royal Asiatic Society*, 1893, Vol. 34.

Oldham, R. D. 'On Probable Changes in the Geography of the Punjab and its Rivers : an Historico-Geographical Study', *Journal of Asiatic Society of Bengal*, 1886, Vol. 55.

Oppenheim, A. L. "Seafaring merchants of Ur," *Journal of the American Oriental Society*, Vol. 74.

Panikker, K.M. *India Through The Ages*, Delhi, 1985. *A Survey of Indian History*, 1977.

Parameswaran. P (Ed), *Bhagavad-Gita and Modern Problems*, Thiruvanantapuram, 2001.

Pargiter, F. E., *Ancient Indian Historical Tradition*, New Delhi, 1997.

Pierre Thuillier, *The Great Implosion - Report on the Collapse of the West, 1999-2002*, Paris, 1995.

Rabindranath Tagore, *Creative Unity*, New Delhi, 1980.

Radhakrishna, B. P. and Merh. S. S. (Ed.), *Vedic Sarasvati : Evolutionary History of a Lost River of North-western India*, Bangalore, 2002.

Radhakrishnan, S. *Indian Philosophy*, 2 Vols, New Delhi, 1989.

Radha Kumud Mookerji, *Ancient Indian Education*, Delhi, 1974. *Chandraguptha Maurya and His Times*, Delhi, 1988.

Raghavan, V. (Ed.), *Founders of Philosophy*, Delhi, 1981.

Rajagopalachari, C. *Kural* (Trans.), Bombay, 1981. *Ramayana*, Mumbai, 2006. *Upanishads*, Bombay, 1982.

Rajesh Kochhar, *The Vedic People*, New Delhi, 2002.

Ranade, R. D. *A Constructive Survey of Upanishadic Philosophy*, Bombay, 1986.

Rao, S. R. *Dawn and Devolution of the Indus Civilization*, New Delhi, 1991. *New Frontiers of Archaeology*, Bombay, 1994.

Rhys Davids, T. W. *Buddhism*, Delhi, 2010.

Robert Ernest Hume, *Thirteen Principal Upanishads*, New Delhi, 2000.

Robert Van De Weyer (Ed.), *366 Readings From Buddhism*, Mumbai, 2006.

Romila Thapar, *Asoka and the Decline of the Mauryan Empire*, New Delhi, 1994. *Interpreting Early India*, New Delhi, 1992.

Romila Thapar and others, *India: Historical Beginnings and the Concept of the Aryan*, New Delhi, 2007.

Roy, B. C. 'Geological Map of Rajasthan', *Geological Survey of India*, Vol. 86; 'Lost Course of Saraswati River in the Indian Desert', *Geographical Journal*, Vol. 145 (3), 1979.

Sarma, R. S. *Material Culture and Social Formations in Ancient India*, Delhi, 2000.

Sarma, Y. D. *Delhi and its Neighbourhood*, New Delhi, 2001.

Sashi Asthana, *History and Archaeology of India's Contact with other Countries*, Delhi, 1976.

Shelley, P. B. *To a Skylark*.

Sircar, D. C. *Inscriptions of Asoka*, New Delhi, 1975.

Surendranath Dasgupta, *A History of Indian Philosophy*, Vol. I, Delhi, 1988.

Swami Tathagatananda, *Journey of the Upanishads to the West*, Calcutta, 2005.

Swami Vivekananda, *Complete Works*, 8 Vols, Kolkata, 2009.

Shriram Sathe, *Dates of the Buddha*, Hyderabad, 1987.

Smith, V. A. *Early History of India*, Oxford, 1924.

Stephen Knapp. *Proof of Vedic Culture's Global Existence*, Michigan, 2000.

Sri Aurobindo, *Hymns to the Mystic Fire*, Pondicherry, 1995. *The Foundations of Indian Culture*, Pondicherry, 1985. *The Human Cycle, The Ideal of Human Unity, War and Self-Determination*, Pondicherry, 1985. *The Secret of the Veda*, Pondicherry, 1987. *The Synthesis of Yoga*, Pondicherry, 1984. *The Upanishads*, Pondicherry, 2000. *Sri Aurobindo Library Centenary Edition.*

Srinivasa Sasri, V. S. *Lectures on the Ramayana*, Madras, 1986.

Sriram Sathe, *Aryans: Who were They*, Mysore, 1991.

Suryanath Kamath and S. B. Deo (Ed.) *The Aryan Problem*, Pune, 1993.

Talboys Wheeler, J. *India : Vedic and Post Vedic*, New Delhi, 2007.

Upinder Singh, *Mysteries of the Past Archaeological Sites in India*, New Delhi, 2002.

Valdia, K. S. *Saraswati : The River that Disappeared*, Orient Longman, Hyderabad, 2002.

Vidyaratnam P N Menon (Ed.), *Viduraniti*, Palghat, 1962.

Wadia, D. N. *Geology of India*, New Delhi, 1984 (First published in 1919.

Warad Pande, N. R. *Aryan Invasion : A Myth*, Nagpur, 1989.

Will Durant, *The Story of Philosophy*, New York, 1961.

Index

N

O

P